ElasticSearch Cookbook

Over 120 advanced recipes to search, analyze, deploy, manage, and monitor data effectively with ElasticSearch

Alberto Paro

BIRMINGHAM - MUMBAI

ElasticSearch Cookbook

Copyright © 2013 Packt Publishing

All rights reserved. No part of this book may be reproduced, stored in a retrieval system, or transmitted in any form or by any means, without the prior written permission of the publisher, except in the case of brief quotations embedded in critical articles or reviews.

Every effort has been made in the preparation of this book to ensure the accuracy of the information presented. However, the information contained in this book is sold without warranty, either express or implied. Neither the author, nor Packt Publishing, and its dealers and distributors will be held liable for any damages caused or alleged to be caused directly or indirectly by this book.

Packt Publishing has endeavored to provide trademark information about all of the companies and products mentioned in this book by the appropriate use of capitals. However, Packt Publishing cannot guarantee the accuracy of this information.

First published: December 2013

Production Reference: 1171213

Published by Packt Publishing Ltd.
Livery Place
35 Livery Street
Birmingham B3 2PB, UK.

ISBN 978-1-78216-662-7

www.packtpub.com

Cover Image by John M. Quick (john.m.quick@gmail.com)

Credits

Author
Alberto Paro

Reviewers
Jettro Coenradie
Henrik Lindström
Richard Louapre
Christian Pietsch

Acquisition Editor
Kevin Colaco

Lead Technical Editor
Arun Nadar

Technical Editors
Pragnesh Bilimoria
Iram Malik
Krishnaveni Haridas
Shruti Rawool

Project Coordinator
Amey Sawant

Proofreader
Bridget Braund

Indexer
Priya Subramani

Graphics
Yuvraj Mannari

Production Coordinator
Pooja Chiplunkar

Cover Work
Pooja Chiplunkar

About the Author

Alberto Paro is an engineer, a project manager, and a software developer. He currently works as a CTO at The Net Planet Europe and as a Freelance Consultant of software engineering on Big Data and NoSQL solutions. He loves studying emerging solutions and applications mainly related to Big Data processing, NoSQL, Natural Language Processing, and neural networks. He started programming in Basic on a Sinclair Spectrum when he was eight years old and in his life he has gained a lot of experience using different operative systems, applications, and programming.

In 2000, he completed Computer Science engineering from Politecnico di Milano with a thesis on designing multi-users and multidevices web applications. He worked as a professor helper at the university for about one year. Then, after coming in contact with The Net Planet company and loving their innovation ideas, he started working on knowledge management solutions and advanced data-mining products.

In his spare time, when he is not playing with his children, he likes working on open source projects. When he was in high school, he started contributing to projects related to the Gnome environment (GTKMM). One of his preferred programming languages was Python and he wrote one of the first NoSQL backend for Django for MongoDB (django-mongodb-engine). In 2010, he started using ElasticSearch to provide search capabilities for some Django e-commerce sites and developed PyES (a pythonic client for ElasticSearch) and the initial part of ElasticSearch MongoDB River.

> I would like to thank my wife and my children for their support. I am indebted to my editors and reviewers for guiding this book to completion. Their professionalism, courtesy, good judgment, and passion for books are much appreciated.

About the Reviewers

Jettro Coenradie likes to try out new stuff. That is why he got his motorcycle drivers license. On a motorbike, you tend to explore different routes to get the best out of your bike and have fun while doing the things you need to do, such as going from A to B. When exploring new technologies, he also likes to explore new routes to find better and more interesting ways to accomplish his goal. Jettro rides an all terrain-bike; he does not like riding on the same ground over and over again. The same is valid for his technical interest; he knows about backend (ElasticSearch, MongoDB, Spring Data, and Spring Integration), as well as frontend (AngularJS, Sass, and Less) and mobile development (iOS and Sencha touch).

Henrik Lindström has worked with enterprise search for the last 10 years and the last two years mainly with ElasticSearch. He was one of the founders of 200 OK AB and the Truffler search service that ran on the top of ElasticSearch. In 2013, 200 OK was acquired by EPiServer AB and at that time, he joined EPiServer and is currently working on their cloud services and mainly the search service EPiServer Find. When Henrik isn't coding or spending time with his family, you might find him in the backcountry with skis on his feet during the winter or with a fly rod in his hand in the summer time.

Richard Louapre is a Technical Consultant with 12 years of experience in content management. He is passionate about exploring new IT technologies, particularly in the field of NoSQL, search engine, and MVC JavaScript framework. He applied those concepts in the open source MongoDB River Plugin for ElasticSearch (`https://github.com/richardwilly98/elasticsearch-river-mongodb`).

Christian Pietsch is a computational linguist with a degree from Saarland University, Germany. His work experience has been mostly research-related. At the Open University, England, he worked as a Java programmer within the Natural Language Generation group. As a Junior Researcher at the Center of Excellence in Cognitive Interaction Technology (CITEC), Germany, he analyzed linguistic data collections using Python and R, and even tried to build a human-like virtual receptionist with his colleagues.

Currently, at the Library Technology and Knowledge Management (LibTec) department of Bielefeld University Library, Germany, his duties include handling bibliographic metadata and research data. For this, his preferred toolkit is the open source modern Perl framework Catmandu that among other things provides easy-to-use wrappers for document stores and search engines such as ElasticSearch. Refer to `http://librecat.org/` for more information about Catmandu.

www.PacktPub.com

Support files, eBooks, discount offers and more

You might want to visit www.PacktPub.com for support files and downloads related to your book.

Did you know that Packt offers eBook versions of every book published, with PDF and ePub files available? You can upgrade to the eBook version at www.PacktPub.com and as a print book customer, you are entitled to a discount on the eBook copy. Get in touch with us at service@packtpub.com for more details.

At www.PacktPub.com, you can also read a collection of free technical articles, sign up for a range of free newsletters and receive exclusive discounts and offers on Packt books and eBooks.

http://PacktLib.PacktPub.com

Do you need instant solutions to your IT questions? PacktLib is Packt's online digital book library. Here, you can access, read and search across Packt's entire library of books.

Why Subscribe?

- Fully searchable across every book published by Packt
- Copy and paste, print and bookmark content
- On demand and accessible via web browser

Free Access for Packt account holders

If you have an account with Packt at www.PacktPub.com, you can use this to access PacktLib today and view nine entirely free books. Simply use your login credentials for immediate access.

To Giulia and Andrea, my extraordinary children.

Table of Contents

Preface   1

Chapter 1: Getting Started   7
- Introduction   7
- Understanding node and cluster   8
- Understanding node services   9
- Managing your data   10
- Understanding cluster, replication, and sharding   12
- Communicating with ElasticSearch   15
- Using the HTTP protocol   16
- Using the Native protocol   18
- Using the Thrift protocol   20

Chapter 2: Downloading and Setting Up ElasticSearch   23
- Introduction   23
- Downloading and installing ElasticSearch   24
- Networking setup   27
- Setting up a node   29
- Setting up ElasticSearch for Linux systems (advanced)   31
- Setting up different node types (advanced)   32
- Installing a plugin   34
- Installing a plugin manually   37
- Removing a plugin   38
- Changing logging settings (advanced)   39

Table of Contents

Chapter 3: Managing Mapping — 41
Introduction — 42
Using explicit mapping creation — 42
Mapping base types — 44
Mapping arrays — 48
Mapping an object — 49
Mapping a document — 51
Using dynamic templates in document mapping — 55
Managing nested objects — 58
Managing a child document — 60
Mapping a multifield — 62
Mapping a GeoPoint field — 64
Mapping a GeoShape field — 67
Mapping an IP field — 68
Mapping an attachment field — 69
Adding generic data to mapping — 72
Mapping different analyzers — 73

Chapter 4: Standard Operations — 75
Introduction — 76
Creating an index — 76
Deleting an index — 79
Opening/closing an index — 80
Putting a mapping in an index — 81
Getting a mapping — 83
Deleting a mapping — 84
Refreshing an index — 86
Flushing an index — 87
Optimizing an index — 89
Checking if an index or type exists — 91
Managing index settings — 92
Using index aliases — 94
Indexing a document — 97
Getting a document — 101
Deleting a document — 104
Updating a document — 106
Speeding up atomic operations (bulk) — 109
Speeding up GET — 111

Chapter 5: Search, Queries, and Filters — 115
- Introduction — 116
- Executing a search — 116
- Sorting a search — 123
- Highlighting results — 126
- Executing a scan query — 129
- Suggesting a correct query — 131
- Counting — 134
- Deleting by query — 135
- Matching all the documents — 137
- Querying/filtering for term — 139
- Querying/filtering for terms — 142
- Using a prefix query/filter — 146
- Using a Boolean query/filter — 148
- Using a range query/filter — 150
- Using span queries — 152
- Using the match query — 156
- Using the IDS query/filter — 158
- Using the has_child query/filter — 160
- Using the top_children query — 162
- Using the has_parent query/filter — 164
- Using a regexp query/filter — 165
- Using exists and missing filters — 167
- Using and/or/not filters — 169
- Using the geo_bounding_box filter — 172
- Using the geo_polygon filter — 173
- Using the geo_distance filter — 174

Chapter 6: Facets — 179
- Introduction — 179
- Executing facets — 180
- Executing terms facets — 183
- Executing range facets — 187
- Executing histogram facets — 190
- Executing date histogram facets — 194
- Executing filter/query facets — 198
- Executing statistical facets — 200
- Executing term statistical facets — 203
- Executing geo distance facets — 206

Chapter 7: Scripting — 211
- Introduction — 211
- Installing additional script plugins — 212
- Sorting using script — 214
- Computing return fields with scripting — 218
- Filtering a search via scripting — 221
- Updating with scripting — 224

Chapter 8: Rivers — 229
- Introduction — 229
- Managing a river — 230
- Using the CouchDB river — 233
- Using the MongoDB river — 236
- Using the RabbitMQ river — 238
- Using the JDBC river — 243
- Using the Twitter river — 247

Chapter 9: Cluster and Nodes Monitoring — 251
- Introduction — 251
- Controlling cluster health via API — 252
- Controlling cluster state via API — 254
- Getting nodes information via API — 259
- Getting node statistic via API — 264
- Installing and using BigDesk — 269
- Installing and using ElasticSearc-head — 275
- Installing and using SemaText SPM — 279

Chapter 10: Java Integration — 283
- Introduction — 283
- Creating an HTTP client — 284
- Creating a native client — 289
- Managing indices with the native client — 292
- Managing mappings — 295
- Managing documents — 298
- Managing bulk action — 302
- Creating a query — 305
- Executing a standard search — 309
- Executing a facet search — 313
- Executing a scroll/scan search — 317

Chapter 11: Python Integration — 323
- Introduction — 323
- Creating a client — 324
- Managing indices — 328
- Managing mappings — 331
- Managing documents — 334
- Executing a standard search — 339
- Executing a facet search — 344

Chapter 12: Plugin Development — 349
- Introduction — 349
- Creating a site plugin — 350
- Creating a simple plugin — 352
- Creating a REST plugin — 362
- Creating a cluster action — 368
- Creating an analyzer plugin — 376
- Creating a river plugin — 379

Index — 391

Preface

One of the main requirements of today applications is the search capability. In the market we can find a lot of solutions to answer this need, both in the commercial and in the open source world. One of the frequently used libraries for searching is Apache Lucene. This library is the base of a large number of search solutions such as Apache Solr, Indextank, and ElasticSearch.

ElasticSearch is one of the younger solutions, written with the cloud, and distributed computing in mind. Its main author, *Shay Banon*, famous for having developed Compass (http://www.compass-project.org), released the first version of ElasticSearch in March 2010.

Thus the main scope of ElasticSearch is to be a search engine; it also provides a lot of features that allows it to be used also as data store and analytic engine via facets.

ElasticSearch contains a lot of innovative features: JSON REST-based, natively distributed in a map/reduce approach, easy to set up, and extensible with plugins. In this book, we will study in depth about these features and many others available in ElasticSearch.

Before ElasticSearch, only Apache Solr was able to provide some of these functionalities, but it was not designed for the cloud and it is not using JSON REST API. In the last year, this situation has changed a bit with the release of Solr Cloud in 2012. For users who want to have a deeper comparison between these two products, I suggest to read posts by *Rafal Kuc* available at http://blog.sematext.com/2012/08/23/solr-vs-elasticsearch-part-1-overview/.

ElasticSearch is also a product in continuous evolution and new functionalities are released both by the ElasticSearch Company (the company founded by *Shay Banon* to provide commercial support for ElasticSearch) and by ElasticSearch users as a plugin (mainly available on GitHub).

In my opinion, ElasticSearch is probably one of the most powerful and easy-to-use search solutions in the market. In writing this book and these recipes, the book reviewers and I have tried to transmit our knowledge, our passion, and the best practices to manage it in a better way.

Preface

What this book covers

Chapter 1, *Getting Started*, gives the reader an overview of the basic concepts of ElasticSearch and the ways to communicate with it.

Chapter 2, *Downloading and Setting Up ElasticSearch*, covers the basic steps to start using ElasticSearch from the simple install to cloud ones.

Chapter 3, *Managing Mapping*, covers the correct definition of the data fields to improve both indexing and searching quality.

Chapter 4, *Standard Operations*, teaches the most common actions that are required to ingest data in ElasticSearch and to manage it.

Chapter 5, *Search, Queries, and Filters*, talks about Search DSL—the core of the search functionalities of ElasticSearch. It is the only way to execute queries in ElasticSearch.

Chapter 6, *Facets,* covers another capability of ElasticSearch—the possibility to execute analytics on search results to improve both user experience and to drill down the information contained in ElasticSearch.

Chapter 7, *Scripting*, shows how to customize ElasticSearch with scripting in different languages.

Chapter 8, *Rivers*, extends ElasticSearch giving the ability to pull data from different sources such as databases, NoSQL solutions, or data streams.

Chapter 9, *Cluster and Nodes Monitoring*, shows how to analyze the behavior of a cluster/node to understand common pitfalls.

Chapter 10, *Java Integration*, describes how to integrate ElasticSearch in Java application using both REST and Native protocols.

Chapter 11, *Python Integration*, covers the usage of the official ElasticSearch Python client and the Pythonic PyES library.

Chapter 12, *Plugin Development*, describes how to create the different types of plugins: site and native. Some examples show the plugin skeletons, the setup process, and their building.

What you need for this book

For this book you will need a computer, of course. In terms of the software required, you don't have to be worried, all the components we use are open source and available for every platform.

For all the REST examples the cURL software (`http://curl.haxx.se/`) is used to simulate a command from the command line. It's commonly preinstalled in Linux and Mac OS X operative systems. For Windows, it can be downloaded from its site and put in a path that can be called from a command line.

For *Chapter 10*, *Java Integration* and *Chapter 12*, *Plugin Development*, the Maven built tool (http://maven.apache.org/) is required, which is a standard for managing build, packaging, and deploy in Java. It is natively supported in Java IDEs such as Eclipse and IntelliJ IDEA.

Chapter 11, *Python Integration*, requires the Python interpreter installed. By default it's available on Linux and Mac OS X. For Windows it can be downloaded from the official Python site (http//www.python.org). For the current examples Version 2.X is used.

Who this book is for

This book is for developers who want to start using both ElasticSearch and at the same time improve their ElasticSearch knowledge. The book covers all aspects of using ElasticSearch and provides solutions and hints for everyday usage. The recipes are reduced in complexity to easily focus the reader on the discussed ElasticSearch aspect and to easily memorize the ElasticSearch functionalities.

The latter chapters that discuss the ElasticSearch integration in JAVA and Python, shows the user how to integrate the power of ElasticSearch in their applications.

The last chapter talks about advanced usage of ElasticSearch and its core extension, so some skilled Java know-how is required.

Conventions

In this book, you will find a number of styles of text that distinguish between different kinds of information. Here are some examples of these styles, and an explanation of their meaning.

Code words in text, database table names, folder names, filenames, file extensions, pathnames, dummy URLs, user input, and Twitter handles are shown as follows: "Open the `config/elasticsearch.yml` file with an editor of your choice."

A block of code is set as follows:

```
path.conf: /opt/data/es/conf
path.data: /opt/data/es/data1,/opt2/data/data2
path.work: /opt/data/work
path.logs: /opt/data/logs
path.plugins: /opt/data/plugins
```

Preface

When we wish to draw your attention to a particular part of a code block, the relevant lines or items are set in bold:

```
{
  "order": {
    "_uid": {
      "store": "yes"
    },
    "_id": {
      "path": "order_id"
    },
    "properties": {
      "order_id": {
        "type": "string",
        "store": "yes",
        "index": "not_analyzed"
      },
```

Any command-line input or output is written as follows:

```
bin/plugin -install elasticsearch/elasticsearch-mapper-attachments/1.9.0
```

New terms and **important words** are shown in bold. Words that you see on the screen, in menus or dialog boxes for example, appear in the text like this: " The **Any Request [+]** tab allows executing custom query. On the left-hand side there are the following options:".

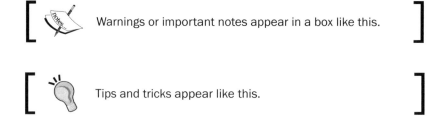

Warnings or important notes appear in a box like this.

Tips and tricks appear like this.

Reader feedback

Feedback from our readers is always welcome. Let us know what you think about this book—what you liked or may have disliked. Reader feedback is important for us to develop titles that you really get the most out of.

To send us general feedback, simply send an e-mail to `feedback@packtpub.com`, and mention the book title via the subject of your message.

If there is a topic that you have expertise in and you are interested in either writing or contributing to a book, see our author guide on `www.packtpub.com/authors`.

Customer support

Now that you are the proud owner of a Packt book, we have a number of things to help you to get the most from your purchase.

Downloading the example code

You can download the example code files for all Packt books you have purchased from your account at http://www.packtpub.com. If you purchased this book elsewhere, you can visit http://www.packtpub.com/support and register to have the files e-mailed directly to you.

Errata

Although we have taken every care to ensure the accuracy of our content, mistakes do happen. If you find a mistake in one of our books—maybe a mistake in the text or the code— we would be grateful if you would report this to us. By doing so, you can save other readers from frustration and help us improve subsequent versions of this book. If you find any errata, please report them by visiting http://www.packtpub.com/submit-errata, selecting your book, clicking on the **errata submission form** link, and entering the details of your errata. Once your errata are verified, your submission will be accepted and the errata will be uploaded on our website, or added to any list of existing errata, under the Errata section of that title. Any existing errata can be viewed by selecting your title from http://www.packtpub.com/support.

Piracy

Piracy of copyright material on the Internet is an ongoing problem across all media. At Packt, we take the protection of our copyright and licenses very seriously. If you come across any illegal copies of our works, in any form, on the Internet, please provide us with the location address or website name immediately so that we can pursue a remedy.

Please contact us at copyright@packtpub.com with a link to the suspected pirated material.

We appreciate your help in protecting our authors, and our ability to bring you valuable content.

Questions

You can contact us at questions@packtpub.com if you are having a problem with any aspect of the book, and we will do our best to address it.

1
Getting Started

In this chapter, we will cover the following topics:

- Understanding node and cluster
- Understanding node services
- Managing your data
- Understanding cluster, replication, and sharding
- Communicating with ElasticSearch
- Using the HTTP protocol
- Using the Native protocol
- Using the Thrift protocol

Introduction

In order to efficiently use ElasticSearch, it is very important to understand how it works. The goal of this chapter is to give the reader an overview of the basic concepts of ElasticSearch such as node, index, shard, type, records, and fields.

ElasticSearch can be used both as a search engine and as a data store. A brief description of the ElasticSearch logic helps the user to improve the performance and quality, and decide when and how to invest in infrastructure to improve scalability and availability. Some details about data replications and base node communication processes are also explained. At the end of this chapter the protocols used to manage ElasticSearch are also discussed.

Understanding node and cluster

Every instance of ElasticSearch is called as node. Several nodes are grouped in a cluster. This is the base of the cloud nature of ElasticSearch.

Getting ready

To better understand the upcoming sections, some knowledge of basic concepts of application node and cluster is required.

How it works...

One or more ElasticSearch nodes can be set up on a physical or a virtual server depending on available resources such as RAM, CPUs, and disk space. A default node allows storing data in it and to process requests and responses. (In *Chapter 2, Downloading and Setting Up ElasticSearch*, we'll see details about how to set up different nodes and cluster topologies). When a node is started, several actions take place during its startup:

- The configuration is read from the environment variables and from the `elasticsearch.yml` configuration file
- A node name is set by a `config` file or chosen from a list of built-in random names
- Internally, the ElasticSearch engine initializes all the modules and plugins that are available in the current installation

After node startup, the node searches for other cluster members and checks its indices and shards status. In order to join two or more nodes in a cluster, the following rules must be matched:

- The version of ElasticSearch must be the same (0.20, 0.9, and so on) otherwise the join is rejected
- The cluster name must be the same
- The network must be configured to support multicast (default) and they can communicate with each other

Refer to the *Networking setup* recipe in the next chapter.

A common approach in cluster management is to have a master node, which is the main reference for all cluster level actions, and the others ones called secondary or slaves, that replicate the master data and actions. All the update actions are first committed in the master node and then replicated in secondary ones.

In a cluster with multiple nodes, if a master node dies, a secondary one is elected to be the new master; this approach allows automatic failover to be set up in an ElasticSearch cluster.

There's more...

There are two important behaviors in an ElasticSearch node, namely the arbiter and the data container.

The arbiter nodes are able to process the REST response and all the other operations of search. During every action execution, ElasticSearch generally executes actions using a MapReduce approach. The arbiter is responsible for distributing the actions to the underlying shards (map) and collecting/aggregating the shard results (redux) to be sent a final response. They may use a huge amount of RAM due to operations such as facets, collecting hits and caching (for example, scan queries).

Data nodes are able to store data in them. They contain the indices shards that store the indexed documents as Lucene indices. All the standard nodes are both arbiter and data container.

In big cluster architectures, having some nodes as simple arbiters with a lot of RAM with no data reduces the resources required by data nodes and improves performance in search using the local memory cache of arbiters.

See also

- *Setting up a node* and *Setting up different node types (advanced)* recipes in the next chapter

Understanding node services

When a node is running, a lot of services are managed by its instance. Services provide additional functionalities to a node and they cover different behaviors such as networking, indexing, analyzing, and so on.

Getting ready

Every ElasticSearch server that is running provides services.

Getting Started

How it works...

ElasticSearch natively provides a large set of functionalities that can be extended with additional plugins. During a node startup, a lot of required services are automatically started. The most important are as follows:

- Cluster services manage cluster state and intra-node communication and synchronization
- Indexing service manages all the index operations, initializing all active indices and shards
- Mapping service that manages the document types stored in the cluster (we'll discuss mapping in *Chapter 3, Managing Mapping*)
- Network services, such as HTTP REST services (default on port 9200), internal ES protocol (on port 9300) and Thrift server (on port 9500 if thrift plugin is installed)
- Plugin service (discussed in *Chapter 2, Downloading and Setting Up ElasticSearch*, for installation and *Chapter 12, Plugin Development*, for detailed usage)
- River service (covered in *Chapter 8, Rivers*)
- Language scripting services that allow adding new language scripting support to ElasticSearch

> Throughout the book, we'll see recipes that interact with ElasticSearch services. Every base functionality or extended functionality is managed in ElasticSearch as a service.

Managing your data

Unless you are using ElasticSearch as a search engine or a distributed data store, it's important to understand concepts on how ElasticSearch stores and manages your data.

Getting ready

To work with ElasticSearch data, a user must know basic concepts of data management and JSON that is the "lingua franca" for working with ElasticSearch data and services.

How it works...

Our main data container is called index (plural indices) and it can be considered as a database in the traditional SQL world. In an index, the data is grouped in data types called mappings in ElasticSearch. A mapping describes how the records are composed (called fields).

Every record, that must be stored in ElasticSearch, must be a JSON object.

Natively, ElasticSearch is a schema-less datastore. When you put records in it, during insert it processes the records, splits them into fields, and updates the schema to manage the inserted data.

To manage huge volumes of records, ElasticSearch uses the common approach to split an index into many shards so that they can be spread on several nodes. The shard management is transparent in usage—all the common record operations are managed automatically in the ElasticSearch application layer.

Every record is stored in only one shard. The sharding algorithm is based on record ID, so many operations that require loading and changing of records can be achieved without hitting all the shards.

The following schema compares ElasticSearch structure with SQL and MongoDB ones:

ElasticSearch	SQL	MongoDB
Index (Indices)	Database	Database
Shard	Shard	Shard
Mapping/Type	Table	Collection
Field	Field	Field
Record (JSON object)	Record (Tuples)	Record (BSON object)

There's more...

ElasticSearch, internally, has rigid rules about how to execute operations to ensure safe operations on index/mapping/records. In ElasticSearch, the operations are divided as follows:

- **Cluster operations**: At cluster level all write ones are locked, first they are applied to the master node and then to the secondary one. The read operations are typically broadcasted.
- **Index management operations**: These operations follow the cluster pattern.
- **Record operations**: These operations are executed on single documents at shard level.

When a record is saved in ElasticSearch, the destination shard is chosen based on the following factors:

- The ID (unique identifier) of the record. If the ID is missing, it is autogenerated by ElasticSearch.
- If the routing or parent (covered while learning the parent/child mapping) parameters are defined, the correct shard is chosen by the hash of these parameters.

Splitting an index into shards allows you to store your data in different nodes, because ElasticSearch tries to do shard balancing.

Every shard can contain up to 2^32 records (about 4.2 billion records), so the real limit to shard size is its storage size.

Shards contain your data and during search process all the shards are used to calculate and retrieve results. ElasticSearch performance in big data scales horizontally with the number of shards.

All native records operations (such as index, search, update, and delete) are managed in shards.

The shard management is completely transparent to the user. Only an advanced user tends to change the default shard routing and management to cover their custom scenarios. A common custom scenario is the requirement to put customer data in the same shard to speed up his/her operations (search/index/analytics).

Best practice

It's best practice not to have a too big shard (over 10 GB) to avoid poor performance in indexing due to continuous merge and resizing of index segments.

It's not good to oversize the number of shards to avoid poor search performance due to native distributed search (it works as MapReduce). Having a huge number of empty shards in an index consumes only memory.

See also

> - Shard on Wikipedia http://en.wikipedia.org/wiki/Shard_(database_architecture)

Understanding cluster, replication, and sharding

Related to shard management, there is the key concept of replication and cluster status.

Getting ready

You need one or more nodes running to have a cluster. To test an effective cluster you need at least two nodes (they can be on the same machine).

How it works...

An index can have one or more replicas—the shards are called primary if they are part of the master index and secondary if they are part of replicas.

To maintain consistency in write operations the following workflow is executed:

1. The write is first executed in the primary shard.
2. If the primary write is successfully done, it is propagated simultaneously in all the secondary shards.
3. If a primary shard dies, a secondary one is elected as primary (if available) and the flow is re-executed.

During search operations, a valid set of shards is chosen randomly between primary and secondary to improve performances.

The following figure shows an example of possible shards configuration:

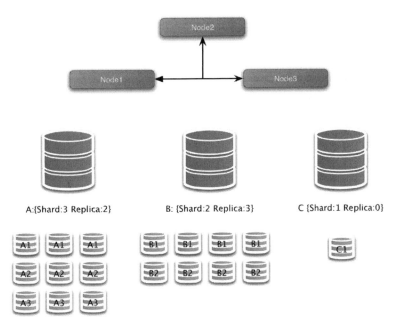

Best practice

In order to prevent data loss and to have High Availability, it's good to have at least one replica so that your system can survive a node failure without downtime and without loss of data.

There's more...

Related to the concept of replication there is the cluster indicator of the health of your cluster.

It can cover three different states:

- **Green**: Everything is ok.
- **Yellow**: Something is missing but you can work.
- **Red**: "Houston, we have a problem". Some primary shards are missing.

How to solve the yellow status

Mainly yellow status is due to some shards that are not allocated. If your cluster is in recovery status, just wait if there is enough space in nodes for your shards.

If your cluster, even after recovery is still in yellow state, it means you don't have enough nodes to contain your replicas so you can either reduce the number of your replicas or add the required number of nodes.

Best practice

The total number of nodes must not be lower than the maximum number of replicas.

How to solve the red status

When you have lost data (that is, one or more shard is missing), you need to try restoring the node(s) that are missing. If your nodes restart and the system goes back to yellow or green status you are safe. Otherwise, you have lost data and your cluster is not usable. In this case, delete the index/indices and restore them from backup (if you have it) or from other sources.

Best practice

To prevent data loss, I suggest having always at least two nodes and the replica set to 1.

> Having one or more replicas on different nodes on different machines allows you to have a live backup of your data, always updated.

See also

- Replica and shard management in this chapter.

Communicating with ElasticSearch

You can communicate with your ElasticSearch server with several protocols. In this recipe we will look at some main protocols.

Getting ready

You need a working ElasticSearch cluster.

How it works...

ElasticSearch is designed to be used as a RESTful server, so the main protocol is HTTP usually on port 9200 and above. Thus, it allows using different protocols such as native and thrift ones. Many others are available as extension plugins, but they are seldom used, such as memcached one.

Every protocol has weak and strong points, it's important to choose the correct one depending on the kind of applications you are developing. If you are in doubt, choose the HTTP protocol layer that is the most standard and easy to use one.

Choosing the right protocol depends on several factors, mainly architectural and performance related. This schema factorizes advantages and disadvantages related to them. If you are using it to communicate with Elasticsearch, the official clients switching from a protocol to another one is generally a simple setting in the client initialization. Refer to the following table which shows protocols and their advantages, disadvantages, and types:

Protocol	Advantages	Disadvantages	Type
HTTP	More often used. API safe and generally compatible with different ES versions. Suggested. JSON	HTTP overhead.	Text
Native	Fast network layer. Programmatic. Best for massive index operations.	API changes and breaks applications. Depends on the same version of ES server.	Binary
Thrift	As HTTP	Related to the thrift plugin.	Binary

Using the HTTP protocol

This recipe shows a sample of using the HTTP protocol.

Getting ready

You need a working ElasticSearch cluster. Using default configuration the 9200 port is open in your server to communicate with.

How to do it...

The standard RESTful protocol, it's easy to integrate.

Now, I'll show how to easily fetch the ElasticSearch greeting API on a running server at 9200 port using several ways and programming languages.

For every language sample, the answer will be the same:

```
{
  "ok" : true,
  "status" : 200,
  "name" : "Payge, Reeva",
  "version" :
  {
    "number" : "0.90.5",
    "snapshot_build" : false
  },
  "tagline" : "You Know, for Search"
}
```

In BASH:

```
curl -XGET http://127.0.0.1:9200
```

In Python:

```
import urllib
result = urllib.open("http://127.0.0.1:9200")
```

In Java:

```java
import java.io.BufferedReader;
import java.io.InputStream;
import java.io.InputStreamReader;
import java.net.URL;

...
try {              // get URL content
  URL url = new URL("http://127.0.0.1:9200");
  URLConnection conn = url.openConnection();//
open the stream and put it into BufferedReader
  BufferedReader br =
  new BufferedReader(new InputStreamReader(conn.getInputStream()));


String inputLine;
while ((inputLine = br.readLine()) != null)
{
    System.out.println(inputLine);
}
br.close();
System.out.println("Done");
} catch (MalformedURLException e) {
e.printStackTrace();
} catch (IOException e) {
e.printStackTrace();
}
```

In Scala:

```scala
scala.io.Source.fromURL("http://127.0.0.1:9200",
  "utf-8").getLines.mkString("\n")
```

How it works...

Every client creates a connection to the server and fetches the answer. The answer is a valid JSON object. You can call ElasticSearch server from any language that you like.

Getting Started

The main advantages of this protocol are as follows:

- **Portability**: It uses web standards so it can be integrated in different languages (Erlang, JavaScript, Python, Ruby, and so on) or called from command-line applications such as curl.
- **Durability**: The REST APIs don't often change. They don't break for minor release changes as Native protocol does.
- **Simple to use**: It speaks JSON to JSON.
- **More supported than other protocols**: Every plugin typically supports a REST endpoint on HTTP.

In this book a lot of examples are used calling the HTTP API via command-line cURL program. This approach is very fast and allows you to test functionalities very quickly.

There's more...

Every language provides drivers to best integrate ElasticSearch or RESTful web services.

ElasticSearch community provides official drivers that support the various services.

Using the Native protocol

ElasticSearch provides a Native protocol, used mainly for low-level communication between nodes, but very useful for fast importing of huge data blocks. This protocol is available only for JVM languages.

Getting ready

You need a working ElasticSearch cluster— the standard port for Native protocol is 9300.

How to do it...

Creating a Java client is quite easy. Take a look at the following code snippet:

```
import net.thenetplanet.common.settings.ImmutableSettings;
import net.thenetplanet.common.settings.Settings;
import net.thenetplanet.client.Client;
import net.thenetplanet.client.transport.TransportClient;
    ...
Settings settings = ImmutableSettings.settingsBuilder()
.put("client.transport.sniff", true).build();
    // we define a new settings
```

```
    // using snif transport allows to autodetect other nodes
Client client = new TransportClient(settings)
            .addTransportAddress(new
InetSocketTransportAddress("127.0.0.1","9300"));
    // a client is created with the settings
```

How it works...

To initialize a native client some settings are required. The important ones are:

- `cluster.name`: This provides the name of the cluster
- `client.transport.sniff`: This allows sniff the rest of the cluster, and add those into its list of machines to use.

With these settings it's possible to initialize a new client giving an IP address and port (default 9300).

There's more...

This is the internal protocol used in ElasticSearch—it's the faster protocol available to talk with ElasticSearch.

The Native protocol is an optimized binary one and works only for JVM languages. To use this protocol, you need to include `elasticsearch.jar` in your JVM project. Because it depends on ElasticSearch implementation, it must be the same version of ElasticSearch cluster.

For this reason, every time you update your ElasticSearch Server/Cluster, you need to update `elasticsearch.jar` of your projects and if there are internal API changes, you need to modify your application code.

To use this protocol you also need to study the internals of ElasticSearch, so it's not so easy to use as HTTP and Thrift protocol.

Native protocol is useful for massive data import. But as ElasticSearch is mainly thought of as a REST HTTP server to communicate with, it lacks support for everything is not standard in ElasticSearch core, such as plugins entry points. Using this protocol you are unable to call entry points made by externals plugins.

See also

The Native protocol is the most used protocol in the Java world and it will be discussed in detail in *Chapter 10*, *Java Integration* and *Chapter 12* , *Plugin Development*.

Getting Started

Using the Thrift protocol

Thrift is an interface definition language, initially developed by Facebook, used to define and create services. This protocol is now in the Apache Software Foundation.

Its usage is similar to HTTP, but it bypasses the limit of HTTP protocol (latency, handshake, and so on) and it's faster.

Getting ready

You need a working ElasticSearch cluster with the thrift plugin installed (https://github.com/elasticsearch/elasticsearch-transport-thrift/) the standard port for thrift protocol is 9500.

How to do it...

In java using ElasticSearch generated classes, creating a client is quite easy as shown in the following code snippet:

```
import org.apache.thrift.protocol.TBinaryProtocol;
import org.apache.thrift.protocol.TProtocol;
import org.apache.thrift.transport.TSocket;
import org.apache.thrift.transport.TTransport;
import org.apache.thrift.transport.TTransportException;
import org.elasticsearch.thrift.*;


TTransport transport = new TSocket("127.0.0.1", 9500);
TProtocol protocol = new TBinaryProtocol(transport);
Rest.Client client = new Rest.Client(protocol);
transport.open();
```

How it works...

To initialize a connection, first we need to open a socket transport. This is done with the TSocket (host/port), using the ElasticSearch thrift standard port 9500.

Then the Socket Transport Protocol must be encapsulated in a Binary Protocol—this is done with the TBinaryProtocol (transport).

Now, a client can be initialized by passing the protocol. The Rest-Client and other utilities classes are generated by elasticsearch.thrift, and live in the org.elasticsearch.thrift namespace.

To have a fully working client, we must open the socket (`transport.open()`).

At the end of program, we should clean the socket closing it (`transport.close()`).

There's more...

Some drivers to connect to ElasticSearch provide a simple to use API to interact with thrift without the boulder that this protocol needs.

For advanced usage, I suggest the use of the Thrift protocol to bypass some problems related with HTTP limits. They are as follows:

- The number of simultaneous connections required in HTTP—thrift transport is less resource angry
- The network traffic is light reduced to its binary nature

A big advantage of this protocol is that on server side it wraps the REST entry points so it can be also used with calls provided by external REST plugins.

See also

- For more details on Thrift, visit the Wikipedia page at `http://en.wikipedia.org/wiki/Apache_Thrift`
- For a complete reference of Thrift ElasticSearch plugin, the official documentation is available at `https://github.com/elasticsearch/elasticsearch-transport-thrift/`

2
Downloading and Setting Up ElasticSearch

In this chapter we will cover the following topics:

- Downloading and installing an ElasticSearch
- Networking setup
- Setting up a node
- Setting up ElasticSearch for Linux systems (advanced)
- Setting up different node types (advanced)
- Installing a plugin
- Installing a plugin manually
- Removing a plugin
- Changing logging settings (advanced)

Introduction

There are different options in installing ElasticSearch and setting up a working environment for development and production.

This chapter explains the installation process and the configuration from a single developer machine to a big cluster, giving hints on how to improve the performance and skip misconfiguration errors.

Downloading and Setting Up ElasticSearch

The setup step is very important, because a bad configuration can bring bad results, poor performances and kill your server.

In this chapter, the management of ElasticSearch plugins is also discussed: installing, configuring, updating, and removing plugins.

Downloading and installing ElasticSearch

ElasticSearch has an active community and the release cycles are very fast.

Because ElasticSearch depends on many common Java libraries (Lucene, Guice, and Jackson are the most famous ones), the ElasticSearch community tries to keep them updated and fix bugs that are discovered in them and in ElasticSearch core.

If it's possible, the best practice is to use the latest available release (usually the more stable one).

Getting ready

A supported ElasticSearch Operative System (Linux/MacOSX/Windows) with installed Java JVM 1.6 or above is required. A web browser is required to download the ElasticSearch binary release.

How to do it...

For downloading and installing an ElasticSearch server, we will perform the steps given as follows:

1. Download ElasticSearch from the Web.

    The latest version is always downloadable from the web address http://www.elasticsearch.org/download/.

    There are versions available for different operative systems:

    - `elasticsearch-{version-number}.zip`: This is for both Linux/Mac OSX, and Windows operating systems
    - `elasticsearch-{version-number}.tar.gz`: This is for Linux/Mac
    - `elasticsearch-{version-number}.deb`: This is for Debian-based Linux distributions (this also covers Ubuntu family)

    These packages contain everything to start ElasticSearch.

    At the time of writing this book, the latest and most stable version of ElasticSearch was 0.90.7. To check out whether this is the latest available or not, please visit http://www.elasticsearch.org/download/.

2. Extract the binary content.

   After downloading the correct release for your platform, the installation consists of expanding the archive in a working directory.

   Choose a working directory that is safe to charset problems and doesn't have a long path to prevent problems when ElasticSearch creates its directories to store the index data.

   For windows platform, a good directory could be `c:\es`, on Unix and MacOSX `/opt/es`.

   To run ElasticSearch, you need a Java Virtual Machine 1.6 or above installed. For better performance, I suggest you use Sun/Oracle 1.7 version.

3. We start ElasticSearch to check if everything is working.

   To start your ElasticSearch server, just go in the install directory and type:

   `# bin/elasticsearch -f`   (for Linux and MacOsX)

   or

   `# bin\elasticserch.bat -f`   (for Windows)

   Now your server should start as shown in the following screenshot:

Downloading and Setting Up ElasticSearch

How it works...

The ElasticSearch package contains three directories:

- `bin`: This contains script to start and manage ElasticSearch. The most important ones are:
    - `elasticsearch(.bat)`: This is the main script to start ElasticSearch
    - `plugin(.bat)`: This is a script to manage plugins
- `config`: This contains the ElasticSearch configs. The most important ones are:
    - `elasticsearch.yml`: This is the main config file for ElasticSearch
    - `logging.yml`: This is the logging config file
- `lib`: This contains all the libraries required to run ElasticSearch

There's more...

During ElasticSearch startup a lot of events happen:

- A node name is chosen automatically (that is Akenaten in the example) if not provided in `elasticsearch.yml`.
- A node name hash is generated for this node (that is, `whqVp_4zQGCgMvJ1CXhcWQ`).
- If there are plugins (internal or sites), they are loaded. In the previous example there are no plugins.
- Automatically if not configured, ElasticSearch binds on all addresses available two ports:
    - 9300 internal, intra node communication, used for discovering other nodes
    - 9200 HTTP REST API port
- After starting, if indices are available, they are checked and put in online mode to be used.

There are more events which are fired during ElasticSearch startup. We'll see them in detail in other recipes.

Networking setup

Correctly setting up a networking is very important for your node and cluster.

As there are a lot of different install scenarios and networking issues in this recipe we will cover two kinds of networking setups:

- Standard installation with autodiscovery working configuration
- Forced IP configuration; used if it is not possible to use autodiscovery

Getting ready

You need a working ElasticSearch installation and to know your current networking configuration (that is, IP).

How to do it...

For configuring networking, we will perform the steps as follows:

1. Open the ElasticSearch configuration file with your favorite text editor.

    Using the standard ElasticSearch configuration file (config/elasticsearch.yml), your node is configured to bind on all your machine interfaces and does autodiscovery broadcasting events, that means it sends "signals" to every machine in the current LAN and waits for a response. If a node responds to it, they can join in a cluster.

    If another node is available in the same LAN, they join in the cluster.

     Only nodes with the same ElasticSearch version and same cluster name (cluster.name option in elasticsearch.yml) can join each other.

2. To customize the network preferences, you need to change some parameters in the elasticsearch.yml file, such as:

    ```
    cluster.name: elasticsearch
    node.name: "My wonderful server"
    network.host: 192.168.0.1
    discovery.zen.ping.unicast.hosts: ["192.168.0.2","192.168.0.3[9300-9400]"]
    ```

> **Downloading the example code**
>
> You can download the example code files for all Packt books you have purchased from your account at http://www.packtpub.com. If you purchased this book elsewhere, you can visit http://www.packtpub.com/support and register to have the files e-mailed directly to you.

This configuration sets the cluster name to elasticsearch, the node name, the network address, and it tries to bind the node to the address given in the discovery section.

3. We can check the configuration during node loading.

    We can now start the server and check if the network is configured:

    ```
    [INFO ][node           ] [Aparo] version[0.90.3], pid[16792], build[5c38d60/2013-08-06T13:18:31Z]
    [INFO ][node           ] [Aparo] initializing ...
    [INFO ][plugins        ] [Aparo] loaded [transport-thrift, river-twitter, mapper-attachments, lang-python, jdbc-river, lang-javascript], sites [bigdesk, head]
    [INFO ][node           ] [Aparo] initialized
    [INFO ][node           ] [Aparo] starting ...
    [INFO ][transport      ] [Aparo] bound_address {inet[/0:0:0:0:0:0:0:0:9300]}, publish_address {inet[/192.168.1.5:9300]}
    [INFO ][cluster.service] [Aparo] new_master [Angela Cairn][yJcbdaPTSgS7ATQszgpSow][inet[/192.168.1.5:9300]], reason: zen-disco-join (elected_as_master)
    [INFO ][discovery      ] [Aparo] elasticsearch/yJcbdaPTSgS7ATQszgpSow
    [INFO ][http           ] [Aparo] bound_address {inet[/0:0:0:0:0:0:0:0:9200]}, publish_address {inet[/192.168.1.5:9200]}
    [INFO ][node           ] [Aparo] started
    ```

    In this case, we have:

    - The transport bounds to 0:0:0:0:0:0:0:0:9300 and 192.168.1.5:9300
    - The REST HTTP interface bounds to 0:0:0:0:0:0:0:0:9200 and 192.168.1.5:9200

How it works...

It works as follows:

- `cluster.name`: This sets up the name of the cluster (only nodes with the same name can join).
- `node.name`: If this is not defined, it is automatically generated by ElasticSearch. It allows defining a name for the node. If you have a lot of nodes on different machines, it is useful to set this name meaningful to easily locate it. Using a valid name is easier to remember than a generated name, such as `whqVp_4zQGCgMvJ1CXhcWQ`.
- `network.host`: This defines the IP of your machine to be used in binding the node. If your server is on different LANs or you want to limit the bind on only a LAN, you must set this value with your server IP.
- `discovery.zen.ping.unicast.hosts`: This allows you to define a list of hosts (with ports or port range) to be used to discover other nodes to join the cluster. This setting allows using the node in LAN where broadcasting is not allowed or autodiscovery is not working (that is, packet filtering routers). The referred port is the transport one, usually 9300. The addresses of the hosts list can be a mix of:
  - host name, that is, myhost1
  - IP address, that is, 192.168.1.2
  - IP address or host name with the port, that is, myhost1:9300 and 192.168.1.2:9300
  - IP address or host name with a range of ports, that is, myhost1:[9300-9400], 192.168.1.2:[9300-9400]

See also

- *Setting up different node types (advanced)*

Setting up a node

ElasticSearch allows you to customize several parameters in an installation. In this recipe, we'll see the most used ones to define where to store our data and to improve general performances.

Getting ready

You need a working ElasticSearch installation.

How to do it...

The steps required for setting up a simple node are as follows:

1. Open the `config/elasticsearch.yml` file with an editor of your choice.
2. Set up the directories that store your server data:

   ```
   path.conf: /opt/data/es/conf
   path.data: /opt/data/es/data1,/opt2/data/data2
   path.work: /opt/data/work
   path.logs: /opt/data/logs
   path.plugins: /opt/data/plugins
   ```

3. Set up parameters to control the standard index creation. These parameters are:

   ```
   index.number_of_shards: 5
   index.number_of_replicas: 1
   ```

How it works...

The `path.conf` file defines the directory that contains your configuration: mainly `elasticsearch.yml` and `logging.yml`. The default location is `$ES_HOME/config` with `ES_HOME` your install directory.

> It's useful to set up the `config` directory outside your application directory so you don't need to copy configuration files every time you update the version or change the ElasticSearch installation directory.

The `path.data` file is the most important one: it allows defining one or more directories where you store index data. When you define more than one directory, they are managed similarly to a RAID 0 configuration (the total space is the sum of all the data directory entry points), favoring locations with the most free space.

The `path.work` file is a location where ElasticSearch puts temporary files.

The `path.log` file is where log files are put. The control how to log is managed in `logging.yml`.

The `path.plugins` file allows overriding the plugins path (default `$ES_HOME/plugins`). It's useful to put "system wide" plugins.

The main parameters used to control the index and shard is `index.number_of_shards`, that controls the standard number of shards for a new created index, and `index.number_of_replicas` that controls the initial number of replicas.

There's more...

There are a lot of other parameters that can be used to customize your ElasticSearch installation and new ones are added with new releases. The most important ones are described in this recipe and in the next one.

See also

- *Setting up ElasticSearch for Linux systems (advanced)*
- The official ElasticSearch documentation at http://www.elasticsearch.org/guide/en/elasticsearch/reference/current/setup-configuration.html

Setting up ElasticSearch for Linux systems (advanced)

If you are using a Linux system, typically on a server, you need to manage extra setup to have a performance gain or to resolve production problems with many indices.

Getting ready

You need a working ElasticSearch installation.

How to do it...

For improving the performance on Linux systems, we will perform the steps given as follows:

1. First you need to change the current limit for the user who runs the ElasticSearch server. In these examples, we call the user as `elasticsearch`.

2. To allow elasticsearch to manage a large number of files, you need to increment the number of file descriptors (number of files) that a user can have. To do so, you must edit your `/etc/security/limits.conf` and add the following lines at the end:

   ```
   elasticsearch      -      nofile      999999
   elasticsearch      -      memlock     unlimited
   ```

   Then a machine restart is required to be sure that changes are taken.

3. For controlling the memory swapping, you need to set up this parameter in `elasticsearch.yml`:

   ```
   bootstrap.mlockall: true
   ```

Downloading and Setting Up ElasticSearch

4. To fix the memory usage size of ElasticSearch server, we need to set up the same value `ES_MIN_MEM` and `ES_MAX_MEM` in `$ES_HOME/bin/elasticsearch.in.sh`. You can otherwise set up `ES_HEAP_SIZE` that automatically initializes `ES_MIN_MEM` and `ES_MAX_MEM` to same `ES_HEAP_SIZE` provided value.

How it works...

The standard limit of file descriptors (max number of open files for a user) is typically 1024. When you store a lot of records in several indices, you run out of file descriptors very quickly, so your ElasticSearch server becomes unresponsive and your indices may become corrupted, losing your data.

Changing the limit to a very high number means that your ElasticSearch doesn't hit the maximum number of open files.

The other settings for the memory prevent ElasticSearch from swapping the memory and give a performance boost in the production environment. These settings are required because during indexing and searching, ElasticSearch creates and destroys a lot of objects in memory. This large number of create/destroy actions fragments the memory, reducing the performances. If you don't set `bootstrap.mlockall: true`, ElasticSearch dumps the memory on disk and defragments it back in memory. With this setting, the defragmentation step is done in memory with huge performance boost.

There's more...

This recipe covers two common errors that happen in production:

- "Too many open files", that can corrupt your indices and your data
- Slow performance in search and indexing due to garbage collector

Setting up different node types (advanced)

ElasticSearch is a native designed for the cloud, so when you need to release a production environment with a huge number of records and you need high availability and good performance, you need to aggregate more nodes in a cluster.

ElasticSearch allows defining different types of nodes to balance and improve overall performances.

Getting ready

You need a working ElasticSearch installation.

How to do it...

For an advance cluster setup, there are some parameters that must be configured to define different node types. These parameters are in `config/elasticsearch.yml` and they can be set with the following steps:

1. Setup if the node can be master or not:

   `node.master: true`

2. Setup if a node must contain data or not:

   `node.data: true`

How it works...

The working of different nodes types is as follows:

- `node.master`: This parameter defines that the node can become master for the cloud. The default value for this parameter is `true`.

  A master node is an arbiter for the cloud: it takes a decision about shard management, it keeps cluster status and it's the main controller of every index action.

- `node.data`: This allows you to store data in the node. The default value for this parameter is `true`. This node will be a worker that indexes and searches data.

Mixing these two parameters, it's possible to have different node types:

node.master	node.data	Node description
true	true	This is a default node. It can be master and contains data.
false	true	This node never becomes a master node, it only holds data. It can be defined as a "workhorse" of your cluster.
true	false	This node only serves as a master: to not store any data and to have free resources. This will be the "coordinator" of your cluster.
false	false	This node acts as a "search load balancer" (fetching data from nodes, aggregating results, and so on).

The more frequently used node type is the first one, but if you have a very big cluster or special needs, you can differentiate the scopes of your nodes to better serve searches and aggregations.

Downloading and Setting Up ElasticSearch

Installing a plugin

One of the main features of ElasticSearch is the possibility to extend it with plugins. Plugins extend ElasticSearch features and functionalities in several ways. There are two kinds of plugins:

- Site plugins: These are used to serve static contents in their entry points. They are mainly used to create management application: monitoring and administration of a cluster.
- Binary plugins: These are jar files that contain application code. They are used for:
    - Rivers (plugins that allow importing data from DBMS or other sources)
    - ScriptEngine (JavaScript, Python, Scala, and Ruby)
    - Custom analyzers and tokenizers
    - REST entry points
    - Supporting new protocols (Thrift, memcache, and so on)
    - Supporting new storages (Hadoop)

Getting ready

You need an installed working ElasticSearch server.

How to do it...

ElasticSearch provides a script for automatically downloading and installing plugins in bin/ directory, called `plugin`.

The steps required to install a plugin are:

1. Call the plugin install the ElasticSearch command with the plugin name reference.

    For installing an administrative interface for Elasticsearch, simply call:

    - on Linux/Mac:

        `plugin -install mobz/elasticsearch-head`

    - on Windows:

        `plugin.bat -install mobz/elasticsearch-head`

2. Check by starting the node that the plugin is correctly loaded.

The following screenshot shows the installation and the initialization of ElasticSearch server with the installed plugin.

```
(pyes)Alberto-MBP:elasticsearch alberto$ bin/plugin -install mobz/elasticsearch-head
-> Installing mobz/elasticsearch-head...
Trying https://github.com/mobz/elasticsearch-head/zipball/master... (assuming site plugin)
Downloading ............DONE
Identified as a _site plugin, moving to _site structure ...
Installed head
(pyes)Alberto-MBP:elasticsearch alberto$ bin/elasticsearch -f
[2013-05-01 15:51:30,427][INFO ][node                     ] [Devil-Slayer] {0.90.0}[15104]: initializing ...
[2013-05-01 15:51:30,433][INFO ][plugins                  ] [Devil-Slayer] loaded [], sites [head]
[2013-05-01 15:51:32,091][INFO ][node                     ] [Devil-Slayer] {0.90.0}[15104]: initialized
[2013-05-01 15:51:32,091][INFO ][node                     ] [Devil-Slayer] {0.90.0}[15104]: starting ...
[2013-05-01 15:51:32,168][INFO ][transport                ] [Devil-Slayer] bound_address {inet[/0:0:0:0:0:0:0:0:9301
]}, publish_address {inet[/192.168.1.46:9301]}
[2013-05-01 15:51:35,250][INFO ][cluster.service          ] [Devil-Slayer] detected_master [du Paris, Bennet][Ux2lz3
l2Q2iM_qtFgwDDoQ][inet[/192.168.1.46:9300]], added {[du Paris, Bennet][Ux2lz3l2Q2iM_qtFgwDDoQ][inet[/192.168.1.46:93
00]],}, reason: zen-disco-receive(from master [[du Paris, Bennet][Ux2lz3l2Q2iM_qtFgwDDoQ][inet[/192.168.1.46:9300]]])
)
[2013-05-01 15:51:35,275][INFO ][discovery                ] [Devil-Slayer] elasticsearch/upVx0siqTE2Ucw1GTbixpg
[2013-05-01 15:51:35,281][INFO ][http                     ] [Devil-Slayer] bound_address {inet[/0:0:0:0:0:0:0:0:9201
]}, publish_address {inet[/192.168.1.46:9201]}
[2013-05-01 15:51:35,281][INFO ][node                     ] [Devil-Slayer] {0.90.0}[15104]: started
```

Remember that a plugin installation requires to restart the ElasticSearch server.

How it works...

The `plugin[.bat]` script is a wrapper for ElasticSearch Plugin Manager. It can be used to install or remove a plugin with the `-remove` options.

To install a plugin, there are two kinds of options:

- Pass the URL of the plugin (zip archive) with the `-url` parameter, that is, `bin/plugin -url http://mywoderfulserve.com/plugins/awesome-plugin.zip`

- Use the `-install` parameter with the Github repository of the plugin.

    The install parameter, that must be given, is formatted in this way:

    `<username>/<repo>[/<version>]`

Downloading and Setting Up ElasticSearch

In the previous example:

- `<username>` was `mobz`
- `<repo>` was `elasticsearch-head`
- `<version>` was not given so master/trunk was used

During the install process, ElasticSearch Plugin Manager is able to:

- Download the plugin
- Create a plugins directory in `ES_HOME` if it's missing
- Unzip the plugin content in the plugin directory
- Remove temporary files

There's more...

There are some hints to remember while installing plugins. The first and most important is that the plugin must be certified for your current ElasticSearch version: some releases can break your plugins. Typically on the plugin developer page, there are the ElasticSearch versions supported by this plugin.

For example, if you look at the Python language plugin page (`https://github.com/elasticsearch/elasticsearch-lang-python`), you'll see a reference table similar to the following table:

Python Plugin	ElasticSearch
master	0.90 -> master
1.2.0	0.90 -> master
1.1.0	0.19 -> 0.20
1.0.0	0.18

You must choose the version working with your current ElasticSearch version.

Updating some plugins in a node environment can cause malfunction due to different plugin versions in different nodes. If you have a big cluster for safety, it's better to check the update in a separate environment to prevent problems.

Note that updating an ElasticSearch server could also break your custom binary plugins due to some internal API changes.

See also

- On the ElasticSearch website, there is an updated list of available plugins (http://www.elasticsearch.org/guide/reference/modules/plugins/).
- *Installing a plugin manually*

Installing a plugin manually

Sometimes your plugin is not available online or the standard installation fails, so you need to install your plugin manually.

Getting ready

You need an installed ElasticSearch server.

How to do it...

We assume that your plugin is named `awesome` and it's packed in a file called `awesome.zip`.

The steps required to execute a manually installed plugin are:

1. Copy your zip file in the plugins directory in your ElasticSearch home installation.
2. If the directory, named `plugins`, doesn't exist, create it.
3. Unzip the contents of the plugin in the plugins directory.
4. Remove the zip archive to clean up unused files.

How it works...

Every ElasticSearch plugin is contained in a directory (usually named as the plugin name).

If the plugin is a site one, the plugin should contain a directory called `_site`, which contains the static files that must be served by the server. If the plugin is a binary one, the plugin directory should be filled with one or more jar files.

When ElasticSearch starts, it scans the plugins directory and loads them. If a plugin is corrupted or broken, the server doesn't start.

Removing a plugin

You have installed some plugins and now you need to remove a plugin because it's not required. Removing an ElasticSearch plugin is easy to uninstall if everything goes right, otherwise you need to manually remove it.

This recipe covers both cases.

Getting ready

You need an installed working ElasticSearch server with an installed plugin. Stop the ElasticSearch server in order to safely remove the plugin.

How to do it...

ElasticSearch Plugin Manager, which comes with its script wrapper (plugin), provides command to automatically remove a plugin.

- On Linux and MacOSX, call:

  `plugin -remove mobz/elasticsearch-head`

  or

  `plugin -remove head`

- On Windows, call:

  `plugin.bat -remove mobz/elasticsearch-head`

  or

  `plugin.bat -remove head`

How it works...

The Plugin Manager `-remove` command tries to detect the correct name of the plugin and remove the directory of the installed plugin.

If there are undeletable files in your plugin directory (or a strange astronomical event that hits your server), the plugin script may fail: to manually remove a plugin, go in to the plugins directory and remove the directory with your plugin name.

Changing logging settings (advanced)

Standard logging settings work very well for general usage.

If you need to debug your ElasticSearch server or change how the logging works (that is, remoting send events), you need to change the `logging.yml` parameters.

Getting ready

You need an installed working ElasticSearch server.

How to do it...

In the config directory in your ElasticSearch, install the directory. There is a `logging.yml` file which controls the working settings. The steps required for changing the logging settings are:

1. To emit every kind of logging ElasticSearch has, you can change the root-level logging from `rootLogger: INFO, console, file` to `rootLogger: DEBUG, console, file`

2. Now if you start ElasticSearch from command-line (with `bin/elasticsearch -f`), you should see a lot of garbage:

```
[2013-05-04 11:50:44,641][DEBUG][index.shard.service      ] [Akhenaten] [text_index][4] scheduling optimizer / merger every 1s
[2013-05-04 11:50:44,641][DEBUG][cluster.service          ] [Akhenaten] processing [shard-started ([text_index][1], node[QX3BfRX7QuSQowUNMJTC-g], [P], s[INITIALIZING]), reason [after recovery from gateway]]: no change in cluster_state
[2013-05-04 11:50:44,641][DEBUG][cluster.action.shard     ] [Akhenaten] processing [reroute post shard-started ([text_index][2], node[QX3BfRX7QuSQowUNMJTC-g], [P], s[INITIALIZING]), reason [after recovery from gateway]]: execute
[2013-05-04 11:50:44,641][DEBUG][index.gateway            ] [Akhenaten] [text_index][4] recovery completed from local, took [4ms]
    index   : files           [3] with total_size [99b], took[1ms]
            : recovered_files [0] with total_size [0b]
            : reusing_files   [3] with total_size [99b]
    start   : took [3ms], check_index [0s]
    translog : number_of_operations [0], took [0s]
[2013-05-04 11:50:44,658][DEBUG][cluster.action.shard     ] [Akhenaten] sending shard started for [text_index][4], node[QX3BfRX7QuSQowUNMJTC-g], [P], s[INITIALIZING], reason [after recovery from gateway]
[2013-05-04 11:50:44,658][DEBUG][cluster.action.shard     ] [Akhenaten] received shard started for [text_index][4], node[QX3BfRX7QuSQowUNMJTC-g], [P], s[INITIALIZING], reason [after recovery from gateway]
[2013-05-04 11:50:44,659][DEBUG][cluster.service          ] [Akhenaten] processing [reroute post shard-started ([text_index][2], node[QX3BfRX7QuSQowUNMJTC-g], [P], s[INITIALIZING]), reason [after recovery from gateway]]: no change in cluster_state
[2013-05-04 11:50:44,659][DEBUG][cluster.service          ] [Akhenaten] processing [shard-started ([text_index][4], node[QX3BfRX7QuSQowUNMJTC-g], [P], s[INITIALIZING]), reason [after recovery from gateway]]: execute
[2013-05-04 11:50:44,659][DEBUG][cluster.action.shard     ] [Akhenaten] applying started shards [[text_index][4], node[QX3BfRX7QuSQowUNMJTC-g], [P], s[INITIALIZING]], reason [after recovery from gateway]
[2013-05-04 11:50:44,660][DEBUG][cluster.service          ] [Akhenaten] cluster state updated, version [6], source [shard-started ([text_index][4], node[QX3BfRX7QuSQowUNMJTC-g], [P], s[INITIALIZING]), reason [after recovery from gateway]]
[2013-05-04 11:50:44,660][DEBUG][river.cluster            ] [Akhenaten] processing [reroute_rivers_node_changed]: execute
[2013-05-04 11:50:44,660][DEBUG][river.cluster            ] [Akhenaten] processing [reroute_rivers_node_changed]: no change in cluster_state
[2013-05-04 11:50:44,661][DEBUG][cluster.service          ] [Akhenaten] processing [shard-started ([text_index][4], node[QX3BfRX7QuSQowUNMJTC-g], [P], s[INITIALIZING]), reason [after recovery from gateway]]: done applying updated cluster_state
[2013-05-04 11:50:44,661][DEBUG][cluster.service          ] [Akhenaten] processing [reroute post shard-started ([text_index][3], node[QX3BfRX7QuSQowUNMJTC-g], [P], s[INITIALIZING]), reason [after recovery from gateway]]: execute
[2013-05-04 11:50:44,662][DEBUG][cluster.service          ] [Akhenaten] processing [reroute post shard-started ([text_index][3], node[QX3BfRX7QuSQowUNMJTC-g], [P], s[INITIALIZING]), reason [after recovery from gateway]]: no change in cluster_state
[2013-05-04 11:50:44,662][DEBUG][cluster.service          ] [Akhenaten] processing [reroute post shard-started ([_percolator][0], node[QX3BfRX7QuSQowUNMJTC-g], [P], s[INITIALIZING]), reason [after recovery from gateway]]: execute
```

How it works...

ElasticSearch logging system is based on the `log4j` library (http://logging.apache.org/log4j/).

Changing the log level can be useful to check for bugs or understanding malfunctions due to bad configuration or strange plugin behaviors. A verbose log can be used from ElasticSearch community to cover the problems.

This is a powerful library to manage logging, covering all the functionalities of it (it's outside the scope of this book). If a user needs advanced usage, there are a lot of books and articles on the Internet for reference.

3
Managing Mapping

In this chapter, we will cover the following topics:

- Using explicit mapping creation
- Mapping base types
- Mapping arrays
- Mapping an object
- Mapping a document
- Using dynamic templates in document mapping
- Managing nested objects
- Managing a child document
- Mapping a multifield
- Mapping a GeoPoint field
- Mapping a GeoShape field
- Mapping an IP field
- Mapping attachment field
- Adding generic data to mapping
- Mapping different analyzers

Introduction

Mapping is the most important concept in ElasticSearch, as it defines how a search engine should process a document.

Search engines are mainly composed of two parts:

- **Indexing**: This action takes a document and stores/indexes/processes it in an index
- **Searching**: This action retrieves the data from the index

These two parts are strictly connected; an error in the indexing step leads to unwanted or missing search results.

ElasticSearch has explicit mapping on an index/type level. When indexing, if mapping is not provided, a default mapping is created, guessing the structure from the data fields that compose the document. Then, this new mapping is automatically propagated to all cluster nodes.

The default type mapping has sensible default values, but when you want to change their behavior you need to provide a new mapping definition.

In this chapter, we'll see all the possible types that compose the mappings.

Using explicit mapping creation

If we consider the index as a database in the SQL world, the mapping is similar to the table definition.

Getting ready

You need a working ElasticSearch cluster, a `test` index (refer to the *Creating an index* recipe in *Chapter 4, Standard Operations*), and basic knowledge of JSON.

How to do it...

For explicit mapping creation, we will perform the following steps:

1. You can explicitly create a mapping by adding a new element in ElasticSearch.

   On bash:

   ```
   #create an index
   curl -XPUT http://127.0.0.1:9200/test
   #{"ok":true,"acknowledged":true}


   #put a record
   curl -XPUT http://127.0.0.1:9200/test/mytype/1 -d '{"name":"Paul","age":35}'
   # {"ok":true,"_index":"test","_type":"mytype","_id":"1","_version":1}


   #get the mapping and pretty print it
   curl -XGET http://127.0.0.1:9200/test/mytype/_mapping?pretty=true
   ```

2. The result mapping auto-created by ElasticSearch should be as follows:

   ```
   {
     "mytype" : {
       "properties" : {
         "age" : {
           "type" : "long"
         },
         "name" : {
           "type" : "string"
         }
       }
     }
   }
   ```

How it works...

The first command line creates the `test` index, decides where to put the document and the type/mapping.

The second command line inserts a document in the index. We'll see the index creation and record indexing in the next chapter.

Managing Mapping

During the document index phase, ElasticSearch controls if the `mytype` type exists, otherwise, it creates an empty one.

ElasticSearch reads all the default properties for the field of the mapping and starts to process them as follows:

- If the field is already present in the mapping and the value of the field is valid, it processes the field
- If the field is already present in the mapping, but the value of the field is of a different type, it processes the field as a new type, migrating the previous field format in a multifield
- If the field is not present, it tries to auto-detect the type of field, it updates the mappings (or adding a new field mapping or converting the actual field in a multifield

There's more...

All the document types go in the same Lucene index, so there isn't full separation between them.

Every document has a unique identifier called UID, stored in the special `uid` field of the document. It's calculated by adding the type of document to the `_id` field.

The `_id` field can be provided at index time or can be assigned automatically by ElasticSearch if it's missing.

ElasticSearch transparently manages the propagation of a type mapping to all the nodes of a cluster, so that all the shards are aligned to processes of that particular type.

Mapping base types

Using explicit mapping allows faster insertion of the data using schema-less approach. Thus to achieve better results and performance in indexing, it's required to manually define mapping.

Fine-tuning mapping brings some advantages such as:

- Reducing the index size on disk
- Indexing only interesting fields (general speed up)
- Precooking data for faster search or real-time analytics (such as facets)

ElasticSearch allows using base fields with a wide range of configurations.

Getting ready

You need a working ElasticSearch cluster and a `test` index where to put mappings.

How to do it...

Let's use a semi real-world example of a shop order for our eBay-like shop.

We initially define an order such as:

Name	Type	Description
`id`	Identifier	Order identifier
`date`	Date (time)	Date of order
`customer_id`	ID reference	Customer ID reference
`name`	String	Name of the item
`quantity`	Integer	Number of items
`vat`	Double	VAT for item
`sent`	Boolean	The order was sent

Our order record must be converted in an ES mapping.

```
{
  "order" : {
    "properties" : {
      "id" : {"type" : "string", "store" : "yes" ,
      "index":"not_analyzed"},
      "date" : {"type" : "date", "store" : "no" ,
      "index":"not_analyzed"},
      "customer_id" : {"type" : "string", "store" : "yes" ,
      "index":"not_analyzed"},
      "sent" : {"type" : "boolean", "index":"not_analyzed"},
      "name" : {"type" : "string",  "index":"analyzed"},
      "quantity" : {"type" : "integer", "index":"not_analyzed"},
      "vat" : {"type" : "double", "index":"no"}
    }
  }
}
```

Now, the mapping is ready to be added in the index. We'll see how to do it in the *Putting a mapping in an index* recipe in *Chapter 4, Standard Operations*.

Managing Mapping

How it works...

The standard field type must be mapped in the correct ElasticSearch field type adding options about how the field must be indexed.

The next table is a reference of the mapping types:

Type	ES type	Description
String, VarChar, text	string	A text field: that is, "a nice text", "CODE0011"
Integer	integer	An integer (32-bit): that is, 1, 2, 3, 4
Long	long	A long value (64-bit)
Float	float	A floating point number (32-bit): that is, 1.2, 4, 5
Double	double	A floating point number (64-bit)
Boolean	boolean	A Boolean value: that is true or false
Date/Datetime	date	A date or datetime value, that is, 2013-12-25, 2013-12-25T22:21:20
Bytes/binary	binary	Some bytes used for binary data, such as a file or a stream of bytes.

Depending on the data type, it's possible to give hints to ElasticSearch on how to process the field for better management. The most used options are as follows:

- `store` (defaults to `no`): This marks that this field has to be stored in a separate index fragment for fast retrieving. Storing a field consumes disk space, but reduces computation if you need to extract it from a document (that is, in scripting and faceting). The possible values for the option are `no` and `yes`.

 Stored fields are faster than others in faceting.

- `index` (defaults to `analyzed`): This configures the field to be indexed. Possible values for this parameter are as follows:
    - `no`: This field is not indexed at all. It is useful to put data that is not searchable.
    - `analyzed`: This field is analyzed with the configured analyzer.
    - `not_analyzed`: This field is processed and indexed, but without being changed by an analyzer.

- `null_value`: defines a default value if the field is missing.
- `boost` (defaults to `1.0`): This is used to change the importance of a field.
- `index_analyzer` (defaults to `null`): This defines an analyzer to be used to process this field. If not defined, the analyzer of the parent object is used.
- `search_analyzer` (defaults to `null`): This defines an analyzer to be used during the search. If not defined, the analyzer of the parent object is used.
- `include_in_all` (defaults to `true`): This marks the current field to be indexed in the special `all` field (a field that contains the text of all fields).

There's more...

In this recipe, we have seen the most used options for the core types, but there are many other options that are useful for borderline usage.

An important parameter, available only for string mapping, is the term vector (a vector of terms that compose a string. Refer to the Lucene documentation for further details at http://lucene.apache.org/core/4_4_0/core/org/apache/lucene/index/Terms.html.):

- `no`: This is a default value and it skips the term vector
- `yes`: This stores the term vector
- `with_offsets`: This stores the term vector with token offset (start and end position in a block of characters)
- `with_positions`: This stores the position of the token in the term vector
- `with_positions_offsets`: This stores all the term vector data

> Term vectors allow fast highlighting, but consume disk space due to the storage of additional text information. It's best practice to be active only in fields that require highlighting, such as title or document content.

See also

- The *Mapping different analyzers* recipe shows alternative analyzers to the standard one.

Managing Mapping

Mapping arrays

Arrays or multi-value fields are very common in data models, but not natively supported in traditional SQL solutions.

In SQL, multi-value fields require the creation of accessory tables that must be joined to gather all the values, resulting in poor performance when the cardinality of records is huge.

Getting ready

You need a working ElasticSearch cluster.

How to do it...

Every field is automatically managed as an array. For example, to store tags for a document, the mapping will be as shown in the following code snippet:

```
{
  "document" : {
    "properties" : {
      "name" : {"type" : "string",  "index":"analyzed"},
      "tag" : {"type" : "string", "store" : "yes" ,
      "index":"not_analyzed"},

    }
  }
}
```

This mapping is valid for indexing the following documents:

```
{"name": "document1", "tag": "awesome"}
```

and

```
{"name": "document2", "tag": ["cool", "awesome", "amazing"] }
```

How it works...

ElasticSearch transparently manages the array; there is no difference if you declare a single value or a multi-value due to its Lucene core nature.

Chapter 3

Multiple values for fields are managed in Lucene, adding them to a document with the same field name (index_name in ElasticSearch). If the `index_name` field is not defined in the mapping, it is taken from the name of the fields. It can also be set to other values for custom behaviors, such as renaming a field at indexing level or merging two or more JSON fields in a single Lucene field. Redefining the `index_name` field must be done with caution as it also affects the search.

For people coming from SQL, this behavior may seem quite strange, but this is a key point in the NoSQL world as it reduces the need for joint query and creating different tables to manage multiple values.

An array of embedded objects has the same behavior as that of simple fields.

Mapping an object

The object is the base structure (also called as record in SQL). ElasticSearch extends the traditional use of object, allowing recursive embedded objects.

Getting ready

You will require a working ElasticSearch cluster.

How to do it...

We can rewrite the order mapping of the *Mapping base types* recipe using an array of items as shown in the following code:

```
{
  "order" : {
    "properties" : {
      "id" : {"type" : "string",
        "store" : "yes", "index":"not_analyzed"},
      "date" : {"type" : "date", "store" : "no",
        "index":"not_analyzed"},
      "customer_id" : {"type" : "string", "store" : "yes",
        "index":"not_analyzed"},
      "sent" : {"type" : "boolean", "store" : "no",
        "index":"not_analyzed"},
      "item" : {
```

Managing Mapping

```
        "type" : "object",
        "properties" : {
          "name" : {"type" : "string", "store" : "no",
            "index":"analyzed"},
          "quantity" : {"type" : "integer",
            "store" : "no",
            "index":"not_analyzed"},
          "vat" : {"type" : "double", "store" : "no",
            "index":"not_analyzed"}
        }
      }
    }
  }
}
```

How it works...

ElasticSearch speaks native JSON. So, every complex JSON structure can be mapped into it.

When ElasticSearch is parsing an object type, it tries to extract fields and processes them as its defined mapping; otherwise, it learns the structure of the object using reflection.

The most important properties for an object are as follows:

- `properties`: This is a collection of fields or objects (we can consider them as columns in the SQL world).
- `enabled` (defaults to `true` if the object should be processed): If this is set to `false`, the data contained in the object is not indexed and it cannot be searched.
- `dynamic` (defaults to `true`): This property allows ElasticSearch to add new field names to the object using reflection on values of inserted data. If it's set to `false`, when you try to index an object contained in a new field type, it'll be rejected silently. If it's set to `strict`, when a new field type is present in the object an error is raised skipping the index process. Control dynamic parameters allows being safe about change in the document structure.
- `include_in_all` (defaults to `true`): This property adds the object values to the special `_all` field (used to aggregate the text of all document fields).

The most used property is `properties` that allows mapping the fields of the object in ElasticSearch fields.

Disabling the indexing part of a document reduces the index size and allows storing data that must not be searched.

There's more...

Also, there are properties that are rarely used, such as `index_name` and `path`, which changes the how Lucene index the object, modifying the inner structure of an index.

See also

- There are special objects that are described in the *Mapping a document*, *Managing a child document*, and *Mapping a nested document* recipes.

Mapping a document

The document, also referred to as root object, has special parameters to control its behavior used to mainly internally perform special processing.

In this recipe we'll see special fields and how to use them.

Getting ready

You need a working ElasticSearch cluster.

How to do it...

We can extend the preceding order example, adding some of the special fields. For example:

```
{
  "order": {
    "_uid": {
      "store": "yes"
    },
    "_id": {
      "path": "order_id"
    },
    "_type": {
      "store": "yes"
    },
    "_source": {
      "store": "yes"
    },
    "_all": {
      "enable": false
    },
```

Managing Mapping

```
"_analyzer": {
  "path": "analyzer_field"
},
"_boost": {
  "null_value": 1.0
},
"_routing": {
  "path": "customer_id",
  "required": true
},
"_index": {
  "enabled": true
},
"_size": {
  "enabled": true,
  "store": "yes"
},
"_timestamp": {
  "enabled": true,
  "store": "yes",
  "path": "date"
},
"_ttl": {
  "enabled": true,
  "default": "3y"
},
"properties": {
  "order_id": {
    "type": "string",
    "store": "yes",
    "index": "not_analyzed"
  },
"date": {
  "type": "date",
  "store": "no",
  "index": "not_analyzed"
},
"analyzer_field": {
  "type": "string",
  "store": "yes",
  "index": "not_analyzed"
},
```

```
      "customer_id": {
        "type": "string",
        "store": "yes",
        "index": "not_analyzed"
      },
      "customer_ip": {
        "type": "ip",
        "store": "yes",
        "index": "yes"
      },
      "customer_location": {
        "type": "geo_point",
        "store": "yes"
      },
      "sent": {
        "type": "boolean",
        "store": "no",
        "index": "not_analyzed"
      }
    }
  }
}
```

How it works...

Every special field has its own parameters and a special meaning, such as:

- `_uid`: This controls the storage of a unique ID, a join between the type and ID of the document. The `_uid` value of a document is unique in the whole index.

- `_id` (defaults to not indexed and not stored): This allows indexing only the id part of the document. It can be associated with a `path` that will be used to extract the ID from the source of the document as shown in the following code:

  ```
  "_id" : {
    "path" : "order_id"
  },
  ```

- `_type` (defaults to indexed and not stored): This allows indexing of type of the document.

- `_index` (defaults to `enabled=false`): This determines whether or not the index should be stored. It can be enabled by setting the `enabled` parameter to `true`.

- `_boost` (defaults to `null_value=1.0`): This controls the boost level of the document. It can be overridden in the `boost` parameter for the field.

Managing Mapping

- _size (defaults to enabled=false): This controls if it stores the size of the source record.
- _timestamp (defaults to enabled=false): This automatically enables the indexing of the document timestamp. If given a parameter path, it can be extracted by the source of document and used. It can be queried as a standard datetime.
- _ttl (defaults to enabled=false): This sets the expiry time of the document. When a document expires, it will be removed from the index. It allows defining an optional default parameter, to provide a default value to the type level.
- _all (defaults to enabled=true): This controls the creation of all fields (a special field that aggregates all the text of all the document fields). It's CPU and storage consumer; so if it is not required, it is better to disable it.
- _source (defaults to enabled=true): This controls the storage of the document source. Storing the source, is very useful, but it's a storage overhead, so it is not required. Thus it's better to turn it off.
- _parent: This defines the parent document (refer to the *Mapping a child document* recipe).
- _routing: This controls in which shard the document should be stored. It supports additional parameters such as:
    - path: This provides a field to be used for routing (especially, customer_id in the example)
    - required (true/false): This forces the presence of the routing value, raising an exception if not provided
- _analyzer: This allows defining a document field that contains the name of the analyzer to be used for fields that do not explicitly define an analyzer or an index_analyzer parameter.

The power to control how to index and processing a document is very important and allows resolution of issues related to complex data types.

Every special field has parameters to set a particular configuration and some of their behavior could change in different releases of ElasticSearch.

See also

- *Using dynamic templates in document mapping*
- *Putting a mapping in an index* in *Chapter 4, Standard Operations*

Using dynamic templates in document mapping

In the *Using explicit mapping creation* recipe, we saw how ElasticSearch is able to guess the field type using reflection. In this recipe we'll see how to help improve its guessing capabilities.

Getting ready

You need a working ElasticSearch cluster.

How to do it...

We can extend the previous mapping adding document-related settings:

```
{
  "order" : {
    "index_analyzer":"standard",
    "search_analyzer":"standard",
    "dynamic_date_formats":["yyyy-MM-dd", "dd-MM-yyyy"],
    "date_detection":true,
    "numeric_detection":true,
    "dynamic_templates":[
    {"template1":{
      "match":"*",
      "match_mapping_type":"long",
      "mapping":{"type":" {dynamic_type}",
      "store":true}
    }}
    ],
    "properties" : {…}
  }
}
```

Managing Mapping

How it works...

The root object (document) controls the behavior of its fields and all its children object fields.

In the document mapping we can define:

- `index_analyzer`: This defines the analyzer to be used for indexing within this document. If `index_analyzer` is not defined in a field, this is considered as default.
- `search_analyzer`: This defines the analyzer to be used for searching. If a field doesn't define an analyzer, `search_analyzer` of the document, if available, is taken.

> If you need to set `index_analyzer` and `search_analyzer` with the same value, you can use the `analyzer` property.

- `date_detection` (defaults to `true`): This enables the extraction of a date from a string.
- `dynamic_date_formats`: This is a list of valid date formats. It is used if `date_detection` is active.
- `numeric_detection` (defaults to `false`): This enables the conversion of strings to numbers if it is possible.
- `dynamic_templates`: This list of templates is used to change the explicit mapping. If one of these templates is matched, the rules defined in it are used to build the final mapping.

A dynamic template is composed of two parts: the matcher and the mapping one.

To match a field for activating the template, several types of matchers are available, such as:

- `match`: This allows defining a match on the field name. The expression is a standard GLOB.
- `unmatch` (optional): This allows defining the expression to be used to exclude matches.
- `match_mapping_type` (optional): This controls the type of matched fields. For example, string, integer, and so on.
- `path_match` (optional): This allows matching the dynamic template against the full dot notation of the field. For example, `obj1.*.value`.
- `path_unmatch` (optional): This does the opposite of `path_match`, excluding the matched fields.
- `match_pattern` (optional): This allows switching the matchers to regex (regular expression); otherwise, the glob pattern match is used.

Chapter 3

The dynamic template mapping part is a standard one, but with the ability to use special placeholders such as:

- `{name}`: This will be replaced with the actual dynamic field name
- `{dynamic_type}`: This will be replaced with the type of the matched field

> The order of dynamic templates is very important, only the first one that is matched is executed. It is good practice to order first the ones with more strict rules and then the other ones.

There's more...

The dynamic template is very handy when you need to set a mapping configuration to all the fields. This action can be done by adding a dynamic template similar to the following code snippet:

```
"dynamic_templates" : [
  {
    "store_generic" : {
      "match" : "*",
      "mapping" : {
        "store" : "yes"
      }
    }
  }
]
```

In this example, all the new fields, which will be added with the explicit mapping, will be stored.

See also

- *Using explicit mapping creation*
- *Mapping a document*
- Glob pattern at `http://en.wikipedia.org/wiki/Glob_pattern`

Managing nested objects

There is a special type of embedded object: the nested one. This resolves a problem related to the Lucene indexing architecture, in which all the fields of embedded objects are viewed as a single object, because during search it is not possible to distinguish values between different embedded objects in the same multi-valued array.

If we consider the previous order example, it's not possible to disguise an item name and its quantity with the same query. We need to index them in different elements and when we join them. This entire trip is managed by nested objects and nested queries.

Getting ready

You need a working ElasticSearch cluster.

How to do it...

A nested object is defined as the standard object with the nested type.

From the example of the *Mapping an object* recipe, we can change the type from `object` to `nested` as shown in the following code:

```
{
  "order" : {
    "properties" : {
      "id" : {"type" : "string",
      "store" : "yes", "index":"not_analyzed"},
      "date" : {"type" : "date", "store" : "no",
      "index":"not_analyzed"},
      "customer_id" : {"type" : "string", "store" : "yes",
      "index":"not_analyzed"},
      "sent" : {"type" : "boolean", "store" : "no",
      "index":"not_analyzed"},
      "item" : {
        "type" : "nested",
        "properties" : {
          "name" : {"type" : "string", "store" : "no",
          "index":"analyzed"},
          "quantity" : {"type" : "integer",
            "store" : "no",
            "index":"not_analyzed"},
          "vat" : {"type" : "double", "store" : "no",
            "index":"not_analyzed"}
        }
      }
    }
  }
}
```

How it works...

When a document is indexed and if an embedded object is marked as nested, it's extracted by the original document and indexed in a new external document.

In the above example, we have reused the mapping of the *Mapping an object recipe*, but we have changed the type of the item from `object` to `nested`. No other required action must be taken to convert an embedded object to a nested object.

The nested objects are special Lucene documents that are saved in the same block of data of its parent. This approach allows fast joining with the parent document.

Nested objects are not searchable with standard queries, but only with the nested one. They are not shown in standard query results.

The lives of nested objects are related to their parents: deleting/updating a parent, automatically deletes/updates all nested children. Changing the parent means ElasticSearch will do the following:

- Delete the old document
- Reindex the old document with less nested data
- Delete the new document
- Reindex the new document with the new nested data

There's more...

Sometimes it is required to propagate information of the nested objects to their parent or root objects, mainly to build simpler queries about their parents. To achieve this goal, there are two special properties of the nested objects, as follows:

- `include_in_parent`: This allows automatic addition of the nested fields to the immediate parent
- `include_in_root`: This adds the nested object fields to the root object

These settings add data replication, but they reduce the complexity of some queries, thus improving performance.

See also

- *Managing a child document*

Managing Mapping

Managing a child document

In the previous recipe we have seen how it's possible to manage relations between objects with the nested object type. The disadvantage of nested objects is their dependence to their parent. If you need to change the value of a nested object, you need to reindex the parent (this brings to a potential performance overhead if the nested objects change too quickly). To solve this problem, ElasticSearch allows defined child documents.

Getting ready

You need a working ElasticSearch cluster.

How to do it...

We can modify the order example indexing the items as separated child documents.

We need to extract the item object and create a new type document item with the `_parent` property set.

```
{
  "order": {
    "properties": {
      "id": {
        "type": "string",
        "store": "yes",
        "index": "not_analyzed"
      },
      "date": {
        "type": "date",
        "store": "no",
        "index": "not_analyzed"
      },
      "customer_id": {
        "type": "string",
        "store": "yes",
        "index": "not_analyzed"
      },
      "sent": {
        "type": "boolean",
        "store": "no",
        "index": "not_analyzed"
      }
    }
  }
```

```
    },
      "item": {
        "_parent": {
          "type": "order"
        },
      "type": "object",
      "properties": {
        "name": {
          "type": "string",
          "store": "no",
          "index": "analyzed"
        },
        "quantity": {
          "type": "integer",
          "store": "no",
          "index": "not_analyzed"
        },
        "vat": {
          "type": "double",
          "store": "no",
          "index": "not_analyzed"
        }
      }
    }
}
```

The above mapping is similar to the ones in the previous recipe. The item object is extracted from the order (in the previous example it was nested) and added as a new mapping. The only difference is that `"type": "nested"` has become `"type": "object"` (it can be omitted), and the new special field, `_parent` that defines the parent/child relation.

How it works...

The child object is a standard root object (document) with an extra `_parent` property defined.

The `type` property of `_parent` refers to the type of the parent document.

The child document must be indexed in the same shard of parent, so that when indexed, an extra parameter must be passed: the parent ID. (We'll see how to do it in the next chapter.)

A child document doesn't require reindexing the parent document when we want to change its values. So it's fast in indexing, reindexing (updating), and deleting.

Managing Mapping

There's more...

In ElasticSearch we have different ways to manage relations between objects:

- **Embedding with type=object**: This is explicitly managed by ElasticSearch. It considers embedding as a part of the main document. It's fast, but you need to reindex the main document for changing a value of the embedded object.
- **Nesting with type=nested**: This allows more accurate search and filtering of parent using nested query on children. Everything works as for embedded object except for query.
- **External children documents**: In this way, children are external documents, with a `_parent` property to bind them to the parent. They must be indexed in the same shard of the parent. The join with the parent is a bit slower than the nested one, because the nested objects are in the same data block of the parent in the Lucene index and they are loaded with the parent, otherwise, the child documents require more read operations.

Choosing how to model the relation from objects depends on your application scenario.

Also, there is another approach that can be used, but on big data documents, bringing poor performances—its decoupling join relation. You do the join query in two steps: first you collect the ID of the children/other documents and then you search them in a field of their parent.

See also

- The *Using has_child query/filter*, *Using top_children query*, and *Using has_parent query/filter* recipes in *Chapter 5, Search, Queries, and Filters*, for more details on child/parent queries

Mapping a multifield

Often, a field must be processed with several core types or in different ways. For example, a string field must be processed as `analyzed` for search and as `not_analyzed` for sorting. To do this, we need to define a multifield.

Multifield is a very powerful feature of mapping, because it allows the use of the same field in different ways.

Getting ready

You need a working ElasticSearch cluster.

Chapter 3

How to do it...

To define a multifield we need to do the following:

1. Use `multi_field` as type.
2. Define a dictionary containing the subfields called `fields`. The subfield with the same name of parent field is the default one.

If we consider the item of our order example, we can index the name as `multi_field` as shown in the following code:

```
"name": {
  "type": "multi_field",
  "fields": {
    "name": {
       "type": "string",
       "index": "not_analyzed"
    },
    "tk": {
      "type": "string",
      "index": "analyzed"
    },
    "code": {
      "type": "string",
      "index": "analyzed",
      "analyzer": "code_analyzer"
    }
  }
},
```

If we already have a mapping stored in ElasticSearch, and if we want to upgrade the field in a multifield, it's enough to save a new mapping with a different type and ElasticSearch provides automatic merging.

How it works...

During indexing, when ElasticSearch processes a `type` field as `multi_field`, it reprocesses the same field for every subfield defined in the mapping.

To access the subfields of `multi_field`, we have a new path built on the base field plus the subfield name. If we consider the preceding example, we have:

- `name`: This points to default multifield subfield (the `not_analyzed` one)
- `name.tk`: This points to the standard analyzed (tokenized) field
- `name.code`: This points to a field analyzed with a code extractor analyzer

Managing Mapping

If you notice in the preceding example, we have changed the analyzer to introduce a code extractor analyzer that allows extraction of the item code from a string.

Using the multifield if we index a string, such as "Good item to buy - ABC1234", we'll have:

- `name` = "Good item to buy - ABC1234" (useful for sorting)
- `name.tk`=["good", "item", "to", "buy", "abc1234"] (useful for searching)
- `name.code` = ["ABC1234"] (useful for searching and faceting)

There's more...

MultiField is very useful in data processing, because it allows you to define several ways to process a field data.

For example, if we are working for document content, we can define them as subfield analyzers to extract names, places, date/time, geo location, and so on. The fields of a multifield are standard core type fields; we can do every process we want on them, such as search, filter, facet, and scripting.

See also

- *Mapping different analyzers*

Mapping a GeoPoint field

ElasticSearch natively supports the use of geolocation types—special types that allow localization of your document in geographic coordinate (latitude and longitude) around the world.

There are two main types used in the geographic world: the point and the shape. In this recipe we'll see the GeoPoint—the base element of a geolocation.

Getting ready

You need a working ElasticSearch cluster.

How to do it...

The type of the field must be set to `geo_point` to define a GeoPoint.

We can extend the order example adding a new field that stores the location of a customer. The following code will be the result:

```
{
  "order": {
    "properties": {
      "id": {
        "type": "string",
        "store": "yes",
        "index": "not_analyzed"
      },
      "date": {
        "type": "date",
        "store": "no",
        "index": "not_analyzed"
      },
      "customer_id": {
        "type": "string",
        "store": "yes",
        "index": "not_analyzed"
      },
      "customer_ip": {
        "type": "ip",
        "store": "yes",
        "index": "yes"
      },
      "customer_location": {
        "type": "geo_point",
        "store": "yes"
      },
      "sent": {
        "type": "boolean",
        "store": "no",
        "index": "not_analyzed"
      }
    }
  }
}
```

Managing Mapping

How it works...

When ElasticSearch indexes a document with a GeoPoint field (such as lat, lon), it processes the latitude and longitude coordinates and creates a special accessory field data to fast query on these coordinates.

It depends on properties, given latitude and a longitude, it's possible to compute a geohash value (http://en.wikipedia.org/wiki/Geohash) and the index process also optimizes these values for special computation such as distance, ranges, and in-shape match.

GeoPoint has special parameters that allow storage of additional geographic data:

- lat_lon (defaults to false): This allows storing the latitude and longitude as a .lat and .lon field. Storing these values improves the performance in many memory algorithms used in distance and in-shape calculus.

   It makes sense to be stored only if there is a single point value for field, for multiple values.

- geohash (defaults to false): This allows storing the computed geohash value.
- geohash_precision (defaults to 12): This defines the precision to be used in geohash calculus.

For example, given a GeoPoint value [45.61752, 9.08363], it will store:

- customer_location = "45.61752, 9.08363"
- customer_location.lat = 45.61752
- customer_location.lon = 9.08363
- customer_location.geohash = "u0n7w8qmrfj"

There's more...

GeoPoint is a special type and can accept several formats as input:

- lat and lon as properties:

  ```
  "customer_location": {
      "lat": 45.61752,
      "lon": 9.08363
  },
  ```

- lat and lon as strings:

  ```
  "customer_location": "45.61752,9.08363",
  ```

- Geohash string

  ```
  "customer_location": "u0n7w8qmrfj",
  ```

- As a GeoJSON array (note in it that `lat` and `lon` are reversed)

  ```
  "customer_location": [9.08363, 45.61752]
  ```

Mapping a GeoShape field

An extension to the concept of point is the shape. ElasticSearch provides a type that facilitates the management of arbitrary polygons—the GeoShape.

Getting ready

You need a working ElasticSearch cluster with Spatial4J (V0.3) and JTS (v1.12) in the classpath to use this type.

How to do it...

To map a `geo_shape` type a user must explicitly provide some parameters:

- `tree` (defaults to `geohash`): It's the name of the `PrefixTree` implementation; *geohash* for `GeohashPrefixTree` and *quadtree* for `QuadPrefixTree`.
- `precision`: It's used instead of `tree_levels` to provide a more human value to be used in the tree level. The precision number can be followed by the unit, that is, 10 m, 10 km, 10 miles, and so on.
- `tree_levels`: It's the maximum number of layers to be used in the `PrefixTree`.
- `distance_error_pct` (defaults to `0,025%` and max `0,5%`): It sets the maximum error allowed in `PrefixTree`.

The `customer_location` mapping that we have seen in the previous recipe using `geo_shape`, will be:

```
"customer_location": {
    "type": "geo_shape",
    "tree": "quadtree",
    "precision": "1m"
},
```

Managing Mapping

How it works...

When a shape is indexed or searched internally, a path tree is created and used.

A path tree is a list of terms that contains geographic information, computed to improve performance in evaluating geo calculus.

The path tree also depends on the shape type: point, linestring, polygon, multipoint, and multipolygon.

See also

- To fully understand the logic behind the GeoShape, visit the ElasticSearch page about GeoShape, and the sites of the libraries used for geographic calculus (https://github.com/spatial4j/spatial4j and http://www.vividsolutions.com/jts/jtshome.htm).

Mapping an IP field

ElasticSearch is used in a lot of networking systems to collect and search logs, such as Kibana (http://kibana.org/) and LogStash (http://logstash.net/). To improve search in these scenarios, it provides the IPv4 type that can be used to store an IP address in an optimized way.

Getting ready

You need a working ElasticSearch cluster.

How to do it...

You need to define the type of the field that contains IP address as `"ip"`.

Using the above order example we can extend it by adding the customer IP address with the following code snippet:

```
"customer_ip": {
  "type": "ip",
  "store": "yes",
  "index": "yes"
}
```

The IP must be in the standard point notation form, as follows:

```
"customer_ip":"19.18.200.201"
```

How it works...

When ElasticSearch is processing a document, if a field is an IP one, it tries to convert its value to a numerical form and generates tokens for fast-value searching.

The IP has the following special properties:

- `index` (defaults to `yes`): This defines if the field must be indexed. Otherwise `no` must be used.
- `precision_step`: (defaults to `4`): This defines how many terms must be generated for its original value.

The other properties (`store`, `boot`, `null_value`, and `include_in_all`) work as other base types.

The advantages of using IP fields versus strings are its faster speed in every range and filter and lower resources usage (disk and memory).

Mapping an attachment field

ElasticSearch allows extending its core types to cover new requirements with native plugins that provide new mapping types. A most used custom field type is the attachment one.

It allows indexing and searching the contents of common documental files, that is, Microsoft office formats, open document formats, PDF, ePub, and many others.

Getting ready

You need a working ElasticSearch cluster with the attachment plugin (`https://github.com/elasticsearch/elasticsearch-mapper-attachments`) installed.

It can be installed from the command line with the following command:

```
bin/plugin -install elasticsearch/elasticsearch-mapper-attachments/1.9.0
```

The plugin version is related to the current ElasticSearch version. Check the GitHub page for further details.

How to do it...

To map a field as an attachment, it's necessary to set the `type` to `attachment`.

Internally the attachment field is a multifield that takes some binary data (encoded base64).

Managing Mapping

If we want to create a mapping for an e-mail storing attachment, it will be:

```
{
  "email": {
    "properties": {
      "sender": {
        "type": "string",
        "store": "yes",
        "index": "not_analyzed"
      },
      "date": {
        "type": "date",
        "store": "no",
        "index": "not_analyzed"
      },
      "document": {
        "type": "attachment",
        "fields": {
          "file": {
            "store": "yes",
            "index": "analyzed"
          },
          "date": {
            "store": "yes"
          },
          "author": {
            "store": "yes"
          },
          "keywords": {
            "store": "yes"
          },
          "content_type": {
            "store": "yes"
          },
          "title": {
            "store": "yes"
          }
        }
      }
    }
  }
}
```

How it works...

The attachment plugin internally uses Apache Tika—a library specialized in text extraction from documents. The list of supported document types is available in the Apache Tika website (http://tika.apache.org/1.3/formats.html), but it covers all common file types.

The attachment type field receives a base64 binary stream that is processed by Tika metadata and text extractor. The field can be seen as a multifield that stores different contents in its subfields:

- `file`: This stores the content of the file
- `date`: This stores the file creation data, extracted by Tika metadata
- `author`: This stores the file author, extracted by Tika metadata
- `keywords`: This stores the file keywords, extracted by Tika metadata
- `content_type`: This stores the file content type
- `title`: This stores the file title, extracted by Tika metadata

> Default settings for attachment plugins are to extract 100000 chars. This value can be changed by globally setting the index settings `index.mappings.attachment.indexed_chars` or when indexing the element passing a value to the `_indexed_chars` property.

There's more...

The attachment type is an example of how it's possible to extend ElasticSearch with its custom types. This is very important when we are managing different types of data that needs custom operations of cooking to be delivered.

The attachment plugin is very useful for indexing documents, e-mails and every type of an unstructured document. A good example of an application that uses it is ScrutMyDocs (http://www.scrutmydocs.org/).

See also

- The official Attachment plugin page available at https://github.com/elasticsearch/elasticsearch-mapper-attachments
- The Tika library page available at http://tika.apache.org
- ScrutMyDocs website available at http://www.scrutmydocs.org/

Managing Mapping

Adding generic data to mapping

Sometimes when we are working with our mapping, it is necessary to store some additional data to be used for display purpose, ORM facilities, permissions, or simply to track them in the mapping.

ElasticSearch allows storing every kind of JSON data we want in the mapping, with the special `_meta` field.

Getting ready

You need a working ElasticSearch cluster

How to do it...

The `_meta` mapping field can be populated with every data we want. For example:

```
{
  "order": {
    "_meta": {
      "attr1": ["value1", "value2"],
      "attr2": {
      "attr3": "value3"
      }
    }
  }
}
```

How it works...

When ElasticSearch processes a mapping and finds a `_meta` field, it stores it in the global mapping status aligned in all the cluster nodes.

The `_meta` field is only for storing purposes; it's not indexed and searchable.

It can be used for:

- Storing the metadata type
- Storing **Object Relational Mapping** (**ORM**) related information
- Storing type permission information
- Storing extra type information (that is, icon filename used to display the type)
- Storing template parts for rendering web interfaces

Mapping different analyzers

In the previous recipes, we have seen how to map different fields and objects in ElasticSearch and we have described how it's easy to change the standard analyzer with the `analyzer`, `index_analyzer`, and `search_analyzer` properties.

Getting ready

You need a working ElasticSearch cluster.

How to do it...

Every core type field allows specifying a custom analyzer for indexing and for searching as field parameters.

For example, if we want that the name field uses a standard analyzer for indexing and a simple analyzer for searching, the mapping will be as follows:

```
{
    "name": {
        "type": "string",
        "index": "analyzed",
        "index_analyzer": "standard",
        "search_analyzer": "simple"
    }
}
```

How it works...

The concept of analyzer comes from Lucene (the core of ElasticSearch). An analyzer is a Lucene element that is composed of a tokenizer, that splits a text in tokens, and one or more token filters that perform token manipulation, such as lowercasing, normalization, removing stopwords, and stemming.

During indexing phase, when ElasticSearch processes a field that must be indexed, an analyzer is chosen, looking first if defined in the field (`index_analyzer`), then in the document, and in the index.

 Choosing the correct analyzer is essential to have good results during query phase.

Managing Mapping

ElasticSearch provides several analyzers in its standard installation. In the following table, the most common ones are described.

Name	Description
standard	It divides a text using a standard tokenizer; normalize tokens, lowercase tokens, and removes unwanted tokens.
simple	It divides text at non-letter and converts them to lowercase.
whitespace	It divides text at spaces.
stop	It processes the text with standard analyzer and then applies custom stopwords.
keyword	It considers the all text as a token.
pattern	It divides the text using a regular expression.
snowball	It works as a standard analyzer plus a stemming at the end of the processing.

For special language purposes, ElasticSearch supports a set of analyzers aimed at analyzing specific language text, such as Arabic, Armenian, Basque, Brazilian, Bulgarian, Catalan, Chinese, Cjk, Czech, Danish, Dutch, English, Finnish, French, Galician, German, Greek, Hindi, Hungarian, Indonesian, Italian, Norwegian, Persian, Portuguese, Romanian, Russian, Spanish, Swedish, Turkish, and Thai.

See also

There are several ElasticSearch plugins that extend the list of available analyzers.

Looking at `GitHub.com`, the most famous ones are as follows:

- ICU Analysis Plugin (`https://github.com/elasticsearch/elasticsearch-analysis-icu`)
- Morphological Analysis Plugin (`https://github.com/imotov/elasticsearch-analysis-morphology`)
- Phonetic Analysis Plugin (`https://github.com/elasticsearch/elasticsearch-analysis-phonetic`)
- Smart Chinese Analysis Plugin (`https://github.com/elasticsearch/elasticsearch-analysis-smartcn`)
- Japanese (kuromoji) Analysis Plugin (`https://github.com/elasticsearch/elasticsearch-analysis-kuromoji`)

4
Standard Operations

In this chapter, we will cover the following topics:

- Creating an index
- Deleting an index
- Opening/closing an index
- Putting a mapping in an index
- Getting a mapping
- Deleting a mapping
- Refreshing an index
- Flushing an index
- Optimizing an index
- Checking if an index or type exists
- Managing index settings
- Using index aliases
- Indexing a document
- Getting a document
- Deleting a document
- Updating a document
- Speeding up atomic operations (bulk)
- Speeding up GET

Standard Operations

Introduction

This chapter covers how to manage indices and operations on documents. We'll start by discussing different operations on indices, such as create, delete, update, open and close.

After indices, we'll see how to manage mappings to complete the discussion on them started in the previous chapter and to create a base for the next chapter mainly centered on search.

In this chapter, a lot of space is given to **CRUD (Create-Read-Update-Delete)** operations on records. For improved performance in indexing, it's also important to understand bulk operations and avoid their common pitfalls.

This chapter doesn't cover operations involving queries which are the main topics of the next chapter.

Also cluster operations will be discussed in the Monitor chapter because they are mainly related to control and monitor the cluster.

Creating an index

The first operation to do before starting indexing data in ElasticSearch is to create an index: the main container of our data.

An index is similar to the concept of a database in SQL.

Getting ready

You need a working ElasticSearch cluster.

How to do it...

The HTTP method to create an index is PUT (but POST also works), the REST URL is the index name, which is written as follows:

```
http://<server>/<index_name>
```

For creating an index, we need to perform the following steps:

1. From command line, we can execute a PUT call as follows:

    ```
    curl -XPUT http://127.0.0.1:9200/myindex -d '{
        "settings" : {
            "index" : {
                "number_of_shards" : 2,
                "number_of_replicas" : 1
            }
        }
    }'
    ```

2. The result returned by ElasticSearch, if everything is all right, should be as follows:

    ```
    {"ok":true,"acknowledged":true}
    ```

3. If the index already exists, a 400 error is returned:

    ```
    {"error":"IndexAlreadyExistsException[[myindex] Already exists]","status":400}
    ```

How it works...

There are some limitations to the index name, due to the following accepted characters:

- ASCII letters [a-z]
- Numbers [0-9]
- Point ".", minus "-", "&", and "_"

 The index name will be mapped in a directory on your storage.

While creating an index, the replication can be set with the following two parameters in `settings/index` object:

- `number_of_shards`: This parameter controls the number of shards that compose an index (every shard can store up to 2^32 documents).
- `number_of_replicas`: This parameter controls the number of replicas (how many times your data is replicated in the cluster for high availability). A good practice is to set this value at least to one.

Standard Operations

The API call initializes a new index, which means:

- The index is created in a primary node level first and then its status is propagated to cluster level
- A default mapping (empty) is created
- All the shards required by the index are initialized and are ready to accept data

The index creation API allows defining the mapping during creation time. The parameter required to define a mapping is `mapping` and accepts multiple mappings. So in a single call it is possible to create an index and to put the required mappings.

There's more...

The create index command allows to pass also the mappings section, which contains the mapping definitions. It's a shortcut to create an index with mappings without executing an extra PUT mapping call.

A common example of this call, using the mapping from the *Putting a mapping in an index* recipe, is as follows:

```
curl -XPOST localhost:9200/myindex -d '{
    "settings" : {
        "number_of_shards" : 2,
        "number_of_replicas" : 1
    },
    "mappings" : {
      "order" : {
          "properties" : {
              "id" : {"type" : "string", "store" : "yes" , "index":"not_analyzed"},
              "date" : {"type" : "date", "store" : "no" , "index":"not_analyzed"},
              "customer_id" : {"type" : "string", "store" : "yes" , "index":"not_analyzed"},
              "sent" : {"type" : "boolean", "index":"not_analyzed"},
              "name" : {"type" : "string", "index":"analyzed"},
              "quantity" : {"type" : "integer", "index":"not_analyzed"},
              "vat" : {"type" : "double", "index":"no"}
          }
      }
   }
}'
```

See also

- The *Understanding cluster, replication, and sharding* recipe in *Chapter 1, Getting Started*
- The *Putting a mapping in an index* recipe in this chapter

Deleting an index

The counterpart of creating an index is deleting one.

Deleting an index means deleting its shards, mappings, and data. There are many common scenarios when we need to delete an index. Some of them are as follows:

- Removing it because the data that it contains is not needed anymore
- Reset an index for a scratch restart
- Delete an index that has some missing shard due to some failure to bring back the cluster in a valid state

Getting ready

You need a working ElasticSearch cluster and the existing index created in the previous recipe.

How to do it...

The HTTP method used to delete an index is DELETE.

The URL contains only the index name, which is as follows:

```
http://<server>/<index_name>
```

For deleting an index, we need to perform the following steps:

1. From command line, we can execute a DELETE call as follows:
   ```
   curl -XDELETE http://127.0.0.1:9200/myindex
   ```

2. The result returned by ElasticSearch, if everything is all right, should be as follows:
   ```
   {"ok":true,"acknowledged":true}
   ```

3. If the index doesn't exist, a 404 error is returned as follows:
   ```
   {"error":"IndexMissingException[[myindex] missing]","status":404}
   ```

 Calling the delete REST entry point without `index_name` deletes all the indices in the cluster.

Standard Operations

How it works...

When an index is deleted, all the data related to the index is removed from the disk and it's lost.

While processing the delete operation, first the cluster is updated, when the shards are deleted from the storage: this operation is very fast, in traditional filesystem it is implemented as a recursive delete.

It's not possible to restore a deleted index, if there is no backup.

Also calling using the special "_all" index names can be used to remove all the indices. In production it is good practice to disable the "all indices deletion" by adding the following line to `elasticsearch.yml`:

```
action.disable_delete_all_indices:true
```

See also

- The *Creating an index* recipe

Opening/closing an index

If you want to keep your data but save resources (memory/CPU), a good alternative to deleting an index is to close them.

ElasticSearch allows to open/close an index for putting it in the online/offline mode.

Getting ready

You need a working ElasticSearch cluster and the index created in the *Creating an index* recipe.

How to do it...

For opening/closing an index, we need to perform the following steps:

1. From command line, we can execute a POST call to close an index as follows:
   ```
   curl -XPOST http://127.0.0.1:9200/myindex/_close
   ```

2. If the call is successfully made, the result returned by ElasticSearch should be as follows:
   ```
   {"ok":true,"acknowledged":true}
   ```

3. To open an index from command line use the following command:

   `curl -XPOST http://127.0.0.1:9200/myindex/_open`

4. If the call is successfully made, the result returned by ElasticSearch should be as follows:

   `{"ok":true,"acknowledged":true}`

How it works...

When an index is closed, there is no overhead on the cluster (except for metadata state): the index shards are off and they don't use file descriptors, memory, and threads.

The following are the use cases for closing an index:

- Disabling date-based indices, for example, when you keep an index for a week, month, or day and you want to keep several online (that is, two months) and some offline (that is, from two months to six months)
- When you do searches on all the active indices of a cluster and don't want to search in some indices, in this case, using alias is the best solution, but you can achieve the same concept of alias with closed indices

When an index is closed, calling the `open` command restores its state.

See also

- The *Creating an index* recipe in this chapter

Putting a mapping in an index

In the previous chapter, we saw how to build a mapping for our data. This recipe shows how to put a type in an index. This kind of operation can be considered as the ElasticSearch version of an SQL create table command.

Getting ready

You need a working ElasticSearch cluster and the index created in the *Creating an index* recipe.

Standard Operations

How to do it...

The HTTP method to put a mapping is `PUT` (POST also works).

The URL format for putting a mapping is as follows:

```
http://<server>/<index_name>/<type_name>/_mapping
```

For putting a mapping in an index, we need to perform the following steps:

1. If we consider the type order of the previous chapter, the call will be as follows:

   ```
   curl -XPUT 'http://localhost:9200/myindex/order/_mapping' -d '{
       "order" : {
           "properties" : {
               "id" : {"type" : "string", "store" : "yes" , "index":"not_analyzed"},
               "date" : {"type" : "date", "store" : "no" , "index":"not_analyzed"},
               "customer_id" : {"type" : "string", "store" : "yes" , "index":"not_analyzed"},
               "sent" : {"type" : "boolean", "index":"not_analyzed"},
               "name" : {"type" : "string", "index":"analyzed"},
               "quantity" : {"type" : "integer", "index":"not_analyzed"},
               "vat" : {"type" : "double", "index":"no"}
           }
       }
   }'
   ```

2. In case of success, the result returned by ElasticSearch should be as follows:

   ```
   {"ok":true,"acknowledged":true}
   ```

How it works...

This call checks if the index exists and then it creates one or more types as described in the mapping. (For the mapping description, refer to the previous chapter).

During mapping insert if there is an existing mapping for this type, it is merged with the new one. If there is a field with different type and the type could not be updated in a multifield, an exception is raised. To prevent exception during the merging mapping phase, it's possible to set the `ignore_conflicts` parameter to `true` (default is `false`).

The PUT mapping call allows to set the type for several indices in one shot: listing the indices comma separated or to apply to all index using the `_all` alias.

See also

- The *Getting a mapping* recipe in this chapter

Getting a mapping

After having set our mappings for processing types, we sometimes need to control or analyze the mapping to prevent issues. The action to get the mapping for a type helps us to understand the structure or its evolution due to some merge and explicit type guessing.

Getting ready

You need a working ElasticSearch cluster and the mapping created in the previous recipe.

How to do it...

The HTTP method to get a mapping is GET.

The URL formats for getting mapping are as follows:

```
http://<server>/_mapping
http://<server>/<index_name>/_mapping
http://<server>/<index_name>/<type_name>/_mapping
```

For getting a mapping from in an index, we need to perform the following steps:

1. If we consider the type order of the previous chapter, the call will be as follows:

   ```
   curl -XGET 'http://localhost:9200/myindex/order/_mapping?pretty=true'
   ```

2. The result returned by ElasticSearch should be as follows:

   ```
   {
       "order": {
           "properties": {
               "customer_id": {
                   "index": "not_analyzed",
                   "index_options": "docs",
                   "omit_norms": true,
                   "store": true,
                   "type": "string"
               },
   ... truncated ...
           }
       }
   }
   ```

Standard Operations

How it works...

The mapping is stored at the cluster level in ElasticSearch. The call checks both the index and type existence and then it returns the stored mapping.

 The returned mapping is in a reduced form, that means the default values for a field are not returned.

ElasticSearch stores only non-default field values to reduce network and memory consumption.

Asking the mapping is very useful for several purposes:

- Debugging template-level mapping
- Checking if explicit mapping is working correctly (good guessing fields)
- Retrieving the mapping metadata, which can be used to store type-related information
- Simply checking if the mapping is correct

If you need to fetch several mappings, it is better to do it at index level or cluster level to reduce the numbers of API calls.

See also

- The *Putting a mapping in an index* recipe in this chapter
- The *Using dynamic templates in document mapping* recipe in *Chapter 3, Managing Mapping*

Deleting a mapping

The last **CRUD (Create, Read, Update, Delete)** operation related to mapping is the delete one.

Deleting a mapping is a destructive operation and must be done with caution to prevent losing your data.

Getting ready

You need a working ElasticSearch cluster and the mapping created in the *Putting a mapping in an index* recipe.

How to do it...

The HTTP method to delete a mapping is DELETE.

The URL formats for getting the mapping are as follows:

```
http://<server>/<index_name>/<type_name>
http://<server>/<index_name>/<type_name>/_mapping
```

For deleting a mapping from in an index, we need to perform the following steps:

1. If we consider the type order of the previous chapter, the call will be as follows:

   ```
   curl -XDELETE 'http://localhost:9200/myindex/order/'
   ```

2. If the call is successfully made, the result returned by ElasticSearch should be an HTTP 200 status code and a message similar to the following one:

   ```
   {"ok":true}
   ```

3. If the mapping/type is missing, the following exception is raised:

   ```
   {"error":"TypeMissingException[[myindex] type[order] missing]","status":404}
   ```

How it works...

ElasticSearch tries to find the mapping for an index-type pair. If it's found, the mapping and all the data related to it are removed. If not found, an exception is raised.

Deleting a mapping removes all the data associated with that mapping: so it's not possible to go back if there is no backup.

The following use cases are used when it's required to delete a mapping:

- **Unused type**: This needs to be deleted to clean the data.
- **Wrong mapping**: You need to change the mapping, but you cannot upgrade it or you can't remove some fields. You need to back up your data, create a new mapping, and reimport the data.
- **Fast cleanup of a type**: You can delete the mapping and recreate it (or you can execute a "delete by query" as explained in further recipe).

See also

- The *Putting a mapping in an index* recipe in this chapter

Standard Operations

Refreshing an index

ElasticSearch allows the user to control the state of the searcher using forced refresh on an index. If not forced, the new indexed document will be only searchable after a fixed time interval (usually 1 second).

Getting ready

You need a working ElasticSearch cluster and the index created in the *Creating an index* recipe.

How to do it...

The HTTP method used for both operations is POST.

The URL formats for refreshing an index is as follows:

```
http://<server>/<index_name(s)>/_refresh
```

The URL format for refreshing all the indices in a cluster is as follows:

```
http://<server>/_refresh
```

For refreshing an index, we need to perform the following steps:

1. If we consider the type order of the previous chapter, the call will be as follows:
   `curl -XPOST 'http://localhost:9200/myindex/_refresh`

2. The result returned by ElasticSearch should be as follows:
   ```
   {"ok":true,"_shards":{"total":4,"successful":2,"failed":0}}
   ```

 The refresh call (as the flush and optimize ones) affects only the primary shards. In the previous example, we have two primary shards and two secondary ones.

How it works...

Near real-time capabilities are automatically managed by ElasticSearch, which automatically refreshes the indices every second if data is changed in them.

You can call the refresh operation on one or more indices (more indices are comma separated) or on all the indices.

ElasticSearch doesn't refresh the state of an index at every inserted document to prevent poor performance due to excessive I/O required in closing and reopening file descriptors.

 You must force the refresh to have your last index data available for searching.

Generally the best time to call the refresh is after having indexed a lot of data to be sure that your records are searchable instantly.

See also

- The *Flushing an index* recipe in this chapter
- The *Optimizing an index* recipe in this chapter

Flushing an index

ElasticSearch for performance reasons stores some data in memory and on a transaction log. If we want to free the memory, empty the translation log and be sure that our data is safely written on the disk we need to flush an index.

Getting ready

You need a working ElasticSearch cluster and the index created in the *Creating an index* recipe.

How to do it...

The HTTP method used for both operations is POST.

The URL format for flushing an index is as follows:

```
http://<server>/<index_name(s)>/_flush[?refresh=True]
```

The URL format for flushing all the indices in a cluster is as follows:

```
http://<server>/_flush[?refresh=True]
```

Standard Operations

For flushing an index, we need to perform the following steps:

1. If we consider the type order of the previous chapter, the call will be as follows:
   ```
   curl -XPOST 'http://localhost:9200/myindex/_flush?refresh=True'
   ```
2. If everything is all right, the result returned by ElasticSearch should be as follows:
   ```
   {"ok":true,"_shards":{"total":4,"successful":2,"failed":0}}
   ```

The result contains the state `ok` and the shard operation status.

How it works...

ElasticSearch tries not to put overhead in I/O operations caching in memory some data to reduce writing: in this way it is able to improve the performance.

To clean up memory and force this data on disk, the flush operation is required.

ElasticSearch automatically provides periodic flush on disk, but forcing flush can be useful in the following instances:

- When we are able to shut down a node to prevent stealing of data
- To have all the data in a safe state (for example after a big indexing operation to have all the data flushed and refreshed)

In the flush call, it is possible to give an extra request parameter, `refresh` to force also the index refresh.

 Flushing too often affects index performances: use it wisely.

See also

- The *Refreshing an index* recipe in this chapter
- The *Optimizing an index* recipe in this chapter

Optimizing an index

ElasticSearch core is based on Lucene, which stores the data in segments on the disk. During an index life, a lot of segments are created and changed. With the increase of segment number the speed of search decreases due to the time required to read all of them. The optimize operation allows to consolidate the index for faster search performance reducing segments.

Getting ready

You need a working ElasticSearch cluster and the index created in the *Creating an index* recipe.

How to do it...

The HTTP method used is POST.

The URL format for optimizing one or more indices, is as follows:

```
http://<server>/<index_name(s)>/_optimize
```

The URL format for optimizing all the indices in a cluster is as follows:

```
http://<server>/_optimize
```

For optimizing an index, we need to perform the following steps:

1. If we consider the index created in the *Creating an index* recipe, the call will be as follows:
   ```
   curl -XPOST 'http://localhost:9200/myindex/_optimize'
   ```

2. The result returned by ElasticSearch should be as follows:
   ```
   {"ok":true,"_shards":{"total":4,"successful":2,"failed":0}}
   ```

The result contains the state `ok` and the shard operation status.

How it works...

Lucene stores your data in several segments on disk. These segments are created when you index a new document/record or when you delete a document. Their numbers can be big (for this reason, in the setup we have increased the file description number for the ElasticSearch process).

Standard Operations

Internally ElasticSearch has a merger, which tries to reduce the number of segments, but it's designed to improve the index performances. The optimize operation in Lucene tries to reduce the segments in a heavy way, removing unused ones, purging deleted documents, and rebuilding the index with minimum number of segments.

The main advantages are as follows:

- Reducing both file descriptors
- Freeing memory used by the segment readers
- Improving performance in search due to less segments management

Optimize is a very heavy operation. The index can be unresponsive while optimizing.

There's more...

You can pass several additional parameters to the optimize call. Some of these are as follows:

- `max_num_segments` (default `autodetect`): This value is set to `1` for complete optimization.
- `only_expunge_deletes` (default `false`): Lucene does not delete documents from segments, but it marks them as deleted. This flag merges only segments that have been deleted.
- `flush` (default `true`): This enables ElasticSearch to perform a flush after optimize.
- `refresh` (default `true`): This enables ElasticSearch to perform a refresh after optimize.
- `wait_for_merge` (default `true`): This helps to determine if the request needs to wait till the merge ends.

See also

- The *Refreshing an index* recipe in this chapter
- The *Optimizing an index* recipe in this chapter

Checking if an index or type exists

During the startup of an application, it's often necessary to check if an index or type exists otherwise we need to create them.

Getting ready

You need a working ElasticSearch cluster and the mapping available in the index as described in the previous recipes.

How to do it...

The HTTP method to check existence is HEAD. The URL format for checking an index is as follows:

```
http://<server>/<index_name>/
```

The URL format for checking a type is as follows:

```
http://<server>/<index_name>/<type>/
```

For checking if an index exists, we need to perform the following steps:

1. If we consider the index created in the *Creating an index* recipe, the call will be as follows:

    ```
    curl -i -XHEAD 'http://localhost:9200/myindex/'
    ```

2. If the index exists an HTTP status code 200 is returned, if missing a 404 is returned. For checking if a type exists, we need to perform the following steps:

    1. If we consider the mapping created in the *Putting a mapping in an index* recipe, the call will be as follows:

        ```
        curl -i -XHEAD 'http://localhost:9200/myindex/order/'
        ```

    2. If the index exists an HTTP status code 200 is returned, if missing a 404 is returned.

How it works...

The checking call is very useful to control if an index or type exists.

This is a typical HEAD REST call to check existence.

 Before every action involved in indexing, generally on application startup, it's good practice to check if an index or type exists to prevent future failures.

Managing index settings

Index settings are more important because they allow to control several important ElasticSearch functionalities such as sharding/replica, caching, term management, routing, and analysis.

Getting ready

You need a working ElasticSearch cluster and the index created in the *Creating an index* recipe

How to do it...

For managing the index settings, we need to perform the following steps:

1. To retrieve the settings of your current index, the URL format is as follows:

    ```
    http://<server>/<index_name>/_settings
    ```

2. We are reading information via the REST API, so the method will be GET and an example of call, using the index create in the *Creating an index* recipe, is as follows:

    ```
    curl -XGET 'http://localhost:9200/myindex/_settings'
    ```

3. The response will be something similar to the following one:

    ```
    {
        "myindex": {
            "settings": {
                "index.number_of_replicas": "1",
                "index.number_of_shards": "2",
                "index.version.created": "900199"
            }
        }
    }
    ```

The response attributes depend on the index settings set. In this case, the response will be the number of replicas (1) and shard (2) and the index creation version (900199).

4. To modify the index settings, we need to use the PUT method. A typical settings change is to increase the replica number:

```
curl -XPUT 'http://localhost:9200/myindex/_settings' -d '
{"index":{"number_of_replicas": "2"}}'
```

How it works...

ElasticSearch provides a lot of options to tune the index behaviors, such as:

- **Replica management**:
    - `index.number_of_replica`: This is the number of replicas each shard has
    - `index.auto_expand_replicas`: This allows to define a dynamic number of replicas related to the number of shards

> Using set `index.auto_expand_replicas` to 0 or all allows creating an index that is replicated in every node (very useful for settings or cluster propagated data such as language options/stopwords).

- **Refresh interval** (default 1s): In the previous *Refreshing an index* recipe we saw how to manually refresh an index. The index settings, `index.refresh_interval` controls the rate of automatic refresh.

- **Cache management**: These settings (`index.cache.*`) control the cache size and life. It is not common to change them; refer to the ElasticSearch documentation for all the available options.at http://www.elasticsearch.org/guide/en/elasticsearch/reference/current/index-modules-cache.html.

- **Write management**: ElasticSearch provides several settings to block a read/write operation in an index and to change metadata. They live in the `index.blocks` settings.

- **Shard allocation management**: These settings control how the shards must be allocated. They live in the `index.routing.allocation.*` namespace.

There are other index settings that can be configured for very specific needs. In every new version of ElasticSearch, the community extends these settings to cover new scenarios.

Standard Operations

There's more...

`refresh_interval` allows several tricks to optimize the indexing speed. As it controls the rate of refresh and refreshing reduces the index performances due to index reopening. A good practice is to disable the refresh interval (set to -1) during a big bulk indexing and restoring the default behavior after it. This can be done with the following steps:

1. We can disable the refresh using the following command:

    ```
    curl -XPOST 'http://localhost:9200/myindex/_settings' -d '
    {"index":{"index_refresh_interval": "-1"}}'
    ```

2. Bulk index some millions of documents.
3. Restore the refresh using the following command:

    ```
    curl -XPOST 'http://localhost:9200/myindex/_settings' -d '
    {"index":{"index_refresh_interval": "1s"}}'
    ```

4. Optionally optimize the index for search performances.

See also

- The *Refreshing an index* recipe in this chapter
- The *Optimizing an index* recipe in this chapter

Using index aliases

Real world applications have a lot of indices and queries that span on more indices. This scenario requires defining all the names of indices on which to we need to perform queries; aliases allow grouping them in a common name.

Some common scenarios of this usage are as follows:

- Log indices divided by date (that is, `log_YYMMDD`) for which we want to create an alias for `the last week`, `the last month`, `today`, `yesterday`, and so on
- "Collecting" website contents in several indices (`New York Times`, `The Guardian`, and so on) for those we want to refer as an index alias "sites"

Getting ready

You need a working ElasticSearch cluster.

How to do it...

The URL format for control aliases are as follows:

`http://<server>/_aliases`

For managing the index aliases, we need to perform the following steps:

1. We are reading aliases status via REST API, so the method will be GET and an example of call is as follows:

   ```
   curl -XGET 'http://localhost:9200/_aliases'
   ```

2. You will get a response similar to the following one:

   ```
   {
       "myindex": {
           "aliases": {}
       },
       "test": {
           "aliases": {}
       }
   }
   ```

   Aliases can be changed with add and delete commands.

3. To add an alias, use the following command:

   ```
   curl -XPOST 'http://localhost:9200/_aliases' -d '
   {
       "actions" : [
           { "add" : { "index":"myindex", "alias":" myalias1" }}
           { "add" : { "index":"test", "alias":" myalias1" }}

       ]
   }'
   ```

   This action adds the `myindex` index to the `myalias1` alias.

4. To delete an alias, use the following command:

   ```
   curl -XPOST 'http://localhost:9200/_aliases' -d '
   {
       "actions" : [
           {"delete":{ "index":"myindex", "alias":" myalias1" }}
       ]
   }'
   ```

   The delete action removes the `myindex` index from the `myalias1` alias.

Standard Operations

How it works...

ElasticSearch, during search operations, automatically expands the alias, so that the required indices are selected.

The alias metadata is kept in the cluster state. When an alias is added/deleted, all the changes are propagated to all the cluster nodes.

Aliases are mainly functional structures to simply index management when data is stored in multiple indices.

There's more...

Alias can also be used to define a filter and routing parameter.

Filters are automatically added to the query to filter out data. Routing via alias allows to determine which shard hits during searching and indexing.

An example of this call is as follows:

```
curl -XPOST 'http://localhost:9200/_aliases' -d '
{
    "actions" : [
        {
            "add" : {
                "index" : "myindex",
                "alias" : " userlalias",
                "filter" : { "term" : { "user" : "user_1" } },
                "search_routing" : "1,2",
                "index_routing" : "2"
            }
        }
    ]
}'
```

In this case we are adding a new alias, `userlalias` to an index `myindex` adding:

- A filter to select only the documents that match a field `user` with term `user_1`
- A list of routing keys to select the shards to be used during search
- A routing key to be used during indexing

> `search_routing` allows multivalued routing keys. `index_routing` has only a single value.

Other than the `_aliases` endpoint there is also the `_alias` one that is related to the defined indices (this functionality is available from ElasticSearch Version 0.90.1 or higher):

`http://<server>/<index>/_alias/<alias_name>`

The previously discussed examples can be converted by using this endpoint.

For getting index aliases, the HTTP method is GET and the preceding example will be as follows:

```
curl -XGET 'http://localhost:9200/myindex/_alias/'
```

The * is a shortcut to allow fetching all the aliases associated with an index. `alias_name` must always be provided, but you can use glob expressions to filter them.

For adding a new alias the HTTP method is PUT and the preceding example will be as follows:

```
curl -XPUT 'http://localhost:9200/myindex/_alias/myalias1'
curl -XPUT 'http://localhost:9200/test/_alias/myalias1'
```

In the call body, it is possible to pass other parameters as we have done in the routing example.

For deleting an alias, the HTTP method is DELETE and the preceding examples will be as follows:

```
curl -XDELETE 'http://localhost:9200/myindex/_alias/myalias1'
curl -XDELETE 'http://localhost:9200/test/_alias/myalias1'
```

The `_alias` index call is very handy to control the aliases for a single index or to automatically manage alias actions after a single index creation.

Indexing a document

In ElasticSearch there are two vital operations: index and search.

Index consists of putting one or more documents in an index: it is similar to the concept of inserting records in a relational database.

In Lucene, the core engine of ElasticSearch, inserting or updating a document has the same cost: in Lucene update means replace.

Standard Operations

Getting ready

You need a working ElasticSearch cluster and the mapping created in the *Putting a mapping in an index* recipe.

How to do it...

For indexing a document, several REST entry points that can be used are as follows:

Method	URL
POST	http://<server>/<index_name>/<type>
PUT/POST	http://<server>/<index_name>/<type> /<id>
PUT/POST	http://<server>/<index_name>/<type> /<id>/_create

For indexing a document, we need to perform the following steps:

1. If we consider the type order of the previous chapter, the call to index a document will be as follows:

```
curl -XPOST 'http://localhost:9200/myindex/
order/2qLrAfPVQvCRMe7Ku8r0Tw' -d '{
    "id" : "1234",
    "date" : "2013-06-07T12:14:54",
    "customer_id" : "customer1",
    "sent" : true,
  "in_stock_items" : 0,
  "items":[
        {"name":"item1", "quantity":3, "vat":20.0},
        {"name":"item2", "quantity":2, "vat":20.0},
        {"name":"item3", "quantity":1, "vat":10.0}
    ]
}'
```

2. If the index is successfully made, the result returned by ElasticSearch should be as follows:

```
{
"ok":true,
"_index":"myindex",
"_type":"order",
"_id":"2qLrAfPVQvCRMe7Ku8r0Tw",
"_version":1
}
```

Some additional information is returned from the index operation, which is as follows:

- The `OK` status
- The autogenerated ID
- The version of the indexed document as per the optimistic concurrency control

How it works...

One of the most used API in ElasticSearch is the index. Basically, index is a JSON document which internally consists of the following steps:

- Routing the call to the correct shard based on the ID or routing/parent metadata. If the ID is missing, a new one is created (refer to *Chapter 1, Getting Started* for more details).
- Validating the sent JSON.
- Processing the JSON according to the mapping. If new fields are present in the document (and the mapping can be updated), new fields are introduced in the mapping.
- Indexing the document in the shard.
- If it contains nested documents, it extracts them and it processes them separately.
- Returning information about the saved document (ID and versioning).

It's important to choose the correct ID for indexing your data. If you don't provide an ID ElasticSearch, during the indexing phase, automatically associates a new one to your document. The ID must generally be of the same length to improve balancing in the data tree and performance. Due to the REST call's nature, it's better to pay attention when using characters other than the ASCII ones due to URL encoding and decoding.

Depending on the mappings, other actions take place during the indexing phase: propagation on replica, nested processing, percolator, and so on.

The document will be available for standard search calls after a refresh (forced with an API call or after the time slice of 1 second – near real time). Every GET API on the document doesn't require a refresh and is instantly available.

There's more...

ElasticSearch allows to pass the index API URL, several query parameters for controlling how the document is indexed. The most used one are as follows:

- `routing`: This controls the shard to be used for indexing. This is as follows:
  ```
  curl -XPOST 'http://localhost:9200/myindex/order?routing=1'
  ```

Standard Operations

- `parent`: This defines the parent of a child document and uses this value to apply routing. The parent object must be specified in the mappings as follows:

    ```
    curl -XPOST 'http://localhost:9200/myindex/order?parent=12'
    ```

- `timestamp`: This is the timestamp to be used in indexing the document. It must be activated in the mappings as follows:

    ```
    curl -XPOST 'http://localhost:9200/myindex/order?timestamp=
    2013-01-25T19%3A22%3A22'
    ```

- `consistency` (one/quorum/all): By default, an index operation succeeds if a quorum (>replica/2+1) of active shards are available. The write consistency value can be changed for index action as follows:

    ```
    curl -XPOST 'http://localhost:9200/myindex/order?consistency=one'
    ```

- `replication` (sync/async): ElasticSearch returns from an index operation when all the shards of the current replication group have executed the operation. Setting the replication to `async` allows executing the index synchronously only on the primary shard and asynchronously on the other shards, returning from the call faster:

    ```
    curl -XPOST 'http://localhost:9200/myindex/
    order?replication=async' …
    ```

- `version`: This allows to use the optimistic concurrency control (http://en.wikipedia.org/wiki/Optimistic_concurrency_control). In the first index of a document, the Version 1 is set on the document. After every update this value is incremented. Optimistic concurrency control is a way to manage concurrency in every insert or update operation. The passed version value is the last seen version (usually returned by a GET or a search). The index happens only if the current index version value is less than or equal to the passed one.

    ```
    curl -XPOST 'http://localhost:9200/myindex/order?version=2' …
    ```

- `op_type`: This can be used to force a create on a document. If a document with the same ID exists, the index fails. An example is as follows:

    ```
    curl -XPOST 'http://localhost:9200/myindex/order?op_type=create'…
    ```

- `ttl`: This allows to define the time to live for a document. All documents, in which the time to live is expired are deleted and purged from the index. This feature is very useful to define records with a fixed life. The value can be a date time or a time value (numeric value ending with s, m, h, d). An example is as follows:

    ```
    curl -XPOST 'http://localhost:9200/myindex/order?ttl=1d'
    ```

- `timeout`: This defines the time to wait for the primary shard to be available. Sometimes the primary shard will not be in a writable status (relocating or recovering from a gateway) and a timeout for the write operation is raised after 1 minute. An example of `timeout` is as follows:

    ```
    curl -XPOST 'http://localhost:9200/myindex/order?timeout=5m' …
    1d'
    ```

See also

- The *Getting a document* recipe in this chapter
- The *Deleting a document* recipe in this chapter
- The *Updating a document* recipe in this chapter
- Refer to optimistic concurrency control at http://en.wikipedia.org/wiki/Optimistic_concurrency_control

Getting a document

After having indexed a document, during your application life it must probably be retrieved.

The GET REST call allows getting a document in real time without the need for a refresh operation.

Getting ready

You need a working ElasticSearch cluster and the indexed document from the *Indexing a document* recipe.

How to do it...

The GET method allows returning a document given its index, type, and ID.

The REST API URL is as follows:

```
http://<server>/<index_name>/<type_name>/<id>
```

For getting a document, we need to perform the following steps:

1. If we consider the document, which we had indexed in the previous recipe, the call will be as follows:

   ```
   curl -XGET http://localhost:9200/myindex/order/2qLrAfPVQvCRMe7Ku8r0Tw?pretty=true
   ```

2. The result returned by ElasticSearch should be the indexed document and it should be as follows:

   ```
   {
   "_index":"myindex","_type":"order","_id":"2qLrAfPVQvCRMe7Ku8r0Tw","_version":1,"exists":true, "_source"
   : {
       "id" : "1234",
       "date" : "2013-06-07T12:14:54",
   ```

Standard Operations

```
            "customer_id" : "customer1",
            "sent" : true,
            "items":[
                {"name":"item1", "quantity":3, "vat":20.0},
                {"name":"item2", "quantity":2, "vat":20.0},
                {"name":"item3", "quantity":1, "vat":10.0}
            ]
        }}
```

Our indexed data is contained in the _source parameter, but the other information returned is as follows:

- _index: This is the index that stores the document
- _type: This is the type of the document
- _id: This is the ID of the document
- _version: This is the version of the document
- exists: This determines whether the document exists

    If the record is missing, a 404 error is returned as the status code and the return JSON will be as follows:

```
{
    "_id": "2qLrAfPVQvCRMe7Ku8r0Tw",
    "_index": "myindex",
    "_type": "order",
    "exists": false
}
```

How it works...

The ElasticSearch GET API on the document doesn't require a refresh: all the GET calls are in real time.

This call is very fast because ElasticSearch is implemented to search only on the shard that contains the record without other overheads. The IDs are often cached in memory for fast lookup.

The source of the document is only available if the _source field is stored (default settings in ElasticSearch).

There are several additional parameters that can be used to control the GET call, which are as follows:

- `fields`: This parameter allows to retrieve only a subset of fields. This is very useful to reduce the bandwidth or to retrieve calculated fields as the attachment mapping ones. This is done using the following command:

    ```
    curl http://localhost:9200/myindex/order/2qLrAfPVQvCRMe7Ku8r0Tw?fields=date,sent
    ```

- `routing`: This parameter allows to specify the shard to be used for the GET operation. This is done using the following command:

    ```
    curl http://localhost:9200/myindex/order/2qLrAfPVQvCRMe7Ku8r0Tw?routing=customer_id
    ```

- `refresh`: This parameter allows to refresh the current shard before doing the GET operation (must be used with care because it slows down indexing and introduces some overhead). This is done using the following command:

    ```
    curl http://localhost:9200/myindex/order/2qLrAfPVQvCRMe7Ku8r0Tw?refresh=true
    ```

- `preference`: This parameter allows to control which shard replica is to be chosen for executing GET. Generally ElasticSearch chooses a random shard for the GET call. Possible values are as follows:
- `_primary`: This is for the primary shard
- `_local`: This is used for trying first the local shard and then fallback to a random choice. Using the local shard can reduce the bandwidth usage and should generally be used with auto-replicating shards (replica set to 0-all)
- `custom`: This is the value for selecting a shard related to a value such as the `customer_id` username

There's more...

The GET API is very fast, so a good practice for developing applications is to try to use the GET call as much as possible. Choosing the correct ID form during application development can increase the performance.

If the shard, which contains the document, is not bound to an ID, to fetch the document a query with an ID filter is required (we will discuss this in the next chapter).

If you don't need to fetch the record but check only its existence, you can replace GET with HEAD and the response will be 200 if it exists or 404 if missing.

The GET call also has a special endpoint `_source` that allows fetching only the source of the document.

Standard Operations

The GET source REST API URL is as follows:

```
http://<server>/<index_name>/<type_name>/<id>/_source
```

To fetch the source of the previous order, we need to execute the following command:

```
curl -XGET http://localhost:9200/myindex/order/2qLrAfPVQvCRMe7Ku8r0Tw/_source
```

See also

- The *Speeding up GET* recipe in this chapter

Deleting a document

Deleting documents in ElasticSearch is possible in two ways: using the delete call or the delete by query, which we'll see in the next chapter.

Getting ready

You need a working ElasticSearch cluster and the indexed document which we have discussed in the *Indexing a document* recipe.

How to do it...

The REST API URL is similar to that of GET calls, but the HTTP method is `DELETE`:

```
http://<server>/<index_name>/<type_name>/<id>
```

For deleting a document, we need to perform the following steps:

1. If we consider the order indexed in the *Indexing a document* recipe, the call to delete a document will be as follows:

   ```
   curl -XDELETE 'http://localhost:9200/myindex/order/2qLrAfPVQvCRMe7Ku8r0Tw'
   ```

2. The result returned by ElasticSearch will be as follows:

   ```
   {
       "_id": "2qLrAfPVQvCRMe7Ku8r0Tw",
       "_index": "myindex",
       "_type": "order",
       "_version": 2,
       "found": true,
       "ok": true
   }
   ```

Chapter 4

The result, a part of the well-known parameter starting from _ returns the `ok` status if the document is found.

3. If the record is missing, a 404 error is returned as the status code and the return JSON will be as follows:

```
{
    "_id": "2qLrAfPVQvCRMe7Ku8r0Tw",
    "_index": "myindex",
    "_type": "order",
    "_version": 2,
    "found": false,
    "ok": true
}
```

How it works...

Deleting record hits only the shards that contain a document, so there is no overhead.

If the document is a child, the parent must be set to look for the correct shard.

There are several additional parameters that can be used to control the delete call. The most important ones are as follows:

- `routing`: This parameter allows to specify the shard to be used for the delete operation
- `version`: This parameter allows defining a version of the document to be deleted to prevent modification of this document
- `parent`: This parameter is similar to routing, and is required if the document is a child one

> The delete operation has no restore functionality. Every document that is deleted is lost forever.

Deleting a record is a fast operation, very easy to use if the IDs of the document to be deleted are available. Otherwise we must use the delete by query call, which we will see in the next chapter.

See also

- The *Deleting by query* recipe in *Chapter 5, Search, Queries, and Filters*

Standard Operations

Updating a document

Documents stored in ElasticSearch can be updated during their lives. There are two available solutions to do this operation in ElasticSearch: repost the new document or use the update call.

The update call can work in the following two ways:

- By providing a script which is the update strategy
- By providing a document that must be merged with the original one

Getting ready

You need a working ElasticSearch cluster and the indexed document which we discussed in the *Indexing a document* recipe.

How to do it...

As we are changing the state of the data the HTTP method is POST and the following is the REST URL:

```
http://<server>/<index_name>/<type_name>/<id>/_update
```

For updating a document, we need to perform the following steps:

1. If we consider the type `order` of the previous recipe, the call to update a document will be as follows:

   ```
   curl -XPOST 'http://localhost:9200/myindex/
   order/2qLrAfPVQvCRMe7Ku8r0Tw/_update' -d '{
   "script" : "ctx._source.in_stock_items += count",
   "params" : {
       "count" : 4
   }}'
   ```

2. If the request is successfully made, the result returned by ElasticSearch will be as follows:

   ```
   {
       "_id": "2qLrAfPVQvCRMe7Ku8r0Tw",
       "_index": "myindex",
       "_type": "order",
       "_version": 3,
       "found": true,
       "ok": true
   }
   ```

3. The record will be as follows:

   ```
   {
       "_id": "2qLrAfPVQvCRMe7Ku8r0Tw",
       "_index": "myindex",
       "_source": {
           "customer_id": "customer1",
           "date": "2013-06-07T12:14:54",
           "id": "1234",
           "in_stock_items": 4,
   ….
           "sent": true
       },
       "_type": "order",
       "_version": 3,
       "exists": true
   }
   ```

The visible changes are as follows:

- The scripted field is changed
- The version is incremented

How it works...

The update operation takes a document, it applies the changes required in the script or in the update document to this document and it will fully re-index the changed document.. In *Chapter 7, Scripting* we will explore the scripting capabilities of ElasticSearch.

The standard language for scripting in ElasticSearch is MVEL (http://mvel.codehaus.org/) and it's used in these examples.

The script can operate on ctx._source: the source of the document (it must be indexed to work) and it can change the document in place.

It's possible to pass parameters to a script by passing a JSON object. These parameters are available in the execution context.

A script can control the ElasticSearch's behavior after the script execution via setting the ctx.op value of the context. Available values are as follows:

- ctx.op="delete": This will delete the document after the script execution.
- ctx.op="none": This will skip the indexing process of the document. A good practice to improve performance is to set ctx.op="none" if the script doesn't update the document to prevent the re-indexing overhead.

In ctx, it is possible to pass also a ttl value to change the time to live of an element setting the ctx._ttl parameter. ctx also manages the timestamp of the record in ctx._timestamp.

Standard Operations

It's also possible to pass an additional object for using if the document is not available in the `upsert` property, which is as follows:

```
curl -XPOST 'http://localhost:9200/myindex/
order/2qLrAfPVQvCRMe7Ku8r0Tw/_update' -d '{
"script" : "ctx._source.in_stock_items += count",
"params" : {
    "count" : 4
},
"upsert" : {"in_stock_items":4}}'
```

If you need to replace some field values, a good solution is to not write complex update script, but to use the special property `doc`, which allows to "overwrite" the values of an object. The document provided in the `doc` parameter will be merged with the original one. This approach is more easy to use, but it cannot set the `ctx.op` parameter, so if the update doesn't change the value of the original document, the following successive phase will always be executed:

```
curl -XPOST 'http://localhost:9200/myindex/
order/2qLrAfPVQvCRMe7Ku8r0Tw/_update' -d '{"doc" : {"in_stock_
items":10}}'
```

If the original document is missing, it is possible to use the provided `doc` for an `upsert` command providing the `doc_as_upsert` parameter:

```
curl -XPOST 'http://localhost:9200/myindex/
order/2qLrAfPVQvCRMe7Ku8r0Tw/_update' -d '{"doc" : {"in_stock_
items":10}, "doc_as_upsert":true}'
```

Using MVEL, it is possible to apply the following advanced operations on fields:

- Removing a field: This is done using `"script" : {"ctx._source.remove("myfield"}}`
- Adding a new field: This is done using `"script" : {"ctx._source.myfield=myvalue"}}`

The update REST call is very useful because it has the following advantages:

- It reduces the bandwidth usage, because the update operation doesn't need a round trip to the client of the data.
- It's safer, because it automatically manages the optimistic concurrent control. If a change happens during script execution, the script is re-executed with the updated data.
- It can be executed in bulk.

See also

- Refer to the *Speeding up atomic operations (bulk)* recipe in this chapter

Speeding up atomic operations (bulk)

When we are inserting/deleting/updating a large number of documents, the HTTP overhead is significant to speed up the process, which ElasticSearch allows executing bulk of calls.

Getting ready

You need a working ElasticSearch cluster.

How to do it...

As we are changing the state of the data the HTTP method is POST and the following is the REST URL:

```
http://<server>/<index_name/_bulk
```

For executing a bulk action, we need to perform the following steps:

1. We need to collect the create/index/delete/update commands in a structure made up of bulk JSON lines, composed by a line of action with metadata and another line optional of data related to the action. Every line must be ended with a newline character "\n".

   A bulk datafile should be as follows:

   ```
   { "index":{ "_index":"myindex", "_type":"order", "_id":"1" } }
   { "field1" : "value1",  "field2" : "value2"  }
   { "delete":{ "_index":"myindex", "_type":"order", "_id":"2" } }
   { "create":{ "_index":"myindex", "_type":"order", "_id":"3" } }
   { "field1" : "value1",  "field2" : "value2"  }
   { "update":{ "_index":"myindex", "_type":"order", "_id":"3" } }
   { "doc":{"field1" : "value1",  "field2" : "value2"   }}
   ```

2. This file can be "bulked" with the following POST command:

   ```
   curl -s -XPOST localhost:9200/_bulk --data-binary @bulkdata;
   ```

3. The result returned by ElasticSearch will collect all the responses of the actions.

Standard Operations

How it works...

The bulk operation allows to aggregate different calls as a single one.

A header part with the action to be performed and an optional body compose every standard operation.

The header is composed by the action name and the object of parameters. Looking at the previous example for index we have:

```
{ "index":{ "_index":"myindex", "_type":"order", "_id":"1" } }
```

For indexing and creating, an extra body is required with the data:

```
{ "field1" : "value1",  "field2" : "value2" }
```

The delete action doesn't require optional data, so only the header composes it:

```
{ "delete":{ "_index":"myindex", "_type":"order", "_id":"1" } }
```

In Version 0.90 or higher versions, ElasticSearch allows to execute bulk update as follows:

```
{ "update":{ "_index":"myindex", "_type":"order", "_id":"3" } }
```

The header accepts all the common parameters of the update action such as `doc`, `upsert`, `doc_as_upsert`, `lang`, `script`, and `params`. For controlling the number of retries in case of concurrency, the bulk update defines the `_retry_on_conflict` parameter set to the number of retries to be performed before raising an exception.

And a possible body for the update, is as follows:

```
{ "doc":{"field1" : "value1",  "field2" : "value2" }}
```

The bulk item can accept the following parameters:

- `routing`: This parameter controls the routing shard.
- `parent`: This parameter is used to select a parent item shard. It's required if you are indexing some child documents.
- `timestamp`: This parameter is used to set the index item timestamp.
- `ttl`: This parameter is used to control the time to live for a document.

Global bulk parameters that can be passed via query arguments are as follows:

- `consistency` (`one`, `quorum`, `all`) (default `quorum`): This parameter controls the number of active shards before executing write operations.
- `refresh` (default `false`): This parameter forces a refresh operation in the shards involved in bulk operations. The new indexed document will be available immediately without waiting the standard refresh interval (`1s`).

Usually ElasticSearch client libraries, that use the ElasticSearch REST API, automatically implement serialization of bulk commands.

The number of commands to be serialized in a bulk is chosen by the user, but these are the following hints to be considered:

- In the standard configuration, ElasticSearch limits the HTTP call to 100 MB in size. If the size is over the limit, the call is rejected.
- A higher number of complex commands take a lot of time to be processed so pay attention to client timeout.
- Small size of commands in a bulk doesn't improve performance.

If the documents aren't big, 500 commands on a bulk can be a good number to start with and it can be tuned depending on the data structures.

The Bulk API can also be used via UDP. Refer to the ElasticSearch documentation for more details at `http://www.elasticsearch.org/guide/en/elasticsearch/reference/current/docs-bulk-udp.html`.

Speeding up GET

The standard GET operation is very fast, but if you need to fetch a lot of IDs, ElasticSearch provides the multi get operation.

Getting ready

You need a working ElasticSearch cluster and the document index explained in the *Indexing a document* recipe.

How to do it...

The following are the multi GET REST URLs:

- `http://<server</_mget`
- `http://<server>/<index_name>/_mget`
- `http://<server>/<index_name>/<type_name>/_mget`

Standard Operations

For executing a multi GET action, we need to perform the following steps:

1. It is the GET method, but it requires a body with IDs and the index/type if they are missing.

   The following is an example which uses the first URL, but we need to provide the `index`, `type`, and `id` parameters:

   ```
   curl 'localhost:9200/_mget' -d '{
       "docs" : [
           {
               "_index" : "myindex",
               "_type" : "order",
               "_id" : "2qLrAfPVQvCRMe7Ku8r0Tw"
           },
           {
               "_index" : "myindex",
               "_type" : "order",
               "_id" : "2"
           }
       ]
   }'
   ```

   This kind of call allows to fetch documents in several different indices and types.

2. If the index and the type is fixed, a call should also be in the following form:

   ```
   curl 'localhost:9200/test/type/_mget' -d '{
       "ids" : ["1", "2"]
   }'
   ```

   The multi GET result is an array of documents.

How it works...

A multi GET call is a shortcut for executing many GET commands in one shot.

ElasticSearch internally spreads the GET operation in parallel on several shards and collects the results to return to the user.

The GET object contains the following parameters:

- `_index`: This parameter is the index that contains the document. It can be omitted if passed in URL.
- `_type`: This parameter defines the type of the document. It can be omitted if passed in URL.
- `_id`: This parameter defines the document ID.
- `fields` (optional): This parameter is a list of fields to be retrieved.
- `routing` (optional): This parameter is the shard routing parameter.

The advantages of a multi GET operation are as follows:

- Reduces networking traffic both internal and external to ElasticSearch
- Speeds up if used in an application: the time of processing a multi GET operation is quite similar to a standard GET operation

See also...

- The *Getting a document* recipe in this chapter

5
Search, Queries, and Filters

In this chapter, we will cover the following topics:

- Executing a search
- Sorting a search
- Highlighting results
- Executing a scan query
- Suggesting a correct query
- Counting
- Deleting by query
- Matching all the documents
- Querying/filtering for term
- Querying/filtering for terms
- Using a prefix query/filter
- Using a Boolean query/filter
- Using a range query/filter
- Using span queries
- Using the match query
- Using the IDS query/filter
- Using the has_child query
- Using the top_children query
- Using a regexp query/filter

Search, Queries, and Filters

- Using exists and missing filters
- Using and/or/not filters
- Using the geo_bounding_box filter
- Using the geo_polygon filter
- Using the geo_distance filter

Introduction

After having the mappings set and the data inserted in the indices, now we can enjoy the search.

In this chapter we will cover the different types of search queries and filters, validate queries, return highlights and limiting fields. This chapter is the core part of the book; and in this chapter the user will understand the difference between query and filter and how to improve quality and speed in search. ElasticSearch allows usage of a rich DSL that covers all common needs: from standard term query to complex GeoShape filtering.

This chapter is divided in to two parts: the first part shows some API calls related search, the second part goes in deep with the query DSL.

To prepare a good base for searching, in online code there are scripts to prepare indices and data for the next recipes.

Executing a search

ElasticSearch was born as a search engine. Its main work is to process queries and give results. As we'll see in this recipe, search in ElasticSearch is not only limited to match some documents, but also to calculate additional information required to improve user experience.

Getting ready

You need a working ElasticSearch cluster and an index populated with the script available in the online code.

How to do it...

For searching and evaluating the results, we will perform the steps given as follows:

1. From command line, we can execute a search using the following command:

   ```
   curl -XGET 'http://127.0.0.1:9200/test-index/test-type/_search' -d
   '{"query":{"match_all":{}}}'
   ```

   In this case we have used a `match_all` query that means "return all the documents". We'll discuss this kind of query in the *Matching all documents* recipe in this chapter.

2. The command, if everything is all right, will return the following result:

   ```
   {
     "took" : 0,
     "timed_out" : false,
     "_shards" : {
       "total" : 5,
       "successful" : 5,
       "failed" : 0
     },
     "hits" : {
       "total" : 3,
       "max_score" : 1.0,
       "hits" : [ {
         "_index" : "test-index",
         "_type" : "test-type",
         "_id" : "1",
         "_score" : 1.0, "_source" : {"position": 1, "parsedtext": "Joe Testere nice guy", "name": "Joe Tester", "uuid": "11111"}
       }, {
         "_index" : "test-index",
         "_type" : "test-type",
         "_id" : "2",
         "_score" : 1.0, "_source" : {"position": 2, "parsedtext": "Bill Testere nice guy", "name": "Bill Baloney", "uuid": "22222"}
       }, {
         "_index" : "test-index",
         "_type" : "test-type",
         "_id" : "3",
         "_score" : 1.0, "_source" : {"position": 3, "parsedtext": "Bill is not\n             nice guy", "name": "Bill Clinton", "uuid": "33333"}
       } ]
     }
   }
   ```

Search, Queries, and Filters

These results contain the following information:

- `took`: This is the time in milliseconds required to execute the query
- `time_out`: This indicates if a timeout was raised during the search and this is related to the timeout parameter of the search
- `_shards`: This is the status of shards divided as follows:
    - `total`: This represents the total number of shards
    - `successful`: This represents the number of shards in which the query was successful
    - `failed`: This represents the number of shards in which the query failed
- `hits`: This represents the results composed, which is divided as follows:
    - `total`: This is the number of documents that match the query
    - `max_score`: This is the score of the first document and is usually 1.0 if score is not involved
    - `hits`: This is a list of result documents

The result document has a lot of fields that are always available and others that depend on search parameters. The most important fields are as follows:

- `_index`: This represents the index that contains the document
- `_type`: This represents the type of the document
- `_id`: This represents the ID of the document
- `_source`: This represents (the default is returned, but can be disabled) the document source
- `_score`: This represents the query score of the document
- `sort`: This represents the values that are used for sorting if the documents are sorted
- `highlight`: This indicates if the highlight is required
- `fields`: This retrieves some fields without fetching all the source objects

How it works...

The HTTP method used to execute a search is GET (but POST also works), the REST URLS are as follows:

- `http://<server>/_search`
- `http://<server>/<index_name(s)>/_search`
- `http://<server>/<index_name(s)>/<type_name(s)>/_search`

Multi indices and types are comma separated. If an index or a type is defined, the search is limited only to them. An alias can be used as the index name.

The core query is usually contained in the body of the GET/POST call, but a lot of options can also be expressed as URI query parameters, which are as follows:

- `q`: This represents the query string to execute simple string queries. One of the example is as follows:
  ```
  curl -XGET 'http://127.0.0.1:9200/test-index/test-type/_search?q=uuid:11111'
  ```
- `df`: This represents the default field to be used within the query. One of the example is as follows:
  ```
  curl -XGET 'http://127.0.0.1:9200/test-index/test-type/_search?df=uuid&q=11111'
  ```
- `from`: This represents (default `0`) the start index of the hits.
- `size`: This represents (default `10`) the number of hits to be returned.
- `analyzer`: This represents the default analyzer to be used.
- `default_operator`: This (default `OR`) can be set to `AND` or `OR`.
- `explain`: This allows to return the information about how the score is calculated as given in the following query:
  ```
  curl -XGET 'http://127.0.0.1:9200/test-index/test-type/_search?q=parsedtext:joe&explain=true'
  ```
- `fields`: This allows to define the fields that must be returned. One example is as follows:
  ```
  curl -XGET 'http://127.0.0.1:9200/test-index/test-type/_search?q=parsedtext:joe&fields=name'
  ```
- `sort`: This (default `score`) allows to change the order of documents. Sort is ascendant by default, if you need to change the order add `desc` to the field as given in the following example:
  ```
  curl -XGET 'http://127.0.0.1:9200/test-index/test-type/_search?sort=name:desc'
  ```
- `timeout`: This (default no active) defines the timeout for the search. ElasticSearch tries to collect results until timeout. If a timeout is fired, all the hits accumulated are returned.
- `search_type`: This allows to define the search strategy. A reference is available on online ElasticSearch's documentation.

Search, Queries, and Filters

Generally the query is contained in the body of the search. The body of the search is the core of ElasticSearch search functionalities. The list of search capabilities extends in every release. For the current Version 1.0 of ElasticSearch, the available parameters are as follows:

- `query`: This contains the query to be executed. Later in this chapter will see how to create different kinds of queries to answer several scenarios.
- `from` (default 0) and `size` (default 10): This allows to control pagination. The `from` parameter is used to define the start position of the hits to be returned.

> The pagination is related to the current search. Firing the same query can give different results if a lot of records have the same score. If you need to process all the resultant documents without repetition, you need to execute scan or scroll queries.

- `sort`: This allows to change the order of matched documents. This is discussed in the *Sorting a search* recipe.
- `filter` (optional): This allows to filter out the query results without affecting the facet count. It's usually used for filtering by facets values.
- `fields` (optional): This controls the fields to be returned.

> Returning only the needed fields reduces the network and memory usage, improving the performance.

- `facets` (optional): This controls the aggregated data that must be computed on results. Using facets improves the user experience on search. This will be discussed in the next chapter.
- `index_boost` (optional): This allows to define a boost value for every index.
- `highlighting` (optional): This allows to define the fields and settings to be used for calculating a query abstract (refer to the *Highlighting results* recipe in this chapter).
- `version` (default `false`): This adds the version of a document in the results.
- `rescore` (optional): This allows to define an extra query to be used in score to improve the quality of results. The rescore query is executed on hits that match the first query and filter.
- `explain` (optional): This returns the information on how the score is calculated for a particular item.
- `script_fields` (optional): This allows to define a script used to calculate the extra fields to be returned with a hit. We'll see this in the *ElasticSearch scripting* recipe in *Chapter 7, Scripting*.

Chapter 5

- `suggest` (optional): This returns the most significant terms related to this query when a query and a field is given. This parameter allows to implement the Google-like "do you mean" functionality (refer to the *Suggesting a correct query* recipe).
- `search_type` (optional): This defines how ElasticSearch should process a query. We'll see the scan query in the *Executing a scan query* recipe in this chapter.
- `scroll` (optional): This controls the scrolling in scroll/scan queries. The scroll allows having an ElasticSearch equivalent of a DBMS cursor.

There's more...

If you are using sort, pay attention to the tokenized fields. The sort order depends on the lower token if ascendant and the high token if descendent. In the previously discussed example the results are as follows:

```
...
"hits" : [ {
      "_index" : "test-index",
      "_type" : "test-type",
      "_id" : "1",
      "_score" : null, "_source" : {"position": 1, "parsedtext":
"Joe Testere nice guy", "name": "Joe Tester", "uuid": "11111"},
      "sort" : [ "tester" ]
  }, {
      "_index" : "test-index",
      "_type" : "test-type",
      "_id" : "3",
      "_score" : null, "_source" : {"position": 3, "parsedtext":
"Bill is not\n              nice guy", "name": "Bill Clinton",
"uuid": "33333"},
      "sort" : [ "clinton" ]
  }, {
      "_index" : "test-index",
      "_type" : "test-type",
      "_id" : "2",
      "_score" : null, "_source" : {"position": 2, "parsedtext":
"Bill Testere nice guy", "name": "Bill Baloney", "uuid": "22222"},
      "sort" : [ "bill" ]
  }
```

Two main concepts are important in search: query and filter. The query means that the matched results are scored using internal Lucene scoring algorithm. In filter, the results are only matched without scoring. Because the filter doesn't need to compute the score it is generally faster.

Search, Queries, and Filters

To improve the quality of the results score, ElasticSearch provides the rescore functionality. This capability allows reordering the top number of documents with another query that it's generally much more expensive, for example if it contains a lot of match queries or scripting. This approach allows executing the rescore only on a small subset of results, reducing overall computation time and resources.

The rescore, as for every query, is executed at shard level so it's automatically distributed.

The following example will show how to execute a fast query (a Boolean one) in the first phase and then to rescore it with a match query in the `rescore` section.

```
curl -s -XPOST 'localhost:9200/_search' -d '{
    "query" : {
        "match" : {
            "parsedtext" : {
                "operator" : "or",
                "query" : "nice guy joe",
                "type" : "boolean"
            }
        }
    },
    "rescore" : {
        "window_size" : 100,
        "query" : {
            "rescore_query" : {
                "match" : {
                    "parsedtext" : {
                        "query" : "joe nice guy",
                        "type" : "phrase",
                        "slop" : 2
                    }
                }
            },
            "query_weight" : 0.8,
            "rescore_query_weight" : 1.5
        }
    }
}'
```

The following are the `rescore` parameters:

- `window_size` (in the example `100`): This parameter controls how many results for shard must be considered in the rescore functionality.
- `query_weight` (default `1.0`) and `rescore_query_weight` (default `1.0`): These parameters are used to compute the final score using the following formula:

*final_score=query_score*query_weight + rescore_score*rescore_query_weight*

If a user wants to keep only the rescore score, he can set the `query_weight` to 0.

See also

- The *Executing facets* recipe in the next chapter
- The *Highlighting results* recipe in this chapter
- The *Executing a scan query* recipe in this chapter
- The *Suggesting a correct query* recipe in this chapter

Sorting a search

While searching for results, the most common criteria in ElasticSearch is the relevance against a text query. Thus the real world applications need to control the sorting criteria. The following are the typical scenarios:

- Sorting a user by surname and name
- Sorting items by stock, price (ascendant, descendent)
- Sorting documents by size, file type, source, and so on

Getting ready

You need a working ElasticSearch cluster and an index populated with the script available in the online code.

Search, Queries, and Filters

How to do it...

For sorting the results, we need to perform the steps given as follows:

1. We need to add a sort section to our query as follows:

   ```
   curl -XGET 'http://127.0.0.1:9200/test-index/test-type/_
   search?pretty=true' -d '{"query":{"match_all":{}},
       "sort" : [
           {"price" : {"order" : "asc", "mode" : "avg", "ignore_
   unmapped":true, "missing":"_last"}},
   "_score"
       ]
   }'
   ```

2. The returned result should be similar to the following one:

   ```
   ...,
     "hits" : {
       "total" : 3,
       "max_score" : null,
       "hits" : [ {
         "_index" : "test-index",
         "_type" : "test-type",
         "_id" : "1",
         "_score" : null, "_source" :{ ... "price":4.0},
         "sort" : [ 4.0 ]
       }, {
          ….
   ```

The sort result is very special: the _score parameter's value is not computed and an extra field sort is created to collect the value used for sorting.

How it works...

The sort is defined as a list that can contain both simple strings and JSON objects.

The sort strings are the names of the fields (that is field1, field2, field3, fields4) used for sorting similar to the order by clause in SQL.

The JSON object allows using the following extra parameters:

- order (asc/desc): This parameter defines if the order must be considered ascendant (default) or descendent.
- ignore_unmapped (true/false): This parameter allows to ignore the fields that don't have mapping in them. This option prevents error during search due to missing mappings.

- `missing(_last/_first)`: This parameter defines how to manage the missing value if we need to put them at the ends (`_last`) of the results or at the start (`_first`).
- `mode`: This parameter defines how to manage multi-valued fields. The possible values are as follows:
    - `min`: This chooses the minimum value (that is in case of an item having multiple prices, it chooses the lowest price in comparison).
    - `max`: This chooses the maximum value.
    - `sum`: The sort value will be computed as the sum of all the values. This mode is only available on numeric fields.
    - `avg`: The sort value will be the average of all the values. This mode is only available on numeric fields.

> If we want add the search score value to the sort list we must use the special sort field, `_score`.

In case you are sorting for a nested object, the following are the two extra parameters that can be used:

- `nested_path`: This defines the nested object to be used for sorting. The field defined for sorting will be relative to the `nested_path` parameter. If we do not define this value, the sorting field will be related to document root. For example, if we have an `address` object nested in a `person` document we can sort for `city.name` using:
    - `address.city.name` without defining the `nested_path` address
    - `city.name` if we define a `nested_path` address
- `nested_filter`: This defines a filter that is used to remove a matching nested document that doesn't match from the sorting value extraction. This filter allows a better selection of values to be used in sorting.

> The sorting process requires that the sorting fields of the all matched query documents are fetched for comparing. To prevent high memory usage it is better to sort on numeric fields and in the case of string sorting, choose short text fields processed with an analyzer that doesn't tokenize the text.

Search, Queries, and Filters

There's more...

There are two special sorting types: geo distance and scripting.

The `_geo_distance` sorting uses the distance from a GeoPoint (location) as a metric to compute the ordering. A sorting example is as follows:

```
...
"sort" : [
        {
            "_geo_distance" : {
                "pin.location" : [-70, 40],
                "order" : "asc",
                "unit" : "km"
            }
        }
    ], ...
```

It accepts the following special parameters:

- `unit`: This defines the metric to be used to compute the distance
- `distance_type` (`plane/arc/factor`): This defines the type of distance to be computed

The name, `_geo_distance` for the field is mandatory.

The point of reference for sorting can be defined in several ways as we have already discussed in the *Mapping a GeoPoint field* recipe in *Chapter 3, Managing Mapping*.

Using the scripts for sorting will be discussed in the *Sorting with scripts* recipe in *Chapter 7, Scripting* after we are introduced to the scripting capabilities of ElasticSearch.

See also

- Refer to the *Mapping a GeoPoint field* recipe in *Chapter 3, Managing Mapping*
- Refer to the *Sorting using script* recipe in *Chapter 7, Scripting*

Highlighting results

ElasticSearch performs a good job on finding results also in large text documents. Thus, for searching text in very large blocks it's very useful, but to improve the user experience it is sometimes required to show the abstract part: a small portion of the text that has matched the query. The highlight functionality in ElasticSearch is designed to do this job.

Getting ready

You need a working ElasticSearch cluster and an index populated with the script available in online code.

How to do it...

For searching and highlighting the results, we need to perform the following steps:

1. From command line, we can execute a search with a `highlight` section as follows:

   ```
   curl -XGET 'http://127.0.0.1:9200/test-index/_
   search?from=0&size=10' -d '
   {
   "query": {"query_string": {"query": "joe"}},
   "highlight": {
   "pre_tags": ["<b>"],
   "fields": {
   "parsedtext": {"order": "score"},
   "name": {"order": "score"}},
      "post_tags": ["</b>"]}}'
   ```

2. If everything is all right, the command will return the following result:

   ```
   {
     ... omissis ...
     "hits" : {
       "total" : 1,
       "max_score" : 0.44194174,
       "hits" : [ {
         "_index" : "test-index",
         "_type" : "test-type",
         "_id" : "1",
         "_score" : 0.44194174, "_source" : {"position": 1,
   "parsedtext": "Joe Testere nice guy", "name": "Joe Tester",
   "uuid": "11111"},
         "highlight" : {
           "name" : [ "<b>Joe</b> Tester" ],
           "parsedtext" : [ "<b>Joe</b> Testere nice guy" ]
         }
       } ]
     }
   }
   ```

As you can see, in the standard result there is a new field, `highlight`, which contains the highlighted fields with an array of fragments.

Search, Queries, and Filters

How it works...

When the `highlight` parameter is passed to the search object, ElasticSearch tries to execute the highlight on document results.

The highlighting phase, which is after the document fetch, tries to extract the highlight following these steps:

- It collects the terms available in the query
- It initializes the highlighter with the parameters given during the query
- It extracts the interested fields: it tries to load them if they are stored, otherwise they are taken from the source
- It executes the query on single fields to detect the more relevant parts
- It adds the found, highlighted fragments to the hit

Using the highlighting functionality is very easy, but there are some important areas where we need to pay attention. They are as follows:

- The field that must be used for highlighting must be available in one of these forms: stored, in source, or in stored term vector

The ElasticSearch highlighter checks the presence of the data field first as term vector (it is the fastest way to execute the highlighting functionality). If the field doesn't have the term vector, it tries to load the field value from the stored fields. If the field is not stored, it finally loads the JSON source, interprets it, and extracts the data value if available. Obviously, the last approach is the slowest one and most resource intensive.

- If a special analyzer is used in search, it should be passed also to the highlighter (this is often automatically managed).

There are several parameters that can be passed in the highlight object to control the highlighting process, and these are as follows:

- `number_of_fragments` (default 5): This parameter controls how many fragments are to be returned. It can be configured globally or for a field.
- `fragment_size` (default 100): This parameter controls the number of characters that the fragments must contain. It can be configured globally or for a field.
- `pre_tags`/`post_tags`: This parameter controls a list of tags to be used for marking the highlighted text.
- `tags_schema="styled"`: This parameter allows defining a tags schema that marks highlighting with different tags with ordered importance. This is a helper to be used to avoid defining a lot of `pre_tags`/`post_tags` tags.

See also

- Refer to the *Executing a search* recipe in this chapter

Executing a scan query

Every time a query is executed, the results are calculated and returned to the user. In ElasticSearch there isn't standard order for records, pagination on a big block of values can bring inconsistencies between results due to added and deleted documents. The scan query tries to resolve these kinds of problems by giving a special cursor that allows to uniquely iterate all the documents. It's often used to back up documents or reindex them.

Getting ready

You need a working ElasticSearch cluster and an index populated with the script available in online code.

How to do it...

For executing a scan query, we need to perform the following steps:

1. From command line, we can execute a search of type scan as follows:

   ```
   curl -XGET 'http://127.0.0.1:9200/test-index/test-type/_search?search_type=scan&scroll=10m&size=50' -d '{"query":{"match_all":{}}}'
   ```

2. If everything is all right, the command will return the following result:

   ```
   {
     "_scroll_id" : "c2Nhbjs1OzQ1Mzp4d1FtcngONlNCYUpVOXh4c0ZiYll3OzQ1Njp4d1FtcngONlNCYUpVOXh4c0ZiYll3OzQ1Nzp4d1FtcngONlNCYUpVOXh4c0ZiYll3OzQ1NDp4d1FtcngONlNCYUpVOXh4c0ZiYll3OzQ1NTp4d1FtcngONlNCYUpVOXh4c0ZiYll3OzE7dG90YWxfaGl0czozOw==",
     "took" : 1,
     "timed_out" : false,
     "_shards" : {
       "total" : 5,
       "successful" : 5,
       "failed" : 0
     },
     "hits" : {
       "total" : 3,
       "max_score" : 0.0,
       "hits" : [ ]
     }
   }
   ```

Search, Queries, and Filters

The result is composed by:

- `scroll_id`: This is the value to be used for scrolling records
- `took`: This is the time required to execute the query
- `timed_out`: This checks if the query was timed out
- `_shards query status`: This gives the information about the status of shards during the query
- `hits`: This gives the other hits that are available after scrolling

3. By having a `scroll_id` parameter, you can use scroll to get the results:

```
curl -XGET 'localhost:9200/_search/scroll?scroll=10m' -d
'c2Nhbjs1OzQ2Mzp4d1FtcngONlNCYUpVOXh4cOZiYll3OzQ2N
jp4d1FtcngONlNCYUpVOXh4cOZiYll3OzQ2Nzp4d1FtcngONlNCYUpVOXh4
cOZiYll3OzQ2NDp4d1FtcngONlNCYUpVOXh4cOZiYll3OzQ2NTp4d1Ftcng
ONlNCYUpVOXh4cOZiYll3OzE7dG90YWxfaGl0czozOw=='
```

4. The result should be something similar to the following one:

```
{
  "_scroll_id" : "c2NhbjswOzE7dG90YWxfaGl0czozOw==",
  "took" : 20,
  "timed_out" : false,
  "_shards" : {
    "total" : 5,
    "successful" : 0,
    "failed" : 5
  },
  "hits" : {
    "total" : 3,
    "max_score" : 0.0,
...}
```

How it works...

The query is interpreted as it is done for search. This kind of search is taught to iterate on a large set of results, so the score and the order are not computed.

During the query phase, every shard takes the state of the IDs in memory until timeout.

Processing a scan query is done in the following two steps:

- The first part executes a query and returns a `scroll_id` parameter which is used to fetch results.
- The second part executes the documents scrolling. You iterate the second step, getting the new `scroll_id` value and fetch other documents.

Chapter 5

 If you need to iterate on a large set of records, scan query must be used, otherwise you will have doubled results.

The scan query is a standard query, but are two special parameters that are passed in the query string, which are as follows:

- `search_type=scan`: This parameter informs ElasticSearch to execute the scan query.
- `scroll=(your timeout)`: This parameter allows defining how long the hits should live. The time can be expressed in seconds using the `s` postfix (that is, `5s`, `10s`, or `15s`) or in minutes using the `m` postfix (that is, `5m`, or `10m`). If you are using a long timeout, you must be sure that your nodes have a lot of RAM to keep them alive. This parameter is mandatory and must be always provided.

 Size is also a bit special as it is treated "per shard" meaning that if you have `size = 10` and 5 shards each scroll will return 50.

See also

- The *Executing a search* recipe in this chapter

Suggesting a correct query

It's very common for users to commit a typewriting error or to need help to complete the words. This scenario is solved by ElasticSearch with the suggest functionality.

Getting ready

You need a working ElasticSearch cluster and an index populated with the script available in online code.

How to do it...

For suggesting a correct term by query, we need to perform the following steps:

1. From command line, we can execute the following suggest call:
   ```
   curl -XGET 'http://127.0.0.1:9200/test-index/_suggest' -d ' {
     "suggest1" : {
   ```

Search, Queries, and Filters

```
          "text" : "we find tester",
          "term" : {
            "field" : "parsedtext"
          }
        }
      }
    }'
```

2. The result returned by ElasticSearch, if everything is all right, should be as follows:

```
{
    "_shards": {
        "failed": 0,
        "successful": 5,
        "total": 5
    },
    "suggest1": [
        {
            "length": 2,
            "offset": 0,
            "options": [],
            "text": "we"
        },
        {
            "length": 4,
            "offset": 3,
            "options": [],
            "text": "find"
        },
        {
            "length": 6,
            "offset": 8,
            "options": [
                {
                    "freq": 2,
                    "score": 0.8333333,
                    "text": "testere"
                }
            ],
            "text": "tester"
        }
    ]
}
```

Chapter 5

The result is composed by:

- The shards status at the time of the query
- The list of tokens with their available candidates

How it works...

The suggest API call works collecting terms statistics on all the index shards. Using the Lucene field statistics it is possible to detect the correct term or complete a term.

The HTTP method used to execute a suggest is GET (but POST also works), the REST URLs are as follows:

- `http://<server>/_suggest`
- `http://<server>/<index_name(s)>/_suggest`

> The suggest can be also embedded in the standard search API call.

There are two types of suggester term and phrase.

The more simple one to configure is the term suggester. It requires only the text and the field to work. It also allows us to set a lot of parameters to set, for example, the minimum size for a word, how to sort results, and the suggester strategy. A complete reference is available on the ElasticSearch website.

The phrase suggester is able to keep relations between terms, which it needs to suggest. The phrase suggester is less efficient than the term one, but it provides better results.

The suggest API is a new feature so parameters and options can change between releases.

See also

- The *Executing a search* recipe in this chapter
- The suggester phrase online documentation is available at `http://www.elasticsearch.org/guide/en/elasticsearch/reference/current/search-suggesters-phrase.html`

Counting

It is often required to return only the count of the matched results and not the results themselves.

There are a lot of scenarios involving counting, some of them are as follows:

- To return a number (for example, how many posts for a blog, how many comments for a post)
- Validating if some items are available: are there posts? are there comments?

Getting ready

You need a working ElasticSearch cluster and an index populated with the script available in online code.

How to do it...

For executing a counting query, we need to perform the following steps:

1. From command line, we will execute the following `count` query:

   ```
   curl -XGET 'http://127.0.0.1:9200/test-index/test-type/_count' -d '{"match_all":{}}'
   ```

2. The result returned by ElasticSearch, if everything is all right, should be as follows:

   ```
   {
      "count" : 3,
      "_shards" : {
        "total" : 5,
        "successful" : 5,
        "failed" : 0
      }
   }
   ```

The result is composed by the count result (a long type) and the shards status at the time of the query.

How it works...

The query is interpreted as it is done for searching. The count is processed and distributed in all the shards, in which it's mapped on Lucene. Every hit shard returns a count that it's aggregated and returned to the user.

Chapter 5

 In ElasticSearch, couting is faster than searching. If the results are not required, it's good practice use it.

The HTTP method to execute a count is GET (but POST also works), the REST URLs are as follows:

- `http://<server>/_count`
- `http://<server>/<index_name(s)>/_count`
- `http://<server>/<index_name(s)>/<type_name(s)>/_count`

Multiple indices and types are comma separated. If an index or a type is defined, the search is limited only to them.

An alias can be used as index name.

Typically a body is used to express a query, but for simple query the `q` (query argument) can be used. For example:

```
curl -XGET 'http://127.0.0.1:9200/test-index/test-type/_count?q=uuid:11111'
```

See also

- The *Executing a search* recipe in this chapter

Deleting by query

In the previous chapter we saw how to delete a document. Deleting a document is very fast but we need to know the document ID.

ElasticSearch provides a call to delete all the documents that match a query.

Getting ready

You need a working ElasticSearch cluster and an index populated with the script available in online code.

Search, Queries, and Filters

How to do it...

For executing a delete by query, we need to perform the following steps:

1. From command line, we need to execute the following query:

   ```
   curl -XDELETE 'http://127.0.0.1:9200/test-index/test-type/_query' -d '{"match_all":{}}'
   ```

2. The result returned by ElasticSearch, if everything is all right, should be as follows:

   ```
   {
     "ok" : true,
     "_indices" : {
       "test-index" : {
         "_shards" : {
           "total" : 5,
           "successful" : 5,
           "failed" : 0
         }
       }
     }
   }
   ```

3. The result is composed by the ok result (a Boolean type) and the shards status at the time of the delete by query.

How it works...

The query is interpreted as it is done for searching. The delete by query is processed and distributed in all the shards.

> When you want remove all the documents without deleting the mapping, a "delete by query" with a "match all query" allows to clean your mapping of all the documents. This call works similar to the truncate table command of the SQL language.

The HTTP method to execute a count is DELETE, the REST URLs are as follows:

- http://<server>/_query
- http://<server>/<index_name(s)>/_query
- http://<server>/<index_name(s)>/<type_name(s)>/_query

Multiple indices and types are comma separated. If an index or a type is defined, the search is limited only to them.

An alias can be used as index name.

Typically a body is used to express a query, but for simple query the q (query argument) can be used. For example:

```
curl -XDELETE 'http://127.0.0.1:9200/test-index/test-type/_query?q=uuid:11111'
```

See also

- The *Executing a search* recipe in this chapter

Matching all the documents

One of the most used queries, usually in conjunction with a filter, is Match All Query. This kind of query allows to returns all the documents.

Getting ready

You need a working ElasticSearch cluster and an index populated with the script available in online code.

How to do it...

For executing the match_all query, we need to perform the following steps:

1. From command line, we execute the following query:

   ```
   curl -XPOST 'http://127.0.0.1:9200/test-index/test-type/_search' -d '{"query":{"match_all":{}}}'
   ```

2. The result returned by ElasticSearch, if everything is all right, should be as follows:

   ```
   {
     "took" : 52,
     "timed_out" : false,
     "_shards" : {
       "total" : 5,
       "successful" : 5,
       "failed" : 0
     },
   ```

Search, Queries, and Filters

```
    "hits" : {
      "total" : 3,
      "max_score" : 1.0,
      "hits" : [ {
        "_index" : "test-index",
        "_type" : "test-type",
        "_id" : "1",
        "_score" : 1.0, "_source" : {"position": 1, "parsedtext":
"Joe Testere nice guy", "name": "Joe Tester", "uuid": "11111"}
      }, {
        "_index" : "test-index",
        "_type" : "test-type",
        "_id" : "2",
        "_score" : 1.0, "_source" : {"position": 2, "parsedtext":
"Bill Testere nice guy", "name": "Bill Baloney", "uuid": "22222"}
      }, {
        "_index" : "test-index",
        "_type" : "test-type",
        "_id" : "3",
        "_score" : 1.0, "_source" : {"position": 3, "parsedtext":
"Bill is not\n                 nice guy", "name": "Bill Clinton",
"uuid": "33333"}
      } ]
    }
  }
```

The result is a standard query result as we have seen in the *Executing a Search* recipe.

How it works...

The `match_all` query is one of the most common ones. It's faster because it doesn't require the score calculus (it's wrapped in Lucene `ConstantScoreQuery`).

The `match_all` query is often used in conjunction with a filter in a filter query. One example is as follows:

```
{
    "filtered" : {
        "match_all" : {},
        "filter" : {
            "term" : { "myfield" : "myterm" }
        }
    }
}
```

See also

> The *Executing a search* recipe in this chapter

Querying/filtering for term

Searching or filtering for a particular term is very frequent. Term query and filter work with exact values and are generally very fast.

Getting ready

You need a working ElasticSearch cluster and an index populated with the script available in online code.

How to do it...

For executing a term query/filter, we need to perform the following steps:

1. We execute a term query, from command line as follows:
   ```
   curl -XPOST 'http://127.0.0.1:9200/test-index/test-type/_search' -d '{
       "query": {
           "term": {
               "uuid": "33333"
           }
       }
   }'
   ```

2. The result returned by ElasticSearch, if everything is all right, should be as follows:
   ```
   {
     "took" : 58,
     "timed_out" : false,
     "_shards" : {
       "total" : 5,
       "successful" : 5,
       "failed" : 0
     },
     "hits" : {
       "total" : 1,
       "max_score" : 0.30685282,
       "hits" : [ {
         "_index" : "test-index",
         "_type" : "test-type",
         "_id" : "3",
   ```

Search, Queries, and Filters

```
        "_score" : 0.30685282, "_source" : {"position": 3,
"parsedtext": "Bill is not\n                 nice guy", "name":
"Bill Clinton", "uuid": "33333"}
    } ]
  }
}
```

The result is similar to the result of a standard query as we have seen in the *Executing a Search* recipe.

3. We will execute a term filter, from command line as follows:

```
curl -XPOST 'http://127.0.0.1:9200/test-index/test-type/_search'
-d '{
    "query": {
        "filtered": {
            "filter": {
                "term": {
                    "uuid": "33333"
                }
            },
            "query": {
                "match_all": {}
            }
        }
    }
}'
```

4. The result will be as follows:

```
{
  "took" : 4,
  "timed_out" : false,
  "_shards" : {
    "total" : 5,
    "successful" : 5,
    "failed" : 0
  },
  "hits" : {
    "total" : 1,
    "max_score" : 1.0,
    "hits" : [ {
      "_index" : "test-index",
      "_type" : "test-type",
      "_id" : "3",
      "_score" : 1.0, "_source" : {"position": 3, "parsedtext":
"Bill is not\n                 nice guy", "name": "Bill Clinton",
"uuid": "33333"}
    } ]
  }
}
```

How it works...

Lucene, due to its inverted index, is one of the fastest engines to search for a term/value in a field.

Every field that is indexed in Lucene is converted in a fast search structure for its particular type:

- Text is split in tokens if analyzed or saved as a single token
- Numeric fields are converted in their fastest binary representation
- Date and Datetime fields are converted in binary forms

In ElasticSearch all these conversions steps are automatically managed. Searching for a term independent of the value, is archived by ElasticSearch using the correct format for the field.

Internally, while executing a term query all the documents matching the term are collected and then they are sorted by score (the scoring depends on the Lucene similarity algorithm chosen). The term filter follows the same iteration, but it doesn't require the score step, so it's much faster.

If we look at the results of the previous searches; for the term query the hit has `0.30685282` as score, the filter has `1.0`. The time required for scoring if the sample is very small is not so relevant, but if you have thousands or millions of documents it takes much more time.

> If the score is not important, prefer to use the term filter.

The filter is preferred to query when the score is not important. Typical scenarios are as follows:

- Filtering permissions
- Filtering numerical values
- Filtering ranges

There's more...

Matching a term is the base of Lucene and ElasticSearch. To correctly use a query/filter you need to pay attention to how the field is indexed.

Search, Queries, and Filters

As we have seen in *Chapter 2, Downloading and Setting Up ElasticSearch*, the terms of an indexed field depends on the analyzer used to index, and to better understand this concept in the following table there is a representation of a phrase which depends on several analyzers. For standard string analyzers the phrase is as follows:

```
Phrase: Peter's house is big.
```

Mapping Index	Analyzer	Tokens
no	(No index)	(No tokens)
not_analyzed	KeywordAnalyzer	[Peter's house is big]
analyzed	StandardAnalyzer	["peter", "s", "house", "is", "big"]

Common pitfalls in running a search are related to misunderstanding the analyzer/mapping configuration.

KeywordAnalyzer, which is used as default for the not_analyzed field, saves the text unchanged as a single token.

StandardAnalyzer, which is the default value for the analyzed field, tokenizes on whitespaces and punctuation. Every token is converted to lowercase. You often use the same analyzer to analyze the query (the default settings), so your query tokens will also be lowercased. In the preceding example if the phrases are analyzed with StandardAnalyzer, you cannot search for the term Peter, but for peter.

> When the same field requires one or more search strategies, you need to use a multifield, setting the different analyzers that you need.

See also

- The *Executing a search* recipe in this chapter

Querying/filtering for terms

The previous type of search works very well for single term search. If you want to achieve a multiterm search, you can process in two ways: by using an and/or filter or using the multiterm query.

Getting ready

You need a working ElasticSearch cluster and an index populated with the script available in online code.

How to do it...

For executing a terms query/filter, we need to perform the following steps:

1. We execute a terms query, from command line as follows:
   ```
   curl -XPOST 'http://127.0.0.1:9200/test-index/test-type/_search' -d '{
       "query": {
           "terms": {
               "uuid": ["33333", "32222"]
           }
       }
   }'
   ```
   The result returned by ElasticSearch, is the same as the previous recipe.

2. If you want use the terms query in a filter. The query should be as follows:
   ```
   curl -XPOST 'http://127.0.0.1:9200/test-index/test-type/_search' -d '{
       "query": {
           "filtered": {
               "filter": {
                   "terms": {
                       "uuid": ["33333", "32222"]
                   }
               },
               "query": {
                   "match_all": {}
               }
           }
       }
   }'
   ```

How it works...

The terms query/filter is related to the previous kind of query. It extends the term query to support multiple values.

This call is very useful because it is a very common concept of filtering on multiple values. In traditional SQL this operation is achieved with the `in` keyword in the `where` clause, for example `Select * from *** where color in ('"red", '"green")`.

In the preceding examples, the query search for `uuid` with values 33333 and 22222.

The terms query/filter are not a mere helper for the term matching function.

Search, Queries, and Filters

The terms query allows to define extra parameters to control the query behavior. Some of the examples are as follows:

- `minimum_match/minimum_should_match`: This parameter controls how many matched terms are required to validate the query, as given in the following code:

    ```
    "terms": {
    "color": ["red", "blue", "white"],
       "minimum_should_match":2
          }
    ```

    The preceding query matches all the documents where in the `color` field has at least two values between `red`, `blue`, and `white`.

- `disable_coord`: This parameter is a boolean value which indicates if the `coord` query must be enabled or disabled. `coord` is a query option used to score better overlapping matching in Lucene. For further details visit http://lucene.apache.org/core/4_0_0/core/org/apache/lucene/search/similarities/Similarity.html.

- `boost`: This parameter gives the standard query boost value used to modify the query weight,

The term filter is very powerful as it allows to define the strategy that must be used in processing the filtering terms. The strategies are passed in the parameter execution and the current available parameters are as follows:

- `plain` (default): This works as a terms query. It generates a bit set with the terms and when is evaluated. This strategy cannot be automatically cached.

- `bool`: This parameter generates a term query for every term and then creates a Boolean filter to be used to filter. This approach allows to reuse the term filters required for Boolean filtering. Performance is increased if the subterm filters are reused.

- `and`: This parameter is the same as `bool`, but the term filter subqueries are wrapped in an `and` filter.

- `or`: This is the same as bool, but the term filter subqueries are wrapped in a `or` filter.

There's more...

Because terms filtering is very powerful, to give some speed in searching, the terms can be fetched by other documents while querying.

This is a very common scenario. Think, for example, a user contains the list of groups in which he is associated and you want to filter the documents that can only be seen by some group. The pseudo code for this should be as follows:

```
curl -XGET localhost:9200/my-index/document/_search -d '{
  "query" : {
    "filtered" : {
      "query":{"match_all":{}},
      "filter" : {
        "terms" : {
          "can_see_groups" : {
            "index" : "my-index",
            "type" : "user",
            "id" : "1bw71LaxSzSp_zV6NB_YGg",
            "path" : "groups"
          }
        }
      }
    }
  }
}'
```

In this example the list of groups is fetched by a document (which always is identified by an index, type, and ID) and the path (field) that contains the values to be inserted in them.

This is a pattern similar to SQL, as shown in the following code:

```
select * from xxx where can_see_group in (select groups from user where user_id='1bw71LaxSzSp_zV6NB_YGg')
```

Generally NoSQL datastores do not support join, so the data must be optimized to enable searching via denormalization or other techniques.

ElasticSearch does not provide the join as in SQL, but it provides similar alternatives. Some of them are as follows:

- Child/parent queries
- Nested queries
- Terms filter with external document term fetching

See also

- The *Executing a search* recipe in this chapter
- The *Querying/filtering for term* recipe in this chapter
- The *Using a Boolean query/filter* recipe in this chapter
- The *Using and/or/not filters* recipe in this chapter

Search, Queries, and Filters

Using a prefix query/filter

The prefix query/filter is used only when the starting part of a term is known. It allows completing truncated or partial terms.

Getting ready

You need a working ElasticSearch cluster and an index populated with the script available in online code.

How to do it...

For executing a `prefix` query/filter, we need to perform the following steps:

1. We execute a `prefix` query, from command line as follows:
   ```
   curl -XPOST 'http://127.0.0.1:9200/test-index/test-type/_search' -d '{
       "query": {
           "prefix": {
               "uuid": "333"
           }
       }
   }'
   ```

2. The result, returned by ElasticSearch, is the same as the previous recipe.

3. If you want use the terms query in a filter, the query should be as follows:
   ```
   curl -XPOST 'http://127.0.0.1:9200/test-index/test-type/_search' -d '{
       "query": {
           "filtered": {
               "filter": {
                   "prefix": {
                       "uuid": "333"
                   }
               },
               "query": {
                   "match_all": {}
               }
           }
       }
   }'
   ```

How it works...

When a prefix query/filter is executed, Lucene has a special method to skip to terms that start with a common prefix: so the execution of a prefix query is very fast.

The prefix query/filter is used, in general, in scenarios where term completion is required. Some of them are as follows:

- Name completion
- Code completion
- On type completion

When a tree structure is designed in ElasticSearch, if the ID of the item is designed to contain the hierarchical relation, it can greatly speed up the application filtering. Some of the examples are as follows:

Id	Element
001	Fruit
00102	Apple
0010201	Green Apple
0010202	Red Apple
00103	Melon
0010301	White Melon
002	Vegetables

In the previous table we have structured ID to contain information about the tree structure, which allows us to create the following queries:

- Filtering by all the fruits is done using the following code:

    "prefix": {"fruit_id": "001" }

- Filtering by all apple types is done by using the following code:

    "prefix": {"fruit_id": "001002" }

- Filtering by all the vegetables is done using the following code:

    "prefix": {"fruit_id": "002" }

If it's compared to a standard SQL `parent_id` table on a very large dataset, the reduction in join and the fast search performance of Lucene can filter the results in a few milliseconds as compared to some seconds/minutes.

> Structuring the data in the correct way can give impressive performance boost!

See also

- Refer to the *Querying/filtering for terms* recipe in this chapter

Using a Boolean query/filter

Every person using a search engine must have sometimes used the syntax with minus (-) and plus (+) to include or exclude some query terms. The Boolean query/filter allows programmatically defining some queries to include or exclude or optionally include (should) in the query.

This kind of query/filter is one of the most important ones, because it allows to aggregate a lot of simple queries/filters that we will see in this chapter to build a big complex one.

Getting ready

You need a working ElasticSearch cluster and an index populated with the script available in online code.

How to do it...

For executing a Boolean query/filter, we need to perform the following steps:

1. We execute a Boolean query, from command line as follows:
   ```
   curl -XPOST 'http://127.0.0.1:9200/test-index/test-type/_search' -d '{
       "query": {
           "bool" : {
           "must" : {
               "term" : { "parsedtext" : "joe" }
           },
           "must_not" : {
               "range" : {
                   "position" : { "from" : 0, "to" : 10 }
               }
           },
           "should" : [
               {
                   "term" : { "uuid" : "11111" }
               },
   ```

```
                {
                    "term" : { "uuid" : "22222" }
                }
            ],
            "minimum_number_should_match" : 1,
            "boost" : 1.0
        }
    }
}'
```

2. The result returned by ElasticSearch is similar to the previous recipes, but in this case should return two records (ID 1 and ID 2).
3. If you want to use a Boolean filter, the query should be as follows:

```
curl -XPOST 'http://127.0.0.1:9200/test-index/test-type/_search'
-d '{
    "query": {
        "filtered": {
            "filter": {
            "bool" : {
            "must" : {
                "term" : { "parsedtext" : "joe" }
            },
            "must_not" : {
                "range" : {
                    "position" : { "from" : 0, "to" : 10 }
                }
            },
            "should" : [
                {
                    "term" : { "uuid" : "11111" }
                },
                {
                    "term" : { "uuid" : "22222" }
                }
            ],
            "minimum_number_should_match" : 1,
            }
            },
            "query": {
                "match_all": {}
            }
        }
    }
}'
```

Search, Queries, and Filters

How it works...

The `bool` query/filter is often one of the most used filters because it allows composing a big query using a lot of simple ones. It has one of the following three parts that are mandatory:

- `must`: This returns a list of queries/filters that must be verified. All the `must` queries must be verified to return the hits. It can be seen as an AND filter with all its subqueries.
- `must_not`: This returns a list of queries/filters that must not be verified. It can be seen as a NOT filter of an AND query.
- `should`: This returns a list of queries that can be verified. The minimum number of these queries must be verified and this value is controlled by `minimum_number_should_match` (default 1).

> The Boolean filter is much faster than a group of and/or/not queries because it is optimized for executing fast Boolean bitwise operations on document bitmap results.

See also

- Refer to the *Querying/filtering for terms* recipe in this chapter

Using a range query/filter

Searching/filtering by range is a very common scenario in a real world application. Some standard cases are as follows:

- Filtering by range numeric value (that is, Price, size, ages, and so on)
- Filtering by date (that is, events of 03/07/12 can be a range query from 03/07/12 00:00:00 and 03/07/12 24:59:59)
- Filtering by term (that is, from A to D)

Getting ready

You need a working ElasticSearch cluster, an index `"test"` (refer to the next chapter to learn how to create an index), and basic knowledge of JSON.

How to do it...

For executing a range query/filter, we need to perform the following step:

1. Considering the sample data of previous examples which contains an integer field `position`. Using it to execute a query for filtering positions between 3 and 5, we will have:

```
curl -XPOST 'http://127.0.0.1:9200/test-index/test-type/_search' 
-d '{
    "query": {
        "filtered": {
            "filter": {
                "range" : {
                   "position" : {
                       "from" : 3,
                       "to" : 4,
                       "include_lower" : true,
                       "include_upper" : false
                   }
                }
            },
            "query": {
                "match_all": {}
            }
        }
    }
}'
```

How it works...

The range query is used because scoring results can cover several interesting scenarios such as:

- Items high in stocks should be presented first
- New items should be boosted
- The most sold item should be boosted

The range filter is very handy with numeric values, as the preceding example shows.

Search, Queries, and Filters

The parameters that a range query/filter accepts are as follows:

- `from` (optional): This parameter defines the starting value for the range
- `to` (optional): This parameter defines the ending value for the range
- `include_in_lower` (optional, default `true`): This parameter includes the starting value in the range
- `include_in_upper` (optional, default `true`): This parameter includes the ending value in the range

In the range filter, the other helper parameters that are available to simplify search are as follows:

- `gt` (greater than): This parameter has the same functionality to set the `from` parameter and the `include_in_lower` parameter to `false`
- `gte` (greater than or equal): This parameter has the same functionality to set the `from` parameter and the `include_in_lower` parameter to `true`
- `lt` (lesser than): This parameter has the same functionality to set the `to` parameter and the `include_in_lower` parameter to `false`
- `lte` (lesser than or equal): This parameter has the same functionality to set the `to` parameter and the `include_in_lower` parameter to `false`

In ElasticSearch, this kind of query/filter covers several types of SQL queries. Some of them are as follows:

- `<, <=, >, >=` on numeric values
- `between` on values and dates

Using span queries

The big difference between standard systems (SQL, but also many NoSQL technologies such as MongoDB, Riak, or CouchDB) and ElasticSearch is the number of facilities to express text queries.

The span query family is a group of queries that control a sequence of text tokens. They allow defining the following queries:

- Exact phrase query
- Exact fragment query (that is, `Take off, give up`)
- Partial exact phrase with a `slop` parameter (other tokens between the searched terms, that is, "the man" with slop 2 can also match "the strong man", "the old wise man", and so on)

Getting ready

You need a working ElasticSearch cluster.

How to do it...

For executing span queries, we need to perform the following steps:

1. The main element in span queries is the `span_term` parameter whose usage is similar to the term of standard query.

    One or more `span_term` parameters can be aggregated to formulate a span query.

    The `span_first` query defines a query in which the `span_term` parameter in the first token or near it. This is an example:

    ```
    curl -XPOST 'http://127.0.0.1:9200/test-index/test-type/_search'
    -d '{
        "query": {
            "span_first" : {
                "match" : {
                    "span_term" : { "parsedtext" : "joe" }
                },
                "end" : 5
            }
        }
    }'
    ```

2. The `span_or` query is used to define multiple values in a span query. This is very handy for simple synonym search.

    ```
    curl -XPOST 'http://127.0.0.1:9200/test-index/test-type/_search'
    -d '{
        "query": {
            "span_or" : {
                "clauses" : [
                    { "span_term" : { "parsedtext" : "nice" } },
                    { "span_term" : { "parsedtext" : "cool" } },
                    { "span_term" : { "parsedtext" : "wonderful"}}
                ]
            }
        }
    }'
    ```

Search, Queries, and Filters

3. Similar to span_or there is a span_multi query, which wraps multiple term queries such as prefix and wildcard ones. For example:

```
curl -XPOST 'http://127.0.0.1:9200/test-index/test-type/_search' -d '{
    "query": {
        "span_multi":{
            "match":{
                "prefix" : { "parsedtext" :  { "value" : "jo" } }
            }
        }
    }
}'
```

4. All these kinds of queries can be used to create the span_near query that allows to control the token sequence of the query, as shown in the following code:

```
curl -XPOST 'http://127.0.0.1:9200/test-index/test-type/_search' -d '{
    "query": {
        "span_near" : {
            "clauses" : [
                { "span_term" : { "parsedtext" : "nice" } },
                { "span_term" : { "parsedtext" : "joe" } },
                { "span_term" : { "parsedtext" : "guy" } }
            ],
            "slop" : 3,
            "in_order" : false,
            "collect_payloads" : false
        }
    }
}'
```

How it works...

Lucene provides the span queries available in ElasticSearch.

The base span query is the span_term parameter that works exactly as the term query. The goal of this span query is to match an exact term (field prefixed by text). It can be composed to formulate other kinds of span queries.

> The main usage of the span query is to match a sequence of terms.

Using a `span_term` parameter in a `span_first` query means to match a term, that must be in the first position. If the end parameter (integer) is defined, it extends the first token matching to the passed value.

One of the most powerful span queries is the `span_or` one that allows to define multiple terms in the same position. It covers several scenarios such as:

- multinames
- synonyms
- several verbal forms

The `span_or` query doesn't have the counterpart, `span` and which doesn't have no meaning.

If the number of terms, that must be passed to a `span_or` query, are many, it can be sometimes reduced with a `span_multi` query with a prefix or a wildcard. This approach allows matching for example all the term play, playing, plays, player, players, and so on using a prefix query with `play`.

Otherwise, the most powerful span query is `span_near`, which allows defining a list of span queries (`clauses`) to be matched in sequence or not. The parameters which can be passed to this span query are as follows:

- `in_order` (default `true`): This parameter defines the order in which the term matched in the clauses must be executed. If you define two span near queries with two span terms to match `joe` and `black`, if `in_order` is true, you will not able to match the `black joe` text.
- `slop` (default 0): This parameter defines the distance between terms that must be matched from the clauses.

By setting slop to 0 and `in_order` to `true` you are creating an "exact phrase" match.

The `span_near` query and `slop` can be used to create a phrase that is able to have some terms that are not known. For example, consider matching an expression such as "the house". If you need to execute an exact match you need to write a similar query as follows:

```
{
    "query": {
        "span_near" : {
            "clauses" : [
                { "span_term" : { "parsedtext" : "the" } },
                { "span_term" : { "parsedtext" : "house" } }
            ],
            "slop" : 0,
            "in_order" : true
        }
    }
}
```

Search, Queries, and Filters

Now, if you have for example an adjective between the article and "house" (that is, the wonderful house, the big house, and so on) the previous query never matches them. To achieve this goal, it is required to set the `slop` value to 1.

Usually slop is set to 1,2, and 3. High values have no meaning.

See also

- Refer to the *Using the match query* recipe in this chapter

Using the match query

ElasticSearch provides a helper to build complex span queries, which depends on simple preconfigured settings. This helper is called the match query.

Getting ready

You need a working ElasticSearch cluster.

How to do it...

For executing a match query, we need to perform the following steps:

1. The standard usage of a `match` query simply requires the field name and the query text. For example:

    ```
    curl -XPOST 'http://127.0.0.1:9200/test-index/test-type/_search'
    -d '{
        "query": {
            "match" : {
                "parsedtext" : "nice guy",
                "operator": "and"
            }
        }
    }'
    ```

2. If you need to execute the same query as a phrase query, the type from `match` changes to `match_phrase`, as given in the following code:

    ```
    curl -XPOST 'http://127.0.0.1:9200/test-index/test-type/_search'
    -d '{
        "query": {
            "match_phrase" : {
                "parsedtext" : "nice guy"
            }
        }
    }'
    ```

3. An extension of the previous query used in text completion or the "search as you type" functionality is the `match_phrase_prefix` query, as given in the following code:

```
curl -XPOST 'http://127.0.0.1:9200/test-index/test-type/_search' -d '{
    "query": {
        "match_phrase_prefix" : {
            "parsedtext" : "nice gu"
        }
    }
}'
```

How it works...

The match query aggregates several queries that cover standard query scenarios.

The standard match query creates a Boolean query that can be controlled by the following parameters:

- operator (default `OR`): This parameter defines how to store and process the terms. If it's set to `OR`, all the terms are converted in the Boolean query with all the terms in "should clauses". If it's set to `AND`, the terms build a list of "must clauses".
- `analyzer` (default based on a mapping or set in a searcher): This parameter allows overriding the default analyzer of the field.
- `fuzziness`: This parameter allows defining fuzzy term search (refer to the *Using a fuzzy query* recipe). Related to this parameter, `prefix_length` and `max_expansion` are available.
- `zero_term_query` (none/all) (default `none`): This parameter controls that is a tokenizer filter removing all the terms from query, the default behavior is to return nothing or all the documents. This is the case when you build an English query searching for "the" or "a" which means that can match all the documents.
- `cutoff_frequency`: This parameter allows handling dynamic stopwords at runtime. During query execution, terms over the `cutoff_frequency` parameter are considered as stopwords. This approach is very useful because it allows converting a general query into a domain-related query, because terms to be skipped depend on the text statistic.

The Boolean query created from the match query is very handy, but it suffers from some common problems related to a Boolean query such as term position. If the term position matters, you need to use another family of match queries, the phrase one.

The `match_phrase` type in the match query builds long span queries from the query text.

Search, Queries, and Filters

The parameters that can be used to improve the quality of phrase query are the analyzers for processing the text and `slop`, which controls the distance between terms (refer to the *Using span queries* recipe in this chapter).

If the last term is partially complete and you want to provide to your users a "query while writing" functionality the phrase type can be set to `match_phrase_prefix`. This type builds a span near the query in which the last clause is a span prefix term.

The match query is a very useful query type or, as I previously defined, it is a helper to build internally several common queries.

See also

- Refer to the *Using span queries* recipe in this chapter
- Refer to the *Using a Boolean query/filter* recipe in this chapter
- Refer to the *Using a prefix query/filter* in this chapter

Using the IDS query/filter

The IDs query and filter allow matching documents by their IDs.

Getting ready

You need a working ElasticSearch cluster.

How to do it...

For executing IDS queries/filters, we need to perform the following steps:

1. The `ids` query for fetching IDs 1, 2, 3 of the `test-type` type is in the following form:

    ```
    curl -XPOST 'http://127.0.0.1:9200/test-index/test-type/_search' -d '{
        "query": {
            "ids" : {
                "type" : "test-type",
                "values" : ["1", "2", "3"]
            }
        }
    }'
    ```

2. The same query can be converted in a filter query similar to the following one:

```
curl -XPOST 'http://127.0.0.1:9200/test-index/test-type/_search'
-d '{
    "query": {
        "filtered": {
            "filter": {
                "ids" : {
                    "type" : "test-type",
                    "values" : ["1", "2", "3"]
                }
            },
            "query": {
                "match_all": {}
            }
        }
    }
}'
```

How it works...

Query and filtering by ID is a very fast operation as IDs are often taken in memory for fast lookup.

The parameters used in this query/filter are as follows:

- `ids` (required): This is a list of IDs that must be matched.
- `type` (optional): This is a string or a list of strings that define the types for searching. If not defined this value is taken from the URL it calls.

 ElasticSearch stores internally the ID of a document in a special field called `_uid` composed by `type#id`. A `_uid` value is unique in an index.

Otherwise, the standard way of using IDs query/filter is to select documents, this query allows to fetch documents without knowing the shard that contains the documents.

The documents are stored in shards based on the hash on their IDs. If a parent ID or a routing is defined, they are used to choose the shard to store the documents. In these cases, the only way to fetch the document knowing its ID is by using the IDs query/filter.

If you need to fetch multiple IDs there are no routing changes (due to `parent_id` or the `routing` parameter at index time), it's better not to use this kind of query, but use a special API call to get documents as they are much faster and also works in real time.

Search, Queries, and Filters

See also

- The *Getting a document* recipe in *Chapter 4, Standard Operations*
- The *Speeding up GET* recipe in *Chapter 4, Standard Operations*

Using the has_child query/filter

ElasticSearch does not provide only simple documents, but it lets you define a hierarchy based on parent and child. The `has_child` query allows querying for parent documents of which the children verify some queries.

Getting ready

You need a working ElasticSearch cluster and the data populated with the populate script.

How to do it...

For executing the `has_child` query/filter, we need to perform the following steps:

1. We need to search the `test-type` parents of which the `test-type2` children have a term in the field value as `value1`. We can create this kind of query as follows:

```
curl -XPOST 'http://127.0.0.1:9200/test-index/test-type/_search' -d '{
    "query": {
        "has_child" : {
            "type" : "test-type2",
            "query" : {
                "term" : {
                    "value" : "value1"
                }
            }
        }
    }
}'
```

2. If scoring is not important, it's better to reformulate the query as a filter in the following way:

```
curl -XPOST 'http://127.0.0.1:9200/test-index/test-type/_search' -d '{
    "query": {
        "filtered": {
            "filter": {
                "has_child" : {
                    "type" : "test-type2",
                    "query" : {
                        "term" : {
                            "value" : "value1"
                        }
                    }
                }
            },
            "query": {
                "match_all": {}
            }
        }
    }
}'
```

How it works...

This kind of query works returning parents that match a children query. The query executed on children can be of every type of query.

The prerequisites of this kind of query are that the children must be correctly indexed in the parent shard.

Internally, this kind of query is a query executed on the children and all the IDs of children are used to filter the parent. A system must have enough memory to store child IDs.

The parameters that are used to control this process are as follows:

- `type`: This parameter defines the type of children. This type is part of the same index of the parent.
- `query`: This parameter defines the query that can be executed for selecting the children. Every kind of query can be used.

ElasticSearch allows that a document has only one parent, because the parent ID is used to choose the shard to which the child should be inserted.

Search, Queries, and Filters

> While working with child documents, it is important to remember that they must be stored in the same shard as their parents. So special precautions must be taken while fetching, modifying, and deleting the ID if the parent is unknown. It's good practice to store the parent_id parameter as a field of the child.

As the parent child relationship can be considered similar to a foreign key of standard SQL, there are some limitations due to the distributed nature of ElasticSearch, which are as follows:

- There must be only a parent for type
- The join part of child/parent is done in a shard and not distributed on all the clusters to reduce networking traffic and increase performance

See also

- Refer to the *Indexing a document* recipe in *Chapter 4*, *Standard Operations*

Using the top_children query

In the previous recipe, the has_child query consumes a large amount of memory because it requires to fetch IDs of all the children. To bypass this limitation in huge data contexts the top_children query allows fetching only the top children results.

Getting ready

You need a working ElasticSearch cluster and the data populated with the populate script.

How to do it...

For executing the top_children query, we need to perform the following steps:

1. We need to search the test-type parents of which the test-type2 top children have a term in the field value as value1. We can create this kind of query as follows:

```
curl -XPOST 'http://127.0.0.1:9200/test-index/test-type/_search' -d '{
    "query": {
        "top_children" : {
            "type" : "test-type2",
            "query" : {
                "term" : {
                    "value" : "value1"
```

```
                }
            },
            "score" : "max",
            "factor" : 5,
            "incremental_factor" : 2
        }
    }
}'
```

How it works...

This kind of query works returning parents that match a child query. The query executed on children can be of every type of query.

Internally this kind of query is a query executed on the children and the top IDs of the children are used to filter the parent. If the number of child IDs are not enough, other IDs are refetched.

The parameters that are used to control this process are as follows:

- `type`: This parameter defines the type of children. This type is part of the same index of the parent.
- `query`: This parameter defines the query that can be executed for selecting the children. Every kind of query can be used.
- `score` (`max`/`sum`/`avg`): This parameter allows controlling the score to be chosen to select the children.
- `factor` (default 5): This parameter defines the multiplicative factor used to fetch the children. Because one parent can have a lot of children and the `parent_id` parameter required for a query is a set of the returned children, you need to fetch more `parent_id` parameters from the children to be sure to have the correct number of result hits. With a factor of 5 and 10 result hits are required, and 50 child IDs must be fetched.
- `incremental_factor` (default 2): This parameter defines the multiplicative factor to be used if there aren't enough child documents fetched by the first query. The equation that controls the number of fetched children is as follows:

*desidered_hits * factor * incremental_factor*

See also

- The *Indexing a document* recipe in *Chapter 4, Standard Operations*
- *Using the has_child query/filter* in this chapter

Search, Queries, and Filters

Using the has_parent query/filter

In the previous recipes, we have seen the `has_child` query. ElasticSearch provides a query to search a child based on the `has_parent` parent query.

Getting ready

You need a working ElasticSearch cluster and the data populated with the populate script.

How to do it...

For executing the `has_parent` query/filter, we need to perform the following steps:

1. We want to search the `test-type2` children of which the `test-type` parents have a term `joe` in the `parsedtext` field. We can create this kind of query as follows:

    ```
    curl -XPOST 'http://127.0.0.1:9200/test-index/test-type2/_search' -d '{
        "query": {
            "has_parent" : {
                "type" : "test-type",
                "query" : {
                    "term" : {
                        "parsedtext" : "joe"
                    }
                }
            }
        }
    }'
    ```

2. If scoring is not important, it's better to reformulate the query as a filter in the following way:

    ```
    curl -XPOST 'http://127.0.0.1:9200/test-index/test-type2/_search' -d '{
        "query": {
            "filtered": {
                "filter": {
                    "has_parent" : {
                        "type" : "test-type",
                        "query" : {
                            "term" : {
                                "parsedtext" : "joe"
    ```

```
                    }
                   }
                  }
                },
                "query": {
                    "match_all": {}
                }
               }
              }
            }'
```

How it works...

This kind of query works returning children that match a parent query.

Internally this subquery is executed on the parents and all the IDs of the matching parents are used to filter the children. A system must have enough memory to store parent IDs.

The parameters that are used to control this process are as follows:

- `type`: This parameter defines the type of the parent.
- `query`: This parameter defines the query that can be executed for selecting the parents. Every kind of query can be used.
- `score_type` (default `none`, available values are `none` and `score`): By using the default configuration of `none`, ElasticSearch ignores the scores for the parent document reducing the memory usage and increasing performance. If it's set to score, the parent query score is aggregated into the children.

See also

- Refer to *Indexing a document* in *Chapter 4, Standard Operations*

Using a regexp query/filter

In the previous recipes we have seen different terms queries (terms, fuzzy, and prefix), another powerful terms query is the `regexp` (regular expression) one.

Getting ready

You need a working ElasticSearch cluster and the data populated with the populate script.

Search, Queries, and Filters

How to do it...

For executing the `regexp` query/filter, we need to perform the following steps:

1. We can execute a `regexp` term query from command line as follows:

    ```
    curl -XPOST 'http://127.0.0.1:9200/test-index/test-type/_search'
    -d '{
        "query": {
            "regexp": {
                "parsedtext": "j.*",
                "flags" : "INTERSECTION|COMPLEMENT|EMPTY"
            }
        }
    }'
    ```

2. If scoring is not important, it's better to reformulate the query as a filter in the following way:

    ```
    curl -XPOST 'http://127.0.0.1:9200/test-index/test-type/_search'
    -d '{
        "query": {
            "filtered": {
                "filter": {
                    "regexp": {
                        "parsedtext": "j.*"
                    }
                },
                "query": {
                    "match_all": {}
                }
            }
        }
    }'
    ```

How it works...

The `regexp` query/filter executes the regular expression against all the document terms. Internally Lucene compiles the regular expression in an automaton to improve the performance. Thus generally the performance of this query/filter is not high, because the performance depends on the regular expression used.

To speed up the `regexp` query/filter, a good approach is to have regular expression that has some known starting characters.

Chapter 5

The parameters that are used to control this process are as follows:

- `boost` (default `1.0`): This parameter defines the values used for boosting the score
- `flags`: This parameter defines a list of one or more flags pipe | delimited. The available flags are as follows:
    - `ALL`: This flag enables all the optional regexp syntax
    - `ANYSTRING`: This flag enables `anystring` (@)
    - `AUTOMATON`: This flag enables the named `automata` (`<identifier>`)
    - `COMPLEMENT`: This flag enables complement (~)
    - `EMPTY`: This flag enables empty language (#)
    - `INTERSECTION`: This flag enables intersection (&)
    - `INTERVAL`: This flag enables numerical intervals (`<n-m>`)
    - `NONE`: This flag doesn't enable the optional regexp syntax

 To avoid poor performance in search don't execute regex starting from `.*..`

See also

- The *Querying/filtering for term* recipe in this chapter

Using exists and missing filters

One of the main characteristics of ElasticSearch is schemaless storage. So due to its schemaless nature two kinds of filters are required to check if a field exists in a document (the `exists` filter) or if it is missing (the `missing` filter).

Getting ready

You need a working ElasticSearch cluster and the data populated with the populate script.

Search, Queries, and Filters

How to do it...

For executing existing and missing filters, we need to perform the following steps:

1. To search all the `test-type` documents that have a field called `parsedtext` the query will be as follows:

    ```
    curl -XPOST 'http://127.0.0.1:9200/test-index/test-type/_search' -d '{
        "query": {
            "filtered": {
                "filter": {
                    "exists": {
                        "field":"parsedtext"
                    }
                },
                "query": {
                    "match_all": {}
                }
            }
        }
    }'
    ```

2. To search all the `test-type` documents that do not have a field called `parsedtext`, the query will be as follows:

    ```
    curl -XPOST 'http://127.0.0.1:9200/test-index/test-type/_search' -d '{
        "query": {
            "filtered": {
                "filter": {
                    "missing": {
                        "field":"parsedtext"
                    }
                },
                "query": {
                    "match_all": {}
                }
            }
        }
    }'
    ```

How it works...

The `exists` and `missing` filters take only the `field` parameter, which contains the name of the field to be checked.

Using simple fields there are no pitfalls, but if you are using a single embedded object or a list of them you need to use a subobject field because of which ElasticSearch/Lucene works.

An example will help you to understand how internally ElasticSearch maps JSON objects to Lucene documents. If you are trying to index such a JSON document, use the following code:

```
{
    "name":"Paul",
    "address":{
        "city":"Sydney",
        "street":"Opera House Road",
        "number":"44"
    }
}
```

ElasticSearch will internally index it as follows:

```
name:paul
address.city:Sydney
address.street:Opera House Road
address.number:44
```

As we can see there is no `address` field indexed, so the `exists` filter on `address` fails. To match documents with an address you must search for a subfield (that is, `address.city`).

Using and/or/not filters

While building complex queries, some typical Boolean operation filters are required, as they allow to construct complex filter relations as in traditional relational world.

Every DSL query cannot be completed if there isn't an and, or, and not filter.

Getting ready

You need a working ElasticSearch cluster and the data populated with the populate script.

Search, Queries, and Filters

How to do it...

For executing and/or/not, we need to perform the following steps:

1. Searching documents with `parsedtext` equal to `joe` and `uuid` equal to `11111` is done by using the following code:

    ```
    curl -XPOST 'http://127.0.0.1:9200/test-index/test-type/_search' 
    -d '{
        "query": {
            "filtered": {
                "filter": {
                    "and": [
                    {
                        "term": {
                            "parsedtext":"joe"
                        }
                    },
                    {
                        "term": {
                            "uuid":"11111"
                        }
                    }]
                },
                "query": {
                    "match_all": {}
                }
            }
        }
    }'
    ```

2. Searching documents with `uuid` equal to `11111` or `22222` can be done with a similar query as follows:

    ```
    curl -XPOST 'http://127.0.0.1:9200/test-index/test-type/_search' 
    -d '{
        "query": {
            "filtered": {
                "filter": {
                    "or": [
                    {
                        "term": {
                            "uuid":"11111"
                        }
                    },
                    {
                        "term": {
                            "uuid":"22222"
                        }
                    }
    ```

```
            }]
        },
        "query": {
            "match_all": {}
        }
    }
}
}'
```

3. Searching documents with `uuid` not equal to `11111` can be done with a similar query as follows:

```
curl -XPOST 'http://127.0.0.1:9200/test-index/test-type/_search' -d '{
    "query": {
        "filtered": {
            "filter": {
                "not": {
                    "term": {
                        "uuid":"11111"
                    }
                }
            },
            "query": {
                "match_all": {}
            }
        }
    }
}'
```

How it works...

The Boolean operator filters are the simplest filters available in ElasticSearch. The `and` and `or` filters accept a list of subfilters which are used for their execution. These kinds of Boolean operator filters are very fast as in Lucene they are converted very efficiently, bit wise on a list of documents IDs.

Also the `not` filter is very fast as the Boolean operators, but it requires only a single filter to be negated.

From a user's point of view we can consider these fields as the following traditional, numerical group operations:

- `and`: This filter returns the documents that match all the subfilters
- `or`: This filter returns the documents that match at least one of the subfields
- `not`: This filter returns the documents that don't match any of the subfield

Search, Queries, and Filters

 For performance reasons, a Boolean filter is faster than a bulk of and/or/not filters.

Using the geo_bounding_box filter

One of the most common operations in geolocalization is searching for a box (square).

Getting ready

You need a working ElasticSearch cluster and the data populated with the geo populate script.

How to do it...

A search to filter documents related to a bounding box of dimensions (40.03, 72.0) and (40.717 * 70.99) can be done by using a similar query as follows:

```
curl -XGET http://127.0.0.1:9200/test-mindex/_search -d '{
    "query": {
        "filtered": {
            "filter": {
                "geo_bounding_box": {
                    "pin.location": {
                        "bottom_right": {
                            "lat": 40.03,
                            "lon": 72.0
                        },
                        "top_left": {
                            "lat": 40.717,
                            "lon": 70.99
                        }
                    }
                }
            },
            "query": {
                "match_all": {}
            }
        }
    }
}'
```

How it works...

ElasticSearch has a lot of optimizations to search for a box shape. The latitude and longitude are indexed only for fast range check, so this kind of filter is executed very quickly.

The parameters required for executing a `geo_bounding_box` filter are `top_left` and `bottom_right` GeoPoint.

It's possible to use several representations of GeoPoints as described in the *Mapping a GeoPoint field* recipe in *Chapter 3, Managing Mapping*.

See also

- The *Mapping a GeoPoint field* recipe in *Chapter 3, Managing Mapping*

Using the geo_polygon filter

The previous recipe, *Using the geo_bounding_box filter* shows how to filter on a square section, which is the most common case. ElasticSearch provides a way to filter the user defined polygonal shapes via the `geo_polygon` filter.

Getting ready

You need a working ElasticSearch cluster and the data populated with the geo populate script.

How to do it...

Searching documents in which `pin.location` is part of a triangle (a shape made up of three GeoPoints), is done by using a similar query as follows:

```
curl -XGET http://127.0.0.1:9200/test-mindex/_search -d '{
    "query": {
        "filtered": {
            "filter": {
                "geo_bounding_box": {
                    "pin.location": {
                        "points": [
                            {
                                "lat": 50,
                                "lon": -30
                            },
                            {
                                "lat": 30,
                                "lon": -80
                            },
```

```
                        {
                            "lat": 80,
                            "lon": -90
                        }
                    ]
                }
            }
        },
        "query": {
            "match_all": {}
        }
    }
}'
```

How it works...

The `geo_polygon` filter allows to define your own shape with a list of GeoPoints so that ElasticSearch can filter documents that are in the polygon.

It can be considered as an extension of the `geo_bounding_box` filter for a generic polygonal form.

See also

- The *Mapping a GeoPoint field* recipe in *Chapter 3, Managing Mapping*
- The *Using the geo_bounding_box filter* recipe in this chapter

Using the geo_distance filter

When you are working with geo locations, one of the common tasks is to filter results based on its distance from a location. The `geo_distance` filter is used to achieve this goal.

Getting ready

You need a working ElasticSearch cluster and the data populated with the geo populate script.

How to do it...

Searching documents in which `pin.location` is `200km` distant from the `lat` value `40` and the `lon` value `70`, is done using a similar query as follows:

```
curl -XGET 'http://127.0.0.1:9200/test-mindex/_search -d '{
    "query": {
        "filtered": {
            "filter": {
                "geo_distance": {
                    "pin.location": {
                        "lat": 40,
                        "lon": 70
                    },
                    "distance": "200km",
                    "optimize_bbox": "memory"
                }
            },
            "query": {
                "match_all": {}
            }
        }
    }
}'
```

How it works...

As we discussed in the *Mapping a GeoPoint field* recipe there are several ways to define GeoPoint and it is internally saved in an optimized way to be searched.

The distance filter executes a distance calculation between a given GeoPoint and the points in documents, returning hits that verify the distance.

The parameters that control the distance filter are as follows:

- The field and the point of reference to be used to calculate the distance. In the preceding example we have `pin.location` and `(40, 70)`.
- `distance`: This parameter defines the distance to be considered. It is usually expressed as a string by a number preceded by a unit.

- Unit (optional): This parameter is the unit of the distance value, if distance is defined as a number. Valid values are as follows:
    - `in` or `inch`
    - `yd` or `yards`
    - `m` or `miles`
    - `km` or `kilometers`
    - `m` or `meters`
    - `mm` or `millimeters`
    - `cm` or `centimeters`
- `distance_type` (default `arc`) (valid choices are `arc/place`): This parameter defines the type of algorithm to calculate the distance.
- `optimize_bbox`: This parameter defines how to filter first with a bounding box to improve performance. This kind of optimization removes a lot of document evaluations limiting the check to values that match a square. Valid values for this parameter are as follows:
    - `memory` (default): This value checks the memory.
    - `indexed`: This value checks using indexing values. It works only if `lat` and `lon` are indexed.
    - `none`: This value disables the bounding box optimization.

There's more...

There is also a range version of this filter that allows filter by range. The `geo_distance_range` filter works as a standard range filter (refer to the *Using range query/filter* recipe) in which the range is defined in `from` and `to` parameters. For example the previously discussed code can be converted into a range without the `from` part as follows:

```
curl -XGET 'http://127.0.0.1:9200/test-mindex/_search -d '{
    "query": {
        "filtered": {
            "filter": {
                "geo_distance_range": {
                    "pin.location": {
                        "lat": 40,
                        "lon": 70
                    },
                    "to": "200km",
                    "optimize_bbox": "memory"
                }
            },
            "query": {
                "match_all": {}
            }
        }
    }
}'
```

See also

- The *Mapping a GeoPoint field* recipe in *Chapter 3, Managing Mapping*
- The *Using a range query/filter* recipe in this chapter

6
Facets

In this chapter, we will cover the following topics:

- Executing facets
- Executing terms facets
- Executing range facets
- Executing histogram facets
- Executing date histogram facets
- Executing filter/query facets
- Executing statistical facets
- Executing term statistical facets
- Executing geo distance facets

Introduction

In developing search solutions not only results are important, but also helpers to improve the quality and the search focus.

ElasticSearch provides a powerful tool to achieve these goals: the facets.

Facets are used not only to improve results, but also to provide additional information on queries, such as counting, folksonomy, histogram, and extra data. Generally, the facets are represented with graphs or a group of filtering options (for example, a list of categories for the search results).

Facets

Because all of them provide some scripting functionalities, they are able to cover a wide spectrum of scenarios. In this chapter, some simple scripting functionalities are shown related to facets, but we will cover in-depth scripting in the next chapter.

Facet is also the base for advanced analytics as shown in the software Kibana (http://www.elasticsearch.org/overview/kibana/) or similar. It's very important to understand how the various types of facets work and when to choose them: to help the user, possible graph representations of some facet results are provided.

Executing facets

ElasticSearch provides several functionalities other than search; it allows executing statistics and real-time analytics on searches via the facets.

Getting ready

You need a working ElasticSearch cluster and an index populated with the script available in the online code.

How to do it...

For executing a facet, we will perform the steps given as follows:

1. From command line:

   ```
   curl -XGET 'http://127.0.0.1:9200/test-index/test-type/_search?pretty=true&size=0' -d '{
     "query": {
       "match_all": {}
     },
     "facets": {
       "tag": {
         "terms": {
           "field": "tag",
           "size": 10
         }
       }
     }
   }'
   ```

   In this case we have used a `match_all` query plus a term facets used to count terms.

2. The result returned by ElasticSearch, if everything is all right, should be:

```
{
  "took" : 2,
  "timed_out" : false,
  "_shards" : {
    "total" : 5,
    "successful" : 5,
    "failed" : 0
  },
  "hits" : {
    "total" : 3,
    "max_score" : 1.0,
    "hits" : [ ]
  },
  "facets" : {
    "tag" : {
      "_type" : "terms",
      "missing" : 0,
      "total" : 3,
      "other" : 0,
      "terms" : [ {
        "term" : "foo",
        "count" : 2
      }, {
        "term" : "bar",
        "count" : 1
      } ]
    }
  }
}
```

The results are not returned because we have fixed the result size to 0. The facet result is contained in the `facets` field. Every type of facet has its own result format (the explanation of this kind of result is in the *Executing terms facets* recipe in this chapter).

How it works...

Every search can return a facet calculation, computed on the query results: facet phase is an additional step in query processing, as for example, the highlighting.

There are several types of facets that can be used in ElasticSearch.

In this chapter, we'll see all standard facets available; additional facet types can be provided with plugin and scripting.

Facets

The facets are the bases for real-time analytics. They allow to execute:

- Counting
- Histogram
- Range aggregation
- Statistic
- Geo distance aggregation

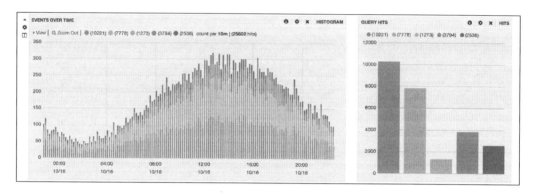

The facets are always executed on search hits; they are usually computed in a map/reduce way. The map step is distributed in shards, meanwhile the reduce step is done in the called search server.

Because, for facet computation, a lot of data should be kept in memory, they usually require a lot of memory to be executed. For example, executing a term facet requires that all unique terms in the field, which is used for faceting, are kept in memory. Executing this operation on million of documents requires perhaps storing a large number of values in memory.

The main usage of facets is to provide additional data to the search results to improve their quality or to extend them with additional information. For example, in searching for news articles, some facets that can be interesting to be calculated could be the authors who wrote the articles and the date histogram of the publishing date.

 It's possible to execute only facet calculation, without returns to search results, to reduce the bandwidth passing the search `size` parameter set to `0`.

See also

- *Executing terms facets*

Chapter 6

Executing terms facets

The terms facet is one of the most used ones. It counts the terms that are in a field of resulting hits. This facet is often used to drill down search.

Getting ready

You need a working ElasticSearch cluster and an index populated with the script available in the online code.

How to do it...

For executing a term facet, we will perform the steps given as follows:

1. We want to calculate the tag count of all the documents: the REST call should be:
   ```
   curl -XGET 'http://127.0.0.1:9200/test-index/test-type/_search?pretty=true&size=0' -d '{
       "query": {
           "match_all": {}
       },
       "facets": {
           "tag": {
               "terms": {
                   "field": "tag",
                   "size": 10
               }
           }
       }
   }'
   ```
   In this example, we need to match all the items, so the `match_all` query is used.

2. The result returned by ElasticSearch, if everything is all right, should be:
   ```
   {
     "took" : 2,
     "timed_out" : false,
     "_shards" : {
       "total" : 5,
       "successful" : 5,
       "failed" : 0
     },
   ```

183

Facets

```
    "hits" : {
      "total" : 3,
      "max_score" : 1.0,
      "hits" : [ ]
    },
    "facets" : {
      "tag" : {
        "_type" : "terms",
        "missing" : 0,
        "total" : 3,
        "other" : 0,
        "terms" : [ {
          "term" : "foo",
          "count" : 2
        }, {
          "term" : "bar",
          "count" : 1
        } ]
      }
    }
}
```

The facet result is composed of several fields:

- `_type`: This is the type of executed facet.
- `missing`: This is the number of results without the term.
- `total`: This is the number of counted terms.
- `other`: This is the number of facet terms computed but not returned.
- `terms`: This is the list of computed facet terms. The terms list is composed of:
  - `term`: This is the term
  - `count`: This is the term count

How it works...

During a search, there are a lot of "phases" that ElasticSearch executes. After the query execution the facets are calculated and aggregated to be returned along with the results.

For the definition of facets during query, there is an optional field called facets, which contains the name to be given to the facet calculation and the facet DSL to be executed.

In this recipe, we will see the `terms` facets that is required as parameters:

- `field`: This is the field to be used to extract facets data. Field value can be a single string (as in the example `"tag"`) or a list of fields (that is, `["field1", "field2", …]`).
- `size` (default `10`): This controls the number of facets value to be returned.
- `order` (optional, default `"count"`): This controls how to calculate the top *n* facet values to be returned. The `order` can be one of these types:
    - `count` (default): This returns the facet values by count
    - `term`: This returns the facet values ordered by term value
    - `reverse_count`: This returns the facet values by count in reverse order
    - `reverse_term`: This returns the facet values ordered by term value in reverse order
- `all_terms` (optional): This gets all terms in query facets, the terms that don't have a hit are set to zero. These kind of settings must not be used if the term number is huge as it consumes a lot of memory and networking. If `all_terms` is used, `size` must not be defined.
- `exclude` (optional): This removes the terms from the results that are contained in the `exclude` list.
- `regex` (optional): This includes all the terms that match the regular expression. The regular expression parameters are controlled by the `regex_flags` parameter.

The `term` facet is very useful to represent sum of values used for further filtering. In graph, they are often shown as a bar chart:

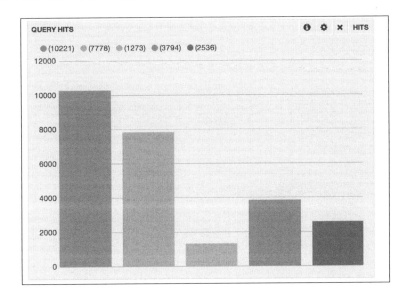

Facets

There's more...

Sometimes we need to have much more control on terms facets: this can be achieved by adding an ElasticSearch script in the `script` field.

With scripting, it is possible to modify the term used for the facet to generate a new value to be used. A simple example, in which we append `123` to all terms, is:

```
{
    "query" : {
        "match_all" : { }
    },
    "facets" : {
        "tag" : {
            "terms" : {
                "field" : "tag",
                "script" : "term + '123'"
            }
        }
    }
}
```

Scripting can also be used to control the inclusion/exclusion of some terms. In this case, a Boolean (true/false) must be returned. If we want a facet with terms that starts with *a*, we can use a similar facet:

```
{
    "query" : {
        "match_all" : { }
    },
    "facets" : {
        "tag" : {
            "terms" : {
                "field" : "tag",
                "script" : "term.startsWith('a')"
            }
        }
    }
}
```

In the previous terms facets examples, we have provided the `field` or `fields` parameter to select the field to be used to compute the facet. It's also possible to pass a `script_field` parameter, which replaces `field` and `fields`, to define the field to be used to extract the data. The `script_field` field can fetch from the `_source` or `_fields` (only if the field is stored) variables in the context. The big advantage of using a `script_field` field is that it can be processed without loading all the hits in memory, so reducing the memory usage, especially for very big datasets. Obviously, the side-effect of using this `script_field` is that it is slower than standard fields.

In the case of `_source`, the first example can be rewritten as:

```
...    "tag": {
           "terms": {
               "script_field": "_source.tag",
               "size": 10
           }
       } ...
```

In the case of using the `_fields` fields:

```
...    "tag": {
           "terms": {
               "script_field": "_fields['tag']",
               "size": 10
           }
       } ...
```

See also

- Chapter 7, Scripting

Executing range facets

The previous recipe describes a facet type that can be very useful if facets are returned on terms or on a limited number of items. Otherwise, it's often required to return the facets aggregated in ranges: the `range` facets answers this requirement. Common scenarios are:

- Price range (used in shops)
- Size range
- Alphabetical range

Facets

Getting ready

You need a working ElasticSearch cluster and an index populated with the script available in the online code.

How to do it...

For executing range facets, we will perform the steps given as follows:

1. We want to provide three types of facet ranges:
    - Price facet, that aggregates the price of items in ranges
    - Age facet, that aggregates the age contained in document in four ranges of 25 years
    - Date facet, the ranges of 6 months of the previous year and all this year

2. To obtain this result, we need to execute a similar query:

```
curl -XGET 'http://127.0.0.1:9200/test-index/test-type/_
search?pretty=true&size=0' -d '{
    "query": {
        "match_all": {}
    },
    "facets": {
        "prices": {
            "range": {
                "field": "price",
                "ranges" : [
                    { "to" : 10.0 },
                    { "from" : 10.0, "to" : 20.0 },
                    { "from" : 20.0, "to" : 100.0 },
                    { "from" : 100.0 }
                ]
            }
        },
        "ages": {
            "range": {
                "field": "age",
                "ranges" : [
                    { "to" : 25 },
                    { "from" : 25, "to" : 50 },
                    { "from" : 50, "to" : 75 },
                    { "from" : 75 }
                ]
            }
```

```
            },
            "range": {
                "terms": {
                    "field": "date",
                    "ranges" : [
                        { "from" : "2012-01-01", "to" : "2012-06-31"
},
                        { "from" : "2012-07-01", "to" : "2012-12-31"
},
                        { "from" : "2013-01-01", "to" : "2013-12-31"
}
                    ]
                }
            }
        }
}'
```

3. The results will be something similar to:

```
{
  "took" : 8,
  "timed_out" : false,
  "_shards" : {
    "total" : 5,
    "successful" : 5,
    "failed" : 0
  },
  "hits" : …,
  "facets" : {
    "prices" : {
      "_type" : "range",
      "ranges" : [ {
        "to" : 10.0,
        "count" : 105,
        "min" : 0.025325332858183724,
        "max" : 9.96176462267223,
        "total_count" : 105,
        "total" : 536.6533630686944,
        "mean" : 5.110984410178042
      }, …]
    }
  }
}
```

Facets

Every facet results has the following fields:

- `to` and `from`: These define the original range of the facet
- `count`: This defines the number of results in this range
- `min`: This defines the minimum value of this facet range
- `max`: This is the maximum value of this facet range
- `total`: This defines the sum of all the values
- `total_count`: This defines the number of value used for computing the facet
- `mean`: This defines the mean of all the values in this range

How it works...

This kind of facet is generally executed against numerical data types (integer, float, long, and dates). This kind of facet can be considered as a list of range filters executed against the result of the query.

The date/datetime values, when used in filter/query, must be expressed in string format: the valid string formats are "yyyy-MM-dd'T'HH:mm:ss" or "yyyy-MM-dd".

Every range is computed separately, so in their definition they can overlap.

See also

- The *Using a range query/filter* recipe in *Chapter 5*, *Search, Queries, and Filters*

Executing histogram facets

ElasticSearch numerical values can be used to process histogram data. The histogram representation of a facet is a very powerful way to show data to end-users.

Getting ready

You need a working ElasticSearch cluster and an index populated with the script available in online code.

Chapter 6

How to do it...

For executing histogram facets, we will perform the steps given as follows:

1. Using the items populated with the script, we want to calculate facets on:
    - Age with interval of 5 years
    - Price with interval of $10
    - Date with interval of 6 months

2. The query will be:

```
curl -XGET 'http://127.0.0.1:9200/test-index/test-type/_search?pretty=true&size=0' -d '{
    "query": {
        "match_all": {}
    },
    "facets": {
        "age" : {
            "histogram" : {
                "field" : "age",
                "interval" : 5
            }
        },
        "price" : {
            "histogram" : {
                "field" : "price",
                "interval" : 10.0
            }
        },
        "date" : {
            "histogram" : {
                "field" : "date",
                "time_interval" : "180d"
            }
        }
    }
}'
```

And the result (stripped) will be:

```
{
  "took" : 3,
  "timed_out" : false,
  "_shards" : {
    "total" : 5, "successful" : 5, "failed" : 0
  },
  "hits" : {
    "total" : 1000,
    ...
```

```
    },
    "facets" : {
      "age" : {
        "_type" : "histogram",
        "entries" : [ {
          "key" : 0, "count" : 34
        }, {
          "key" : 5, "count" : 41
        }, {
          "key" : 10, "count" : 42
        }, {
          "key" : 15, "count" : 43
        }, {
          ...
          "key" : 100, "count" : 9
        } ]
      },
      "price" : {
        "_type" : "histogram",
        "entries" : [ {
          "key" : 0, "count" : 105
        }, {
          "key" : 10, "count" : 107
        }, {
          ...
        }, {
          "key" : 90, "count" : 99
        } ]
      },
      "date" : {
        "_type" : "histogram",
        "entries" : [ {
          "key" : 1275264000000, "count" : 19
        }, {
          "key" : 1290816000000, "count" : 94
        }, {
          ...
        }, {
          "key" : 1446336000000, "count" : 68
        } ]
      }
    }
  }
}
```

The facet result is composed of several fields:

- `_type`: This gives the type of executed facet (histogram in the example)
- `entries`: This gives a list of facet results. These results are composed of:
  - `key`: This gives the value that is always on the x axis in the histogram graph
  - `count`: This gives the value

If a datetime value is used, the key result is returned as epoch value (https://en.wikipedia.org/wiki/Epoch_(reference_date)).

How it works...

This kind of facet is calculated and distributed in every shard with search results and then the facet results are aggregated in the search node server (arbiter) and returned to the user.

The histogram facet works only on numerical fields (boolean, integer, long integer, and float) and the `date/datetime` fields (that are internally represented as a long).

To control the histogram generation on a defined field, a parameter (`interval`) is required, which is used to generate interval to aggregate the hits.

For numerical fields, this value is a number (in the previous example, we have done numerical calculus on age and price), for the `datetime` fields it can be also expressed using ElasticSearch date strings and it must be defined in the `time_interval` parameter (see the date facet in the example).

The standard representation of a histogram is a bar chart as similar to the following one:

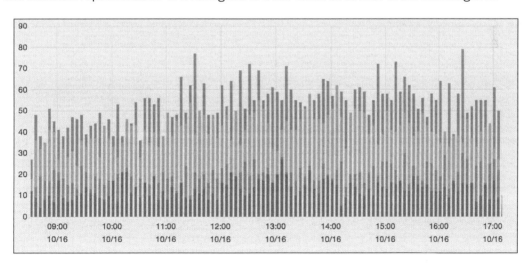

Facets

There's more...

The histogram facet can also be improved using ElasticSearch scripting functionalities. It is possible to script both the key (`key_script`) and value (`value_script`).

If key is provided by script, it is not required to set the interval, because it can be easily computed in the `key_script` key.

If additional parameters need to be sent to `key_script` and `value_script`, they can be passed via the `params` parameter as usually done in ElasticSearch scripting.

An example of scripted facet histogram is:

```
..."facets" : {
        "my_histogram" : {
            "histogram" : {
                "key_script" : "doc['date'].date.minuteOfHour * param1",
                "value_script" : "doc['numericValue1'].value + param2",
                "params" : {
                    "param1" : 1,
                    "param2" : 2
                }
            }
        }
    }....
```

See also

- *Executing date histogram facets*

Executing date histogram facets

The previous recipe works mainly on numeric fields, ElasticSearch provides a custom date histogram facet to operate on date/datetime values.

This facet is required because date values need a deeper customization to solve problems, such as timezone conversion and special time intervals.

Getting ready

You need a working ElasticSearch cluster and an index populated with the script available in online code.

How to do it...

For executing date histogram facets, we will perform the steps given as follows:

1. We need two different date/time facets, which are:
    - an annual facet
    - a quarter facet, but with time zone +1:00

2. The query will be:
    ```
    curl -XGET 'http://127.0.0.1:9200/test-index/test-type/_search?from=0&pretty=true&size=10' -d '
    {
        "query": {
            "match_all": {}
        },
        "facets": {
            "date_year": {
                "date_histogram": {
                    "field": "date",
                    "interval": "year"
                }
            },
            "date_quarter": {
                "date_histogram": {
                    "field": "date",
                    "interval": "quarter" ,
                    "time_zone": "+01:00"
                }
            }


        }
    }'
    ```

3. The corresponding result will be:
    ```
    {
      "took" : 3,
      "timed_out" : false,
      "_shards" : {
        "total" : 5,
        "successful" : 5,
        "failed" : 0
      },
    ```

Facets

```
      "hits" : {
        "total" : 1000,
        "max_score" : 1.0,
        "hits" : [ ]
      },
      "facets" : {
        "date_year" : {
          "_type" : "date_histogram",
          "entries" : [ {
            "time" : 1262304000000,
            "count" : 40
          }, {
            "time" : 1293840000000,
            "count" : 182
          }, {
          ….. .
"time" : 1451606400000,
            "count" : 42
          } ]
        },
        "date_quarter" : {
          "_type" : "date_histogram",
          "entries" : [ {
            "time" : 1285891200000,
            "count" : 40
          }, {
            "time" : 1293840000000,
            "count" : 42
          }, {
…
          }, {
            "time" : 1459468800000,
            "count" : 2
          } ]
        }
      }
    }
```

The facet result is composed of several fields:

- `type`: This gives the type of executed facet (`date_histogram` in the example).
- `entries`: This gives a list of facet results. These results are composed by:
    - `time`: This gives the value in epoch
    - `count`: This gives the value

How it works...

The date histogram is computed by ElasticSearch similarly as the previous recipe histogram type. The main difference from the standard one is that the interval is not numerical, but date intervals are defined constants. The `interval` parameter allows using several values, such as:

- year
- quarter
- month
- week
- day
- hour
- minute

While working with date values, it's important to use the correct time zone to prevent query errors.

By default, ElasticSearch uses the UTC milliseconds since the epoch to store the `datetime` values. To better handle the correct timestamp, there are some parameters that can be tricked:

- `time_zone` (or `pre_zone`) (optional): This allows defining a time zone offset to be used in value calculation. This value is used to preprocess the `datetime` value for the facet aggregation. The value can be expressed in numeric form (that is, `-3`) or if minutes must be defined in the time zone, a string representation can be used (that is, `+07:30`)
- `post_zone` (optional): This takes the result and applies the time zone offset.
- `pre_zone_adjust_large_interval` (default `false`) (optional): This applies the `hour` interval also for `day` or above intervals.

There's more...

The data histogram facet allows returning other fields other than date. By using the `key_field` parameter it is possible to define the key field to be used in pair with the `value_field` (the value to be returned). For example, we want to compute the statistics on prices against their date. We can achieve this result using:

```
{
  "date_price": {
    "date_histogram": {
      "key_field": "date",
      "value_field": "price",
      "interval": "day"
    }
  }
}
```

Facets

It will trigger a similar facet results:

```
"date_price" : {
    "_type" : "date_histogram",
    "entries" : [ {
      "time" : 1287446400000,
      "count" : 1,
      "min" : 57.17903733037952,
      "max" : 57.17903733037952,
      "total" : 57.17903733037952,
      "total_count" : 1,
      "mean" : 57.17903733037952
    }, {
      ...
```

Executing filter/query facets

Sometimes, we don't need complex computation, but only the number of hits that verifies a particular query or filter. To obtain this result, the filter/query facet is used.

Getting ready

You need a working ElasticSearch cluster and an index populated with the script available in the online code.

How to do it...

For executing filter/query facets, we will perform the steps given as follows:

1. We need to compute two different filter facets, which are:
   - The count of documents that have `ullam` as tag
   - The count of documents that have age equal to 37

2. The query to execute these facets is:
```
curl -XGET 'http://127.0.0.1:9200/test-index/test-type/_search?from=0&pretty=true&size=0' -d '
{
    "query": {
        "match_all": {}
    },
    "facets": {
        "ullam_docs": {
            "filter" : {
```

Chapter 6

```
                    "term" : { "tag" : "ullam" }
        }
            },
            "age37_docs": {
                "filter" : {
                    "term" : { "age" : 37 }
        }
            }
        }
    }
}'
```

In this case we have used simple filters, but they can be of every complexity needed.

 To improve performance, a user should always prefer filter to query.

3. The results of the previous query with facets will be:

```
{
  "took" : 6,
  "timed_out" : false,
  "_shards" : {
    "total" : 5,
    "successful" : 5,
    "failed" : 0
  },
  "hits" : {
    "total" : 1000,
    "max_score" : 1.0,
    "hits" : [ ]
  },
  "facets" : {
    "ullam_docs" : {
      "_type" : "filter",
      "count" : 17
    },
    "age37_docs" : {
      "_type" : "filter",
      "count" : 6
    }
  }
}
```

Facets

How it works...

The filter/query facet is very trivial: it executes a count on a filter/query on matched element. You can consider this facet as a count query on the results.

As we can see from the previous result, the facet contains only two values:

- `_type`: This gives the type of facet
- `count`: This gives the count result

It could seem a very simple facet: generally, users tend not to use it as they prefer the statistic one, which also provides a count or in the worst cases they execute another search generating more server workload.

The big advantage of this kind of facet is that the count, if possible, is executed via a filter/query, that is, by far faster than iterating all the results.

Another important advantage is that the filter/query can be composed by every possible valid Query DSL element.

See also

- The *Counting* recipe in *Chapter 5, Search, Queries, and Filters*
- The *Querying/filtering for term* recipe in *Chapter 5, Search, Queries, and Filters*

Executing statistical facets

The core of real-time analytics is the statistical facet. It works on numerical fields and in one-shot is able to compute several numerical metrics.

Getting ready

You need a working ElasticSearch cluster and an index populated with the script available in online code.

How to do it...

For executing statistical facets, we will perform the steps given as follows:

1. We need to compute two different statistical facets, that are:
    - price statistic
    - age statistic

2. The query to execute these facets is:
```
curl -XGET 'http://127.0.0.1:9200/test-index/test-type/_search?pretty=true&size=0' -d '{
    "query": {
        "match_all": {}
    },
    "facets": {
        "age" : {
            "statistical" : {
                "field" : "age",
            }
        },
        "price" : {
            "statistical" : {
                "field" : "price",
            }
        }
    }
}'
```

3. The result will be:
```
{
  "took" : 12,
  "timed_out" : false,
  "_shards" : {
    "total" : 5,
    "successful" : 5,
    "failed" : 0
  },
  "hits" : {
    "total" : 1000,
    "max_score" : 1.0,
    "hits" : [ ]
  },
  "facets" : {
    "age" : {
      "_type" : "statistical",
      "count" : 1000,
      "total" : 53243.0,
      "min" : 1.0,
      "max" : 100.0,
      "mean" : 53.243,
      "sum_of_squares" : 3653701.0,
      "variance" : 818.8839509999999,
      "std_deviation" : 28.616148430562767
    },
```

Facets

```
      "price" : {
        "_type" : "statistical",
        "count" : 1000,
        "total" : 50295.451273305494,
        "min" : 0.025325332858183724,
        "max" : 99.98302508488757,
        "mean" : 50.295451273305495,
        "sum_of_squares" : 3363069.573351521,
        "variance" : 833.4371545660738,
        "std_deviation" : 28.869311639976345
      }
    }
  }
```

The facet result is composed of several fields:

- `type`: This gives the type of executed facet (that is, statistical)
- `count`: This gives the number of total collected facets
- `total`: This gives the sum of all facet values
- `min`: This gives the minimum facet value
- `max`: This gives the maximum facet value
- `mean`: This gives the mean of the values
- `sum_of_squares`: This gives the sum of squares of values
- `variance`: This gives the variance of values
- `std_deviation`: This gives the standard deviation of values

How it works...

This kind of facet is calculated and distributed in every shard (when possible), then the facet results are aggregated and completed in the search server to be returned to the user.

The only required parameter is the `field` parameter, which can be one or more fields that must be used for executing the facet.

The facet iterates on all matched documents and increments the values required to execute these statistics. Obviously, the final results can only be computed using the results of all the shards.

There's more...

Sometimes the value used for computing the statistic facet needs to be "prepared" to obtain a valid result. As the other facets types, the statistical facet allows defining the `script` and `params` parameters for using ElasticSearch scripting.

A common case is, for example, to add some VAT to a price and this action can be easily done with the following code:

```
{
    "query" : {
        "match_all" : {}
    },
    "facets" : {
        "stat1" : {
            "statistical" : {
                "script" : "doc['price'].value*(1.0+vat/100)",
                "params" : {
                    "vat" : 8.5
                }
            }
        }
    }
}
```

Executing term statistical facets

The term statistical facets unifies both term and statistical facets in a single one. This kind of facet is used to aggregate values using a field and compute statistic on another one.

This covers a lot of common scenarios required in facets that are generally referred as value X for feature Y.

Getting ready

You need a working ElasticSearch cluster and an index populated with the script available in online code.

Facets

How to do it...

For executing term statistical facets, we will perform the steps given as follows:

1. We need to compute the price as the function of available tags.
2. To reach our goal we need to write a request similar to the following code:
   ```
   curl -XGET 'http://127.0.0.1:9200/test-index/test-type/_
   search?pretty=true&size=0' -d '{
       "query": {
           "match_all": {}
       },
       "facets": {
           "price_for_tag" : {
               "terms_stats" : {
                   "key_field" : "tag",
                   "value_field" : "price"
               }
           }
       }
   }'
   ```
3. The result will be:
   ```
   {
     "took" : 120,
     "timed_out" : false,
     "_shards" : {
       "total" : 5,
       "successful" : 5,
       "failed" : 0
     },
     "hits" : {
       "total" : 1000,
       "max_score" : 1.0,
       "hits" : [ ]
     },
     "facets" : {
       "price_for_tag" : {
         "_type" : "terms_stats",
         "missing" : 0,
         "terms" : [ {
           "term" : "laborum",
           "count" : 25,
           "total_count" : 25,
           "min" : 1.0338029265616777,
   ```

```
            "max" : 97.16465968170533,
            "total" : 1110.2372482622998,
            "mean" : 44.40948993049199
        }, ….
    }
  }
}
```

How it works...

The terms statistical facets are designed to cover a very common pattern, counting (compute statistic) on a field referred by another one.

The `key_field` field is used to aggregate the results of the query, the `value_field` field is used to select the value to compute on.

Because it is based on the term facet, it is possible to control the number of facet using the `size` parameter. The default value is `10` facet results, but you can set it to `0` for retrieving all the results (if the facet set is not too big).

To better control the quality of returned facets, it is possible to define the `shard_size` parameter, which controls the number of facets that must be returned by every shard.

This parameter is very important when working with fields with high cardinality. Due to map/reduce approach, usually only the `size` facets are fetched by every shard. This fetching is done separately and then aggregated before it returns the results. In the case of high facet cardinality, the accuracy could be low due to the impossibility to "guess" the correct champions due to a sparse distribution. Increasing the `shard_size` parameter permits to mitigate this numerical effect.

> Increasing the `shard_size` parameter improves the accuracy but it also means to add more overheads in computation due to the increase of memory, networking, and CPU usage.

It's possible to control the order of returned terms via the `order` parameter. Possible values are:

- `count` (the default) and `reverse_count`
- `term` and `reverse_term`
- `total` and `reverse_total`
- `min` and `reverse_min`
- `max` and `reverse_max`
- `mean` and `reverse_mean`

The term statistical facets also allow using scripting as we have already seen for the statistical facets.

Facets

See also

- *Executing terms facets*
- *Executing statistical facets*

Executing geo distance facets

Other than standard types that we have seen in the previous facets, ElasticSearch allows executing facets against a GeoPoint: the geo distance facets. This is an evolution of the previously discussed range facets built to work on geo locations.

Getting ready

You need a working ElasticSearch cluster and an index populated with the script available in online code.

How to do it...

For executing geo distance facets, we will perform the steps given as follows:

1. Using the `position` field available in documents, we want to aggregate the other documents in four ranges:
    - Less then 10 kilometers
    - From 10 kilometers to 20
    - From 20 kilometers to 50
    - From 50 kilometers to 100
    - Above 100 kilometers

2. To achieve these goals, we create a geo distance facet with a code similar to this one:
```
curl -XGET 'http://127.0.0.1:9200/test-index/test-type/_search?pretty=true&size=0' -d ' {
    "query" : {
        "match_all" : {}
    },
    "facets" : {
        "position" : {
            "geo_distance" : {
                "position" : {
                    "lat": 83.76,
                    "lon": -81.20
                },
```

```
                        "ranges" : [
                            { "to" : 10 },
                            { "from" : 10, "to" : 20 },
                            { "from" : 20, "to" : 50 },
                            { "from" : 50, "to" : 100 },
                            { "from" : 100 }
                        ]
                    }
                }
            }
}'
```

3. The result will be:

```
{
    "took" : 23,
    "timed_out" : false,
    "_shards" : {
        "total" : 5,
        "successful" : 5,
        "failed" : 0
    },
    "hits" : {
        "total" : 1000,
        "max_score" : 1.0,
        "hits" : [ ]
    },
    "facets" : {
        "posistion" : {
            "_type" : "geo_distance",
            "ranges" : [ {
                "to" : 10.0,
                "count" : 1,
                "min" : 0.2903123939621829,
                "max" : 0.2903123939621829,
                "total_count" : 1,
                "total" : 0.2903123939621829,
                "mean" : 0.2903123939621829
            },… {
                "from" : 100.0,
                "count" : 999,
                "min" : 133.32803268700687,
                "max" : 19716.372410118485,
                "total_count" : 999,
                "total" : 9691323.833150115,
                "mean" : 9701.024858008122
            } ]
        }
    }
}
```

Facets

How it works...

The geo range facets is an extension of the range facets that works on geo localizations. It works only if a field is mapped as a `geo_point` field.

The field can contain a single or a multi-valued GeoPoints.

The facet requires two parameters:

- The GeoPoints to be used to compute the distances
- A list of ranges to collect documents based on their distance from the target point.

The GeoPoints can be defined in one of the following accepted formats:

- Latitude and longitude as properties, that is `{"lat": 83.76, "lon": -81.20 }`
- Longitude and latitude as array, that is `[-81.20, 83.76]`
- Latitude and longitude as string, that is `"83.76, -81.20"`
- Geohash, that is `"fnyk80"`

The ranges are defined as a couple of `from/to` values. If one of them is missing, they are considered unbound.

The value used for the range is by default set to kilometers, but using the property unit it's possible to set to:

- `mi` or `miles`
- `in` or `inch`
- `yd` or `yard`
- `km` or `kilometers`
- `m` or `meters`
- `cm` or `centimeter`
- `mm` or `millimeters`

It's also possible to set how the distance is computed with the `distance_type` parameter. Valid values for this parameter are:

- `arc` (default): This uses the Arc Length formula. It is the most precise.
- `plane`: This uses the plane distance formula. It is the fastest and most CPU intensive, but it's also the less precise.

As for the range filter, the range values are treated separately, so the overlapping ranges are allowed. When the results are returned, this facet provides a lot of information in its fields:

- `from/to`: This defines the analyzed range
- `min/max/mean`: This defines the minimum distance, the maximum distance, and the mean of the distances
- `count/total_count`: This defines the number of documents that match the range
- `total`: This defines the total of matched distances

There's more...

This facet also allows setting a `value_field` field, which is used to compute the facet results in place of the start GeoPoint. For example, if we want the age statistics in function of range distance from the point, the facet will become:

```
curl -XGET 'http://127.0.0.1:9200/test-index/test-type/_search?pretty=true&size=0' -d ' {
    "query" : {
        "match_all" : {}
    },
    "facets" : {
        "position" : {
            "geo_distance" : {
                "position" : {
                    "lat": 83.76,
                    "lon": -81.20
                },
                "value_field":"age",
                "ranges" : ...
            }
        }
    }
}'
```

Facets

If more control is needed on the value, it is possible to use the `value_script` parameter and pass optional parameters via `params` field to the script, similar to the previous recipe. For example, the previous facets become:

```
curl -XGET 'http://127.0.0.1:9200/test-index/test-type/_
search?pretty=true&size=0' -d ' {
    "query" : {
        "match_all" : {}
    },
    "facets" : {
        "position" : {
            "geo_distance" : {
                "position" : {
                    "lat": 83.76,
                    "lon": -81.20
                },
                "value_script":"doc['age'] * param1",
                "params" : {
                    "param1" : 1.5
                }
                "ranges" : ...
            }
        }
    }
}'
```

See also

- *Executing range facets*
- The *Mapping a GeoPoint field* recipe, in *Chapter 3, Managing Mapping*

7
Scripting

In this chapter, we will cover the following topics:

- Installing additional script plugins
- Sorting using script
- Computing return fields with scripting
- Filtering a search via scripting
- Updating with scripting

Introduction

ElasticSearch has a powerful way to extend its capabilities with custom scripts that can be written in several programming languages. The most common ones are MVEL, JavaScript, and Python.

We already have a taste of the scripting capabilities of ElasticSearch, in the previous chapter, using scripting for facets. In this chapter we will see how it's possible to create custom scoring algorithms, special processed return fields, custom sorting or complex update operations on records.

The scripting concept of ElasticSearch can be seen as an advanced stored procedures system in the NoSQL world; so, for an advanced use of ElasticSearch, it is very important to master it.

Scripting

Installing additional script plugins

ElasticSearch provides native scripting (a Java code compiled in JAR) and MVEL, but a lot of interesting languages are available, such as JavaScript and Python. These languages must be installed as plugins.

Getting ready

You need a working ElasticSearch cluster.

How to do it...

For installing a JavaScript language support for Elasticsearch, we will perform the following steps:

1. From the command line, simply call the following command:

   ```
   bin/plugin --install elasticsearch/elasticsearch-lang-javascript/1.4.0
   ```

2. It will fire as results:

   ```
   -> Installing elasticsearch/elasticsearch-lang-javascript/1.4.0...
   Trying http://download.elasticsearch.org/elasticsearch/elasticsearch-lang-javascript/elasticsearch-lang-javascript-1.4.0.zip...
   Downloading ....DONE
   Installed lang-javascript
   ```

   If the installation is successful, the output will end with Installed; otherwise, an error is returned.

3. For installing a Python language support for Elasticsearch, just call the following command:

   ```
   bin/plugin -install elasticsearch/elasticsearch-lang-python/1.2.0
   ```

    The version number depends on the ElasticSearch version. Take a look at the plugin web page to choose the correct version.

How it works...

Language plugins allow the extension of the number of supported languages to be used in scripting.

During the ElasticSearch start-up, PluginService loads all the installed language plugins. Thus, installing or upgrading a plugin requires a node restart.

The ElasticSearch community provides common scripting languages (a list is available on the ElasticSearch site plugin page); others are available in GitHub repositories (a simple search on GitHub allows us to find them).

The most used languages for scripting are as follows:

- **MVEL** (http://mvel.codehaus.org/): This language, embedded in ElasticSearch, is a simple language to provide scripting functionalities. This is one of the fast available language extensions.
- **JavaScript** (https://github.com/elasticsearch/elasticsearch-lang-javascript): This is an external plugin. The JavaScript implementation is based on Java Rhino (https://developer.mozilla.org/en-US/docs/Rhino) and it's very fast.
- **Python** (https://github.com/elasticsearch/elasticsearch-lang-python): This is an external plugin, based on Jython (http://jython.org). It allows Python to be used as a script engine. From several benchmarks, it's slower than languages.
- **Groovy** (https://github.com/elasticsearch/elasticsearch-lang-groovy): This is another external plugin. It enables the use of Groovy (http://groovy.codehaus.org/) as a scripting language.

There's more...

MVEL is a preferred choice to be used if the script is not too complex.

> The performance of every language is different; the faster one is the native Java. In the case of dynamic scripting languages, MVEL is faster, as compared to JavaScript and Python.

Scripting

For accessing document properties in MVEL scripts, the same approach works similarly to other scripting languages, you can use:

- `doc.score`: This stores the document score.
- `doc['field_name'].value`: This extracts the value of the `field_name` field from the document. If the value is an array or if you want to extract the value as an array, you can use `doc['field_name'].values`.
- `doc['field_name'].empty`: This returns `true` if the `field_name` field has no value in the document.
- `doc['field_name'].multivalue`: This returns `true` if the `field_name` field contains multiple values.

If the field contains a GeoPoint value, additional methods are available, such as:

- `doc['field_name'].lat`: This returns the latitude of a GeoPoint. If you need the value as an array, you can use `doc['field_name'].lats`.
- `doc['field_name'].lon`: This returns the longitude of a GeoPoint. If you need the value as an array, you can use `doc['field_name'].lons`
- `doc['field_name'].distance(lat,lon)`: This returns the plane distance in miles given a lat/lon point. If you need to calculate the distance in kilometers, you should use `doc['field_name'].distanceInKm(lat,lon)`.
- `doc['field_name'].arcDistance(lat,lon)`: This returns the arc distance in miles given a lat/lon point. If you need to calculate the distance in kilometers, you should use `doc['field_name'].arcDistanceInKm(lat,lon)`.
- `doc['field_name'].geohashDistance(geohash)`: This returns the distance in miles given a geohash value. If you need to calculate the same distance in kilometers, you should use `doc['field_name']` and `geohashDistanceInKm(lat,lon)`.

By using these helper methods it is possible to create advanced scripts to boost a document by a distance that can be very handy in developing geolocalized centered applications.

Sorting using script

ElasticSearch provides scripting support for sorting functionality. In real-world applications, there is often a need to modify the score using an algorithm that depends on the context and some external variables. Some common scenarios are as follows:

- Sorting places near a point
- Sorting by most read articles
- Sorting items by custom customer logic
- Sorting items with more revenue

Getting ready

You need a working ElasticSearch cluster and an index populated with the script used for facet processing, available in the online code.

How to do it...

For sorting using scripting, we will perform the following steps:

1. If we want to order our documents by the price field multiplied by a factor parameter (usually VAT), the search will be as shown in the following code:

    ```
    curl -XGET 'http://127.0.0.1:9200/test-index/test-type/_
    search?&pretty=true&size=3' -d '{
      "query": {
        "match_all": {}
      },
      "sort": {
        "_script" : {
          "script" : "doc[\"price\"].value * factor",
          "type" : "number",
          "ignore_unmapped" : true,
          "params" : {
            "factor" : 1.1
          },
              "order" : "asc"
            }
        }
    }'
    ```

    In this case we have used a match_all query and a sort script.

2. If everything is correct, the result returned by ElasticSearch should be as shown in the following code:

    ```
    {
      "took" : 7,
      "timed_out" : false,
      "_shards" : {
        "total" : 5,
        "successful" : 5,
        "failed" : 0
      },
      "hits" : {
        "total" : 1000,
        "max_score" : null,
        "hits" : [ {
          "_index" : "test-index",
          "_type" : "test-type",
    ```

Scripting

```
            "_id" : "161",
            "_score" : null, "_source" : …,
            "sort" : [ 0.0278578661440021 ]
        }, {
            "_index" : "test-index",
            "_type" : "test-type",
            "_id" : "634",
            "_score" : null, "_source" : …,
            "sort" : [ 0.08131364254827411 ]
        }, {
            "_index" : "test-index",
            "_type" : "test-type",
            "_id" : "465",
            "_score" : null, "_source" : …,
            "sort" : [ 0.1094966959069832 ]
        } ]
    }
}
```

How it works...

The `sort` parameter, which we discussed in *Chapter 5, Search, Queries, and Filters*, can be extended with the help of scripting.

The `sort` scripting allows defining several parameters, such as:

- `order (default "asc") ("asc" or "desc")`: This determines whether the order must be ascending or descending.
- `script`: This contains the code to be executed.
- `type`: This defines the type to convert the value.
- `params` (optional, a JSON object): This defines the parameters to be passed to.
- `ignore_unmapped` (optional): This ignores unmapped fields in sort. This flag allows us to skip problems due to missing fields in shards.

Extending the sort with scripting allows the use of a broader approach in scoring your hits.

ElasticSearch scripting permits the use of every code that you want. You can create custom complex algorithms for scoring your documents.

There's more...

MVEL provides a lot of built-in functions that can be used in scripts such as:

Function	Description
time()	The current time in milliseconds
sin(a)	Returns the trigonometric sine of an angle
cos(a)	Returns the trigonometric cosine of an angle
tan(a)	Returns the trigonometric tangent of an angle
asin(a)	Returns the arc sine of a value
acos(a)	Returns the arc cosine of a value
atan(a)	Returns the arc tangent of a value
toRadians(angdeg)	Converts an angle measured in degrees to an approximately equivalent angle measured in radians
toDegrees(angrad)	Converts an angle measured in radians to an approximately equivalent angle measured in degrees
exp(a)	Returns Euler's number raised to the power of a value
log(a)	Returns the natural logarithm (base e) of a value
log10(a)	Returns the base 10 logarithm of a value
sqrt(a)	Returns the correctly rounded positive square root of a value
cbrt(a)	Returns the cube root of a double value
IEEEremainder(f1, f2)	Computes the remainder operation on two arguments as prescribed by the IEEE 754 standard
ceil(a)	Returns the smallest (closest to negative infinity) value that is greater than or equal to the argument and is equal to a mathematical integer
floor(a)	Returns the largest (closest to positive infinity) value that is less than or equal to the argument and is equal to a mathematical integer
rint(a)	Returns the value that is closest in value to the argument and is equal to a mathematical integer
atan2(y, x)	Returns the angle, theta from the conversion of rectangular coordinates (x,y_) to polar coordinates (r,_theta)
pow(a, b)	Returns the value of the first argument raised to the power of the second argument
round(a)	Returns the closest integer to the argument
random()	Returns a random double value
abs(a)	Returns the absolute value of a value
max(a, b)	Returns the greater of two values

Scripting

Function	Description
`min(a, b)`	Returns the smaller of two values
`ulp(d)`	Returns the size of the unit in the last place of the argument
`signum(d)`	Returns the signum function of the argument
`sinh(x)`	Returns the hyperbolic sine of a value
`cosh(x)`	Returns the hyperbolic cosine of a value
`tanh(x)`	Returns the hyperbolic tangent of a value
`hypot(x,y)`	Returns sqrt(x^2+y^2) without intermediate overflow or underflow
`acos(a)`	Returns the arc cosine of a value
`atan(a)`	Returns the arc tangent of a value

If you want to retrieve records in a random order, you can use a script with a random method as shown in the following code:

```
curl -XGET 'http://127.0.0.1:9200/test-index/test-type/_
search?&pretty=true&size=3' -d '{
    "query": {
        "match_all": {}
    },
    "sort": {
        "_script" : {
            "script" : "Math.random()",
            "type" : "number",
            "params" : {}
        }
    }
}'
```

Computing return fields with scripting

ElasticSearch allows us to define complex expressions that can be used to return a new calculated field value.

These special fields are called `script_fields`, and they can be expressed with a script in every available ElasticSearch scripting language.

Getting ready

You need a working ElasticSearch cluster and an index populated with the script used for facet processing, available in the online code.

Chapter 7

How to do it...

For computing return fields with scripting, we will perform the following steps:

1. Return the following script fields:
    - "my_calc_field": This concatenates the texts of the "name" and "description" fields
    - "my_calc_field2": This multiplies the "price" value by the "discount" parameter

2. From the command-line, we will execute the following code:
    ```
    curl -XGET 'http://127.0.0.1:9200/test-index/test-type/_
    search?&pretty=true&size=3' -d '{
      "query": {
        "match_all": {}
      },
      "script_fields" : {
        "my_calc_field" : {
          "script" : "doc[\"name\"].value + \" -- \" +
            doc[\"description\"].value"
        },
        "my_calc_field2" : {
          "script" : "doc[\"price\"].value * discount",
          "params" : {
            "discount" : 0.8
          }
        }
      }
    }'
    ```

3. If everything is all right, the result returned by ElasticSearch should be:
    ```
    {
      "took" : 4,
      "timed_out" : false,
      "_shards" : {
        "total" : 5,
        "successful" : 5,
        "failed" : 0
      },
      "hits" : {
        "total" : 1000,
        "max_score" : 1.0,
    ```

```
          "hits" : [ {
            "_index" : "test-index",
            "_type" : "test-type",
            "_id" : "4",
            "_score" : 1.0,
            "fields" : {
              "my_calc_field" : "entropic -- accusantium",
              "my_calc_field2" : 5.480038242170081
            }
          }, {
            "_index" : "test-index",
            "_type" : "test-type",
            "_id" : "9",
            "_score" : 1.0,
            "fields" : {
              "my_calc_field" : "frankie -- accusantium",
              "my_calc_field2" : 34.79852410178313
            }
          }, {
            "_index" : "test-index",
            "_type" : "test-type",
            "_id" : "11",
            "_score" : 1.0,
            "fields" : {
              "my_calc_field" : "johansson -- accusamus",
              "my_calc_field2" : 11.824173084636591
            }
          } ]
        }
      }
```

How it works...

The script fields are similar to executing an SQL function on a field during a select.

In ElasticSearch, after a search phase is executed and hits to be returned are calculated, if some fields (standard or script) are defined, they are calculated and returned.

The script field, which can be written with all supported languages, is processed by passing a value to the source of the document and, if some other parameters are defined in the script (in the example factor), they are passed to the script function.

The script function is a code snippet, so it can contain everything that a language allows to write, but it must be evaluated to a value (or a list of values).

See also

- The *Installing additional script plugins* recipe in this chapter to install additional languages for scripting
- The *Sorting using script* recipe to have a reference of extra built-in functions to be used in MVEL scripts

Filtering a search via scripting

In *Chapter 5, Search, Queries, and Filters*, we have seen many filters. ElasticSearch scripting allows extending the traditional filter with custom script.

Using scripting to create a custom filter is a convenient way to write scripting rules not provided by Lucene or ElasticSearch and to create business rules not available in query DSL.

Getting ready

You need a working ElasticSearch cluster and an index, populated with the script used for facet processing, available in the online code.

How to do it...

For filtering a search using a scripting, we will perform the following steps:

1. We'll write a search with a filter that filters out a document with an age value less than a parameter value:

    ```
    curl -XGET 'http://127.0.0.1:9200/test-index/test-type/_
    search?&pretty=true&size=3' -d '{
      "query": {
        "filtered": {
          "filter": {
            "script": {
              "script": "doc[\"age\"].value > param1",
              "params" : {
                "param1" : 80
              }
            }
          },
          "query": {
            "match_all": {}
          }
        }
      }
    }'
    ```

    In this example, all documents, in which the age value is upper than `param1`, are taken as valid ones.

Scripting

2. If everything is correct, the result returned by ElasticSearch should be as shown in the following code:

```
{
  "took" : 30,
  "timed_out" : false,
  "_shards" : {
    "total" : 5,
    "successful" : 5,
    "failed" : 0
  },
  "hits" : {
    "total" : 237,
    "max_score" : 1.0,
    "hits" : [ {
      "_index" : "test-index",
      "_type" : "test-type",
      "_id" : "9",
      "_score" : 1.0, "_source" :{ ... "age": 83, ... }
    }, {
      "_index" : "test-index",
      "_type" : "test-type",
      "_id" : "23",
      "_score" : 1.0, "_source" : { ... "age": 87, ... }
    }, {
      "_index" : "test-index",
      "_type" : "test-type",
      "_id" : "47",
      "_score" : 1.0, "_source" : {.... "age": 98, ...}
    } ]
  }
}
```

How it works...

The script filter is a language script that returns a Boolean value (true/false). For every hit, the script is evaluated and if it returns true, the hit passes the filter. Scripting can only be used as Lucene filters, not as queries, because it doesn't interact with search (exceptions are constant_score and custom_filters_score).

The scripting fields are as follows:

- script: This contains the code to be executed
- params: These are optional parameters to be passed to the script
- lang (defaults to MVEL): This defines the language of the script

The script code can be every code in your preferred, supported scripting language that returns a Boolean value.

There's more...

Using others language is very similar to MVEL.

For the current example, I have chosen a standard comparison that works for several languages. To execute the same script using the JavaScript language, the code is:

```
curl -XGET 'http://127.0.0.1:9200/test-index/test-type/_
search?&pretty=true&size=3' -d '{
  "query": {
    "filtered": {
      "filter": {
        "script": {
          "script": "doc[\"age\"].value > param1",
          "lang":"javascript",
          "params" : {
            "param1" : 80
          }
        }
      },
      "query": {
        "match_all": {}
      }
    }
  }
}'
```

For Python, we have the following code:

```
curl -XGET 'http://127.0.0.1:9200/test-index/test-type/_
search?&pretty=true&size=3' -d '{
  "query": {
    "filtered": {
      "filter": {
        "script": {
          "script": "doc[\"age\"].value > param1",
          "lang":"python",
          "params" : {
            "param1" : 80
          }
        }
      },
      "query": {
        "match_all": {}
      }
    }
  }
}'
```

Scripting

See also

- The *Installing additional script plugins* recipe in this chapter to install additional languages for scripting
- The *Sorting using script* recipe to have a reference of extra built-in functions to be used in MVEL scripts

Updating with scripting

ElasticSearch allows updating a document in-place.

Updating a document via scripting reduces networking traffic (otherwise, you need to fetch the document, change the field, and send it back) and allows improving performance when you need to process a huge amount of documents.

Getting ready

You need a working ElasticSearch cluster and an index populated with the script used for facet processing, available in the online code.

How to do it...

For updating using a scripting, we will perform the following steps:

1. We'll write an update action that adds a tag value to a list of tags available in the source of a document. It should look as shown in the following code:

    ```
    curl -XPOST 'http://127.0.0.1:9200/test-index/test-type/9/_update?&pretty=true' -d '{
        "script" : "ctx._source.tag += tag",
        "params" : {
            "tag" : "cool"
        }
    }'
    ```

2. If everything is correct, the result returned by ElasticSearch should be:

    ```
    {
      "ok" : true,
      "_index" : "test-index",
      "_type" : "test-type",
      "_id" : "9",
      "_version" : 2
    }
    ```

How it works...

The REST HTTP method used to update a document is **POST**.

The URL contains only the index name, the type, and the document ID, as follows:

    http://<server>/<index_name>/<type>/<document_id>/_update

The update action is composed of three different steps:

- **Get operation, very fast**: This operation works on real-time data (no need to refresh) and retrieves the record
- **Script execution**: The script is executed on the document and, if required, the document is updated
- **Saving the document**: The document, if required, is saved

The script execution follows the workflow in the following manner:

- The script is compiled and the result is cached to improve re-execution. The compilation depends on the scripting language; it allows detecting errors in the script such as typographical errors, syntax errors and language-related errors. The compilation step can be CPU bound, so ElasticSearch caches the compilation results for further execution.
- The document is executed in the script context. The document data is available in the ctx variable in the script.

The update script can set several parameters in the ctx variable. The most important parameters are:

- ctx._source: This contains the source of the document
- ctx._timestamp: If it's defined, this value is set to the document timestamp
- ctx.op: This defines the main operation type to be executed. There are several available values, such as:
    - index: The default value is nothing is defined: the record is re-indexed with the update values
    - delete: The document is deleted after the update
    - none: The document is skipped without re-indexing the document

 If you need to execute a large number of update operations, it's better to perform them in bulk to improve your application's performance.

Scripting

There's more...

The previous example can be rewritten using the JavaScript language, and it looks as shown in the following code:

```
curl -XPOST 'http://127.0.0.1:9200/test-index/test-type/9/_update?&pretty=true' -d '{
    "script" : "ctx._source.tag += tag",
    "lang":"js",
    "params" : {
        "tag" : "cool"
    }
}'
```

The previous example can be written using the Python language, as follows:

```
curl -XPOST 'http://127.0.0.1:9200/test-index/test-type/9/_update?&pretty=true' -d '{
    "script" : "ctx[\"_source\"][\"tag\"] = list(ctx[\"_source\"][\"tag\"]) + [tag]",
    "lang":"python",
    "params" : {
        "tag" : "cool"
    }
}'
```

In the Python example, the Java list must be converted into a Python list to allow add elements; the back conversion is automatically done.

> To improve the performance if a field is not changed, it's a good practice to set the ctx._op variable equal to none to disable the indexing of the unchanged document.

In the following example we will execute an update that adds new "tags" and "labels" to an object, but we will mark for indexing the document only if the tags or labels values are changed.

```
curl -XPOST 'http://127.0.0.1:9200/test-index/test-type/9/_update?&pretty=true' -d '{
  "script" : "ctx.op = "none";
  if(ctx._source.containsValue("tags")){
    foreach(item:new_tags){
      if(!ctx._source.tags.contains(item)){
        ctx._source.tags += item;
        ctx.op = "index";
      }
    }
```

```
    }else{
      ctx._source.tags=new_tags;
      ctx.op = "index";
    };
    if(ctx._source.containsValue("labels")){
      foreach(item:new_labels){
        if(!ctx._source.labels.contains(item)){
          ctx._source.labels += item;
          ctx.op = "index";
        }
      }
    }else{
      ctx._source.labels=new_labels;
      ctx.op = "index";
    };",
    "params" : {
      "new_tags" : ["cool", "nice"],
      "new_labels" : ["red", "blue", "green"]
    }
  }
}'
```

The preceding script uses the following steps:

1. It marks the operation to none to prevent indexing if in the following steps the original source is not changed.
2. It checks if the tags field is available in the source object.
3. If the tags field is available in the source object, it iterates all the values of the new_tags list. If the value is not available in the current tags list, it adds it and updates the operation to index.
4. It the tags field doesn't exist in the source object, it simply adds it to the source and marks the operation to index.
5. The steps from 2 to 4 are repeated for the labels value. The repetition is present in this example to show the ElasticSearch user how it is possible to update multiple values in a single update operation.

This script could be quite complex, but it shows the powerful capabilities of scripting in ElasticSearch.

8
Rivers

In this chapter, we will cover the following topics:

- Managing a river
- Using the CouchDB river
- Using the MongoDB river
- Using the RabbitMQ river
- Using the JDBC river
- Using the Twitter river

Introduction

There are two ways to insert your data in ElasticSearch. In the previous chapters we have seen the index API, which allows storing documents in ElasticSearch via the PUT/POST API or the bulk shortcut. The other way is to use a service that fetches the data from an external source (one shot or periodically) and puts the data into the cluster.

ElasticSearch names these services as `Rivers` and the ElasticSearch community provides several rivers to connect to the following data sources:

- CouchDB
- MongoDB
- RabbitMQ
- SQL DBMS (Oracle, MySQL, PostgreSQL and so on)
- Redis
- Twitter
- Wikipedia

Rivers

The rivers are available as external plugins.

In this chapter we'll discuss how to manage a river (creating, checking, and deleting) and how to configure the most common ones.

Managing a river

In ElasticSearch, the following are the two main action-related river setups:

- Creating a river
- Deleting a river

Getting ready

You need a working ElasticSearch cluster.

How to do it...

For managing a river, we need to perform the following steps:

1. A river is uniquely defined by a name and a type. The type of the river is the type name defined in the loaded river plugins.

2. After the `name` and the `type` parameters, usually a river requires an extra configuration that can be passed in the `_meta` property.

3. To create a river, the HTTP method is PUT (POST also works):

    ```
    curl -XPUT 'http://127.0.0.1:9200/_river/my_river/_meta' -d '{
        "type" : "dummy"
    }'
    ```

    The `dummy` type is a "fake" river always installed in ElasticSearch.

4. The result will be as follows:

    ```
    {"ok":true,"_index":"_river","_type":"my_river","_id":"_meta","_version":1}
    ```

5. If you look at ElasticSearch logs, you'll see some new lines, which are as follows:

    ```
    [2013-08-03 20:48:39,206][INFO ][cluster.metadata         ] [Elsie-Dee] [_river] creating index, cause [auto(index api)], shards [1]/[1], mappings []
    [2013-08-03 20:48:39,272][INFO ][cluster.metadata         ] [Elsie-Dee] [_river] update_mapping [my_river] (dynamic)
    [2013-08-03 20:48:39,286][INFO ][river.dummy              ]
    ```

```
[Elsie-Dee] [dummy][my_river] create
[2013-08-03 20:48:39,287][INFO ][river.dummy             ]
[Elsie-Dee] [dummy][my_river] start
[2013-08-03 20:48:39,292][INFO ][cluster.metadata        ]
[Elsie-Dee] [_river] update_mapping [my_river] (dynamic)
```

6. To remove a river, we will use the HTTP method DELETE. If we consider the previous created river, the REST call is as follows:

    `curl -XDELETE 'http://127.0.0.1:9200/_river/my_river/'`

7. The result will be as follows:

    `{"ok":true}`

8. If you look to ElasticSearch logs, you'll see some new lines:

```
[2013-08-03 20:48:39,292][INFO ][cluster.metadata        ]
[Elsie-Dee] [_river] update_mapping [my_river] (dynamic)
[2013-08-03 20:56:19,706][INFO ][cluster.metadata        ]
[Elsie-Dee] [[_river]] remove_mapping [my_river]
[2013-08-03 20:56:19,706][INFO ][river.dummy             ]
[Elsie-Dee] [dummy][my_river] close
```

How it works...

When the ElasticSearch node starts up, the river service is automatically activated.

Generally depending on the implementation of river, there are two different usages, which are as follows:

- `one shot`: Here, the river is created with some parameters. It executes its work and then it removes itself. This approach is mainly used for processing files, dumps, and every source that need to be processed only for a single time as the data in it does not change.
- `cyclic`: Here, the river after processing all the data, the river waits for some time and then it restarts, processing new data if available. This case is typical of data sources that evolve in time such as DBMS, MongoDB, RabbitMQ, and Redis.

The rivers are stored in a special index `_river` (in ElasticSearch all special indices start with `_` character), the document type name becomes the river name and the `_meta` document is where the river configuration is stored.

Rivers

When ElasticSearch receives a creation river call, it creates the new river mapping and starts the river. Generally the river is composed by the following components:

- **A producer thread**: This collects the documents to be indexed and sends them to a consumer (thread).
- **A consumer thread**: This executes bulk insert of documents sent by the producer.

When the river is started, these threads are started and the data is processed and sent to the cluster.

In our example, we can see that a river is started by looking to ElasticSearch logfiles.

When we want to remove a river, the DELETE call removes it from execution. At server level, ElasticSearch stops the river, flushes the stale data, and removes it from the `_river` index.

ElasticSearch always guarantees that a single river instance is running in the cluster (singleton). If the river is executed in a node and this node should "die", the river is rescheduled on another cluster node.

There's more...

When a river is executed a special document _status is available under the river name. This is a standard ElasticSearch document that can be fetched with the GET API.

For the preceding example it's possible to check the status using the following command:

```
curl -XGET 'http://127.0.0.1:9200/_river/my_river/_status'
```

The answer will be something similar to the following one:

```
{
    "_id": "_status",
    "_index": "_river",
    "_source": {
        "node": {
            "id": "BbeoKc-CQpSFicQF6rvgNQ",
            "name": "Alyssa Moy",
            "transport_address": "inet[/192.168.1.14:9300]"
        },
        "ok": true
    },
    "_type": "my_river",
    "_version": 1,
    "exists": true
}
```

In the `_source`, the node attribute defines in which node the river is in execution. The status can also contain special river fields describing the current river position in the process (for example, number of document processed, last river cycle, ...).

See also

- The *Installing a plugin* recipe in *Chapter 2, Downloading and Setting Up ElasticSearch*

Using the CouchDB river

CouchDB is a NoSQL data store that stores data in the JSON format, similar to ElasticSearch. It can query with map/reduce tasks and it's RESTful, so every operation can be done via HTTP API calls.

Using ElasticSearch to search the CouchDB data is very handy as it extends CouchDB data store with Lucene search capabilities.

Getting ready

You need a working ElasticSearch cluster and a working CouchDB Server to connect to.

How to do it...

For using the CouchDB river, we need to perform the following steps:

1. Firstly, we need to install the CouchDB river plugin, which is available on GitHub and maintained by the ElasticSearch company. We can install the river plugin in the following way:

   ```
   bin/plugin -install elasticsearch/elasticsearch-river-couchdb/1.2.0
   ```

   > The CouchDB river plugin uses the attachment plugin and sometimes JavaScript scripting language, it is good practice to install them.

2. After restarting the node, we are able to create a configuration (config.json) for our CouchDB river as follows:

   ```
   {
       "type": "couchdb",
       "couchdb": {
           "host": "localhost",
           "port": 5984,
           "db": "my_db",
           "filter": null
       },
   ```

Rivers

```
        "index": {
            "index": "my_db",
            "type": "my_db",
            "bulk_size": "100",
            "bulk_timeout": "10ms"
        }
    }
```

3. Now we can create the river with the current configuration as follows:

   ```
   curl -XPUT 'http://127.0.0.1:9200/_river/couchriver/_meta' -d @ config.json
   ```

4. The result will be as follows:

   ```
   {"ok":true,"_index":"_river","_type":" couchriver ","_id":"_meta","_version":1}
   ```

How it works...

The CouchDB river is designed to be fast in detecting changes and propagating them from CouchDB to ElasticSearch. To avoid creating overhead in polling the server and to consume less resources, it is designed to hook the `_changes` feed of CouchDB.

This approach prevents to execute a lot of map/reduce queries on CouchDB to retrieve the new or changed documents.

To create a CouchDB river the type must be set to `couchdb`. The following parameters must be passed to the `couchdb` object:

- `protocol` (default `http`, valid values are `http` and `https`): This parameter defines the protocol to be used.
- `no_verify` (default `false`): This parameter if `true`, the river will skip HTTPS certificate validation.
- `host` (default `localhost`): This parameter defines the host server to be used.
- `port`: (default `5984`): This parameter defines the CouchDB port number.
- `db` (default the river name): This parameter defines the name of database to be monitored.
- `filter`: This parameter defines some filters to be applied to remove the unwanted documents.
- `filter_parameters`: This parameter defines a list of keys/values used to filter out documents.
- `ignore_attachments` (default `false`): This parameter if `true`, the document containing an attachment will be skipped by the river. It requires the attachment plugin installed.

- **user** and **password**: These parameters if defined, are used to authenticate to CouchDB.
- **script**: This is an optional script to be executed on documents.
- **scriptType** (default `js`): This is the scripting language used to process the provided script. It requires the JavaScript language plugin installed.

The CouchDB river also provides a good tuning on indexing, letting the user set the following index parameters in the `index` object:

- **index**: This parameter defines the index name to be used.
- **type**: This parameter defines the type to be used.
- **bulk_size** (default `100`): This parameter defines the number of bulk actions to be collected before sending them as bulk.
- **bulk_timeout** (default 10 ms): If changes are detected within `bulk_timeout`, they are packed up to `bulk_size` before sending them.

When the river starts, it initializes the following threads:

- The slurper thread manages the connection between the ElasticSearch and CouchDB server. It continuously fetch changes in CouchDB and inserts them in a queue to be read by the indexer. Generally, this thread is called a producer.
- The indexer thread collects items from the queue and prepares the bulk to be indexed. It is often referred as a consumer.

There's more...

The CouchDB river is a very fast and well designed river. There are two important tools to improve the quality of your documents: filter and script.

The filter, if applicable, allows to filters documents in CouchDB `_change` stream reducing the bandwidth and the documents that must be indexed. The filter can also be used for partitioning your CouchDB database: for example it allows creating rivers that index user documents in their own ElasticSearch index.

The script allows document manipulation before indexing them. Typical scenarios cover adding/cloning/editing/joining fields, but other document manipulations are available though limited to the capabilities of the chosen scripting language.

See also

- The CouchDB river plugin home page at https://github.com/elasticsearch/elasticsearch-river-couchdb

Using the MongoDB river

MongoDB is a very common NoSQL tool used all over the world. One of its main drawbacks is that it was not designed for text searching.

Thus, the latest MongoDB version provides full text search, its completeness, and functionality are far more limited than the current ElasticSearch version. So it's quite common to use MongoDB as the data store and ElasticSearch for searching. The MongoDB river, which initially was developed by me and now is maintained by *Richard Louapre*, helps to create a bridge between these two applications.

Getting ready

You need a working ElasticSearch cluster and a working MongoDB instance installed in the same machine of ElasticSearch in replica set (http://docs.mongodb.org/manual/tutorial/deploy-replica-set/ and http://docs.mongodb.org/manual/tutorial/convert-standalone-to-replica-set/). You need to restore the sample data available in mongodb/data using the following command:

```
mongorestore -d escookbook escookbook
```

How to do it...

For using the MongoDB river, we need to perform the following steps:

1. Firstly, we need to install the MongoDB river plugin, which is available on GitHub (https://github.com/richardwilly98/elasticsearch-river-mongodb). We can install the river plugin in the following way:

   ```
   bin/plugin -install richardwilly98/elasticsearch-river-mongodb/1.6.11
   ```

    As internal the MongoDB river plugin uses the attachment plugin and sometimes the JavaScript scripting language, it is good practice to install them.

2. Restart your ElasticSearch node to be sure that the river plugin is loaded. In the log you should see the following result:

   ```
   [2013-08-04 15:39:29,705][INFO ][plugins                  ] [Dirtnap] loaded [river-twitter, transport-thrift, river-mongodb, mapper-attachments, lang-python, lang-javascript], sites [bigdesk, head]
   ```

3. We need to create a `config(.json)` file to configure the river. In this case we will define a database and a collection to fetch the data as follows:

```
{
  "type" : "mongodb",
  "mongodb" : {
   "servers" : [
    { "host" : "localhost", "port" : 27017 }
   ],
   "db" : "escookbook",
   "collection" : "items"
  },
  "index" : {
   "name" : "items"
  }
}
```

4. Now we can create the river with the following configuration:

   `curl -XPUT 'http://127.0.0.1:9200/_river/mongodbriver/_meta' -d @ config.json`

5. The result will be as follows:

   `{"ok":true,"_index":"_river","_type":"mongodbriver","_id":"_meta","_version":1}`

How it works...

The current MongoDB river allows to fetch data from a MongoDB instance and insert it in the current cluster. It's important that the MongoDB instance is correctly configured in replica set as the river works on the **oplog (Operation log)** collection. The oplog collection is a special collection used to keep every MongoDB change. The river interprets the log actions and replicates them in ElasticSearch. Using this approach it's not required to continue polling the MongoDB cluster and doesn't require searches that can reduce the performance significantly.

The ElasticSearch configuration used in the previous example is quite simple. These are the following sections in the configuration:

- `mongodb`: This contains MongoDB related parameters. The most important ones are as follows:
    - `servers`: This is a list of hosts and ports to connect to.
    - `credentials`: This is a list of database credentials (`db`, `user`, `password`). For example:

      `{"db":"mydatabase", "user":"username", "password":"myseceret"}`

Rivers

- `db`: This defines the database to be monitored.
- `collection`: This defines the collection to be monitored.
- `gridfs`: This defines a Boolean indicating if the collection is a gridfs.
- `filter`: This defines an extra filter to filter out records.

▶ `index`: This defines where to store documents in ElasticSearch. The most important parameters that can be passed are as follows:

- `name`: This is the index name to be used.
- `type`: This is the type to be used.
- `throttle_size`: This is the size of the bulk.

If no mappings are defined, the river auto detects the format from the MongoDB document.

One of the main advantages of using this plugin is that, because it works on oplog, it always keeps the data updated without MongoDB overhead.

See also

▶ The MongoDB river plugin home page at `https://github.com/richardwilly98/elasticsearch-river-mongodb`

Using the RabbitMQ river

RabbitMQ is a fast message broker, which can handle thousands of messages in a second. It can be very handy to be used in conjunction with ElasticSearch to bulk index records.

The RabbitMQ river plugin is designed to wait for messages that store bulk operations and index them.

Getting ready

You need a working ElasticSearch cluster and a working RabbitMQ instance installed in the same machine of ElasticSearch.

How to do it...

For using the RabbitMQ river, we need to perform the following steps:

1. Firstly, we need to install the RabbitMQ river plugin, which is available on GitHub (https://github.com/elasticsearch/elasticsearch-river-rabbitmq). We can install the river plugin in the following way:

   ```
   bin/plugin -install elasticsearch/elasticsearch-river-rabbitmq/1.6.0
   ```

2. The result should be as follows:

   ```
   -> Installing elasticsearch/elasticsearch-river-rabbitmq/1.6.0...
   Trying http://download.elasticsearch.org/elasticsearch/elasticsearch-river-rabbitmq/elasticsearch-river-rabbitmq-1.6.0.zip...
   Downloading ...................DONE
   Installed river-rabbitmq
   ```

3. Restart your ElasticSearch node to ensure that the river plugin is properly loaded. In the log you should see the following result:

   ```
   [2013-08-12 23:08:43,639][INFO ][plugins                  ] [Fault Zone] loaded [river-rabbitmq, river-twitter, transport-thrift, river-mongodb, mapper-attachments, lang-python, river-couchdb, lang-javascript], sites [bigdesk, head]
   ```

4. We need to create a config(.json) file, to configure the river, as follows:

   ```
   {
     "type" : "rabbitmq",
     "rabbitmq" : {
           "host" : "localhost",
           "port" : 5672,
           "user" : "guest",
           "pass" : "guest",
           "vhost" : "/",
           "queue" : "elasticsearch",
           "exchange" : "elasticsearch",
           "routing_key" : "elasticsearch",
           "exchange_declare" : true,
           "exchange_type" : "direct",
           "exchange_durable" : true,
           "queue_declare" : true,
           "queue_bind" : true,
           "queue_durable" : true,
           "queue_auto_delete" : false,
           "heartbeat" : "30m"
   ```

Rivers

```
        },
        "index" : {
            "bulk_size" : 100,
            "bulk_timeout" : "10ms",
            "ordered" : false
        }
    }
```

5. Now we can create the river with the current configuration as follows:

    ```
    curl -XPUT 'http://127.0.0.1:9200/_river/rabbitriver/_meta' -d @
    config.json
    ```

6. The result will be as follows:

    ```
    {"ok":true,"_index":"_river","_type":" rabbitriver ","_id":"_
    meta","_version":1}
    ```

How it works...

The RabbitMQ river instantiates a connection to the RabbitMQ server and waits for messages to process. The only kind of messages, that the plugin is able to process, are bulk operation.

 Every bulk operation must terminate with a new line character \n otherwise the last operation will be shallowed.

Typically, the connection is a direct one, that means that as fast as the message is sent to the server, it is redirected to the client.

The river type is `rabbitmq` and all client configurations live on the `rabbitmq` object. The most common parameters are as follows:

- `host` (default `localhost`): This defines the RabbitMQ server address.
- `port` (default `5672`): This defines the RabbitMQ server port.
- `user` and `pass`: This defines the the username and password credentials required to access the RabbitMQ server.
- `vhost` (default `/`): This defines the RabbitMQ host to be used.
- `exchange_declare` (`false/true`) and `exchange` (default `elasticsearch`): These control if an exchange must be bound and the exchange name.
- `exchange_type` (default `direct`): This defines the type of exchange to be used.
- `exchange_durable` (default `true`): This defines a durable exchange that survives the RabbitMQ broker restart, otherwise it is transient.

- `queue_declare` (false/true) and `queue` (default `elasticsearch`): These control if a queue must be bound and the queue name.
- `queue_durable` (default `true`): This defines a durable queue that survives the RabbitMQ broker restart, otherwise it is transient.
- `queue_auto_delete` (default `false`): This defines that a queue, where consumers finish all the messages, is automatically deleted.
- `heartbeat`: This sends the hearbeat delay to the connection. It's used to prevent connection dropping if there are network inactivities.

Sometimes the RabbitMQ server is configured in the cluster mode for higher availability. In this configuration there is no a single host, but a list of hosts. They can be defined as a list of addresses in the following way:

```
{
    "rabbitmq" : {
        "addresses" : [
            {
                "host" : "host1",
                "port" : 5672
            },
            {
                "host" : "host2",
                "port" : 5672
            }
        ]
    }
    ...
}
```

There's more...

The RabbitMQ river plugin allows to control with scripting two important aspects of bulk processing: the global bulk with the `bulk_scripting_filter` and every single document with `script_filter` that must be indexed or created.

The definition of these two script filters is given by the following standards:

- `script`: This is the code of the script
- `script_lang`: This is the language to be used to interpret the code
- `script_params`: This is a dictionary/map/key-value containing the additional parameter to be passed to the script.

The `bulk_script_filter` will receive a block of text (body) that is the text consisting of a list of actions. The script must return another block of text to be processed by ElasticSearch. If the script returns a null, the bulk is skipped.

An example of the `bulk_script_filter` declaration is as follows:

```
{
    "type" : "rabbitmq",
    "rabbitmq" : {
        ...
    },
    "index" : {
        ...
    },
    "bulk_script_filter" : {
        "script" : "myscript",
        "script_lang" : "native",
        "script_params" : {
            "param1" : "val1",
            "param2" : "val2"
            ...
        }
    }
}
```

If a `script_filter` is defined, a `ctx` context is passed to the script for every document, which must be indexed or created.

An example of the `script_filter` declaration is as follows:

```
{
    "type" : "rabbitmq",
    "rabbitmq" : {
        ...
    },
    "index" : {
        ...
    },
    "script_filter" : {
        "script" : "ctx.type1.field1 += param1",
        "script_lang" : "mvel",
        "script_params" : {
          "param1" : 1
        }
    }
}
```

Using the RabbitMQ broker can be a very powerful tool, which allows to support high load and balancing, moving the load peak on to the RabbitMQ message queue. The performance of a message queue as RabbitMQ is far faster than ElasticSearch in processing INSERT because it doesn't require indexing the data. So, it can be a good frontend to resolve ElasticSearch index peaks, and also to allow executing delayed bulk if an ElasticSearch node is down.

See also

- The RabbitMQ river documentation at https://github.com/elasticsearch/elasticsearch-river-rabbitmq
- The *Managing a river* recipe in this chapter

Using the JDBC river

Generally application data is stored in a DBMS of some kind (Oracle, MySQL, PostgreSql, Microsoft SQL Server, SQLite, and so on), to power up traditional application with advanced search capabilities of ElasticSearch and Lucene. All this data must be imported in ElasticSearch. The JDBC river by *Jörg Prante* allows to connect to these DBMSs, executes some queries and indexes the results.

Getting ready

You need a working ElasticSearch.

How to do it...

For using the JDBC river, we need to perform the following steps:

1. Firstly, we need to install the JDBC river plugin, which is available on GitHub (https://github.com/jprante/elasticsearch-river-jdbc). We can install the river plugin in the following way:

   ```
   bin/plugin -url http://bit.ly/145e9Ly -install river-jdbc
   ```

2. The result should be as follows:

   ```
   -> Installing river-jdbc...
   Trying http://bit.ly/145e9Ly...
   Downloading ... .....DONE
   Installed river-jdbc into .../elasticsearch/plugins/river-jdbc
   ```

> The JDBC river plugin does not bundle DBMS drivers, so you need to download them and place in the `plugin` directory.

3. If you need to use PostgreSQL, you need to download the driver at `http://jdbc.postgresql.org/download.html`. The current driver is `http://jdbc.postgresql.org/download/postgresql-9.2-1003.jdbc4.jar`.

4. If you need to use MySql, you need to download the driver at `http://dev.mysql.com`. Current driver is `http://dev.mysql.com/get/Downloads/Connector-J/mysql-connector-java-5.1.26.zip/from/http://cdn.mysql.com/`.

5. Restart your ElasticSearch node to be sure that the river plugin is loaded. In the log you should see the following result:

   ```
   [2013-08-18 14:59:10,143][INFO ][node                     ]
   [Fight-Man] initializing ...
   [2013-08-18 14:59:10,163][INFO ][plugins                  ]
   [Fight-Man] loaded [river-twitter, transport-thrift, jdbc-river],
   sites []
   ```

6. We need to create a `config(.json)` file to configure the river. In this case we define a PostgreSQL database, `items` and a table `items` to fetch the data.

   ```
   {
       "type" : "jdbc",
       "jdbc" :{
           "strategy" : "oneshot",
           "driver" : "org.postgresql.Driver",
           "url" : "jdbc:postgresql://localhost:5432/items",
           "user" : "username",
           "password" : "password",
           "sql" : "select * from items",
           "poll" : "1h",
           "scale" : 0,
           "autocommit" : false,
           "fetchsize" : 100,
           "max_rows" : 0,
           "max_retries" : 3,
           "max_retries_wait" : "10s",
           "locale" : "it,
           "digesting" : true,
       },
       "index" : {
           "index" : "jdbc",
           "type" : "jdbc",
           "bulk_size" : 100,
           "max_bulk_requests" : 30,
           "versioning" : false,
           "acknowledge" : false
       }
   }
   ```

7. Now we can create the river with the current configuration as follows:

   ```
   curl -XPUT 'http://127.0.0.1:9200/_river/jdbcriver/_meta' -d @
   config.json
   ```

8. The result will be as follows:

   ```
   {"ok":true,"_index":"_river","_type":"jdbcriver","_id":"_meta","_version":1}
   ```

How it works...

The JDBC river is a very versatile river, which has a lot of options to cover a large number of common scenarios related database issues. As it works for every DBMS which provides JDBC drivers, it comes without a built-in driver. They must be installed, usually in the river directory, before using them.

The common flow for using the JDBC river is to provide a connection and a SQL query to fetch SQL records that will be converted into ElasticSearch ones.

The river type is `jdbc` and all the client configurations live on the `jdbc` object. The most common parameters are as follows:

- `strategy` (default `simple`): This is the strategy of the JDBC river, currently the following ones are implemented:
  - `simple`: This fetches data with the SQL query, indexes the data in ElasticSearch, waits for the next poll interval, and then it restarts the loop
  - `oneshot`: This has a similar workflow to simple strategy, but it ends after the first loop
  - `table`: This fetches all the records of a table without using SQL
- `driver`: This is the JDBC driver class. Every JDBC driver defines its own class. The classes are as follows:
  - `mysql`: `com.mysql.jdbc.Driver`
  - `postgresql`: `org.postgresql.Driver`
  - `oracle`: `oracle.jdbc.OracleDriver`
  - `sql server`: `com.microsoft.sqlserver.jdbc.SQLServerDriver`
- `url`: This is the JDBC URL for the driver.
- `user`: This is the database username.
- `password`: This is the database user password.
- `sql`: This is the SQL statement. Typically this is a SELECT statement. If it ends with `.sql`, the statement is looked up in the ElasticSearch filesystem.
- `sqlparams`: These are the bind parameters for the SQL statement (in order).

Rivers

- `poll`: This is the time interval for repetitions (ignored in the "oneshot" strategy).
- `rounding`: This determines the rounding mode for numeric values: `ceiling, down, floor, halfdown, halfeven, halfup, unnecessary, up`.
- `scale`: This gives the precision of the numeric values.
- `autocommit`: This is true if each statement should be automatically executed.
- `fetchsize`: This defines the fetch size for large result sets, most drivers implement `fetchsize` to control the amount of rows in the buffer while iterating through the result set.
- `max_rows`: This limits the number of rows fetches by a statement, the rest of the rows are ignored.
- `max_retries`: This defines the number of retries to (re)connect to a database. This is often used when there are problems with the DBMS to automatically reconnect if the connection is dropped.
- `max_retries_wait`: This defines the time to wait between retries.
- `locale`: This is the default locale (used for parsing numerical values and floating point character).
- `digesting`: This determines if a checksum should be used for the data indexed by each run (required for updates by versioning).
- `acksql`: This is an INSERT/UPDATE acknowledge SQL statement that is executed after a result set has been fetched.
- `acksqlparams`: These are the bind parameters for acknowledging the SQL statement.

The JDBC river also provides a good tuning on indexing, letting the user set the following index parameters in the `index` object:

- `index`: This defines the Elasticsearch index used for indexing the data from JDBC.
- `type`: This defines the Elasticsearch type of the index used for indexing the data from JDBC.
- `bulk_size`: This defines the length of each bulk index request submitted.
- `max_bulk_requests`: This defines the maximum number of concurrent bulk requests. This setting allows to control the rate of bulk operations to prevent DBMS or ElasticSearch overhead for too high fetch and index cycles.
- `index_settings`: These are the optional settings for the Elasticsearch index.
- `type_mapping`: This is an optional mapping for the Elasticsearch index type.
- `versioning`: This is `true` if versioning should be used in the Elasticsearch indexed documents.
- `acknowledge`: This is `true` if Elasticsearch bulk responses should be acknowledged to a database table ("table" strategy only).

The JDBC river plugin has a lot of options, choosing the correct ones depends on a particular scenario.

It's a very handy tool to import data from traditional relational databases without too much effort. If complex data manipulation on databases is required, it's better to implement custom river plugin to do the job.

See also

- The JDBC plugin river home page and documentation at https://github.com/jprante/elasticsearch-river-jdbc
- The *Managing a river* recipe in this chapter

Using the Twitter river

In the previous recipes, we have seen rivers that fetch data from data stores, both SQL and NoSQL. In this recipe, we'll discuss how to use the Twitter river to collect tweets from Twitter and store them in ElasticSearch.

Getting ready

You need a working ElasticSearch and OAuth Twitter token. To obtain it, you need to log in to Twitter (https://dev.twitter.com/apps/) and create a new app at https://dev.twitter.com/apps/new.

How to do it...

For using the Twitter river, we need to perform the following steps:

1. Firstly, we need to install the Twitter river plugin, which is available on Github (https://github.com/elasticsearch/elasticsearch-river-twitter). We can install the river plugin in the usual way as follows:

   ```
   bin/plugin -install elasticsearch/elasticsearch-river-twitter/1.4.0
   ```

2. The result should be as follows:

   ```
   -> Installing elasticsearch/elasticsearch-river-twitter/1.4.0...
   Trying http://download.elasticsearch.org/elasticsearch/elasticsearch-river-twitter/elasticsearch-river-twitter-1.4.0.zip...
   Downloading ......DONE
   Installed river-twitter into .../elasticsearch/plugins/river-twitter
   ```

Rivers

3. Restart your ElasticSearch node to be sure that the river plugin is loaded. In the log, you should see the following result:

   ```
   ...
   [2013-08-18 14:59:10,143][INFO ][node                     ]
   [Fight-Man] initializing ...
   [2013-08-18 14:59:10,163][INFO ][plugins                  ]
   [Fight-Man] loaded [river-twitter, transport-thrift, jdbc-river],
   sites []
   ```

4. We need to create a `config(.json)` file to configure the river, as follows:

   ```
   {
       "type" : "twitter",
       "twitter" : {
           "oauth" : {
               "consumer_key" : "*** YOUR Consumer key HERE ***",
               "consumer_secret" : "*** YOUR Consumer secret HERE ***",
               "access_token" : "*** YOUR Access token HERE ***",
               "access_token_secret" : "*** YOUR Access token secret HERE ***"
           },
           "type" : "sample",
           "ignore_retweet" : true
       },
       "index" : {
           "index" : "my_twitter_river",
           "type" : "status",
           "bulk_size" : 100
       }
   }
   ```

5. Now we can create the river with the current configuration as follows:

   ```
   curl -XPUT 'http://127.0.0.1:9200/_river/twitterriver/_meta' -d @
   config.json
   ```

6. The result will be as follows:

   ```
   {"ok":true,"_index":"_river","_type":"twitterriver",
   "_id":"_meta","_version":1}
   ```

How it works...

The Twitter river, after having logged into Twitter, starts collecting tweets and sends them in bulk to ElasticSearch.

The river type is `twitter` and all client configurations live on the `twitter` object. The following are the most common parameters:

- `oauth`: This parameter is an object containing four keys to access the Twitter API. These are generated when you create a Twitter application, and these keys are as follows:
    - `consumer_key`
    - `consumer_secret`
    - `access_token`
    - `access_token_secret`
- `type`: This can be one of the following three allowed by the Twitter API:
    - `sample`
    - `filter` (refer to https://dev.twitter.com/docs/api/1.1/post/statuses/filter)
    - `firehose`
- `raw` (default `false`): This parameter if `true`, the tweets are indexed in ElasticSearch without any change.
- `ignore_retweet` (default `false`): This parameter if `true`, retweets are skipped.

There's more...

To control the Twitter flow, we need to define an additional filter object.

Defining a filter automatically switches the type to filter. The Twitter filter API allows to define the following additional parameters to filter:

- `tracks`: This is used to track the keywords.
- `follow`: This follows the IDs of Twitter users.
- `locations`: This tracks a set of bounding box.

These are the filter capabilities allowed by Twitter to reduce the number of tweets sent to you and to focus the search on some particular targets.

Rivers

A filter river config file will look as follows:

```
{
    "type" : "twitter",
    "twitter" : {
        "oauth" : {
            "consumer_key" : "*** YOUR Consumer key HERE ***",
            "consumer_secret" : "*** YOUR Consumer secret HERE ***",
            "access_token" : "*** YOUR Access token HERE ***",
            "access_token_secret" : "*** YOUR Access token secret HERE ***"
        },
        "filter" : {
            "tracks" : ["elasticsearch", "cookbook", "packtpub"],
        }
    }
}
```

See also

- The Twitter plugin river home page and documentation available at https://github.com/elasticsearch/elasticsearch-river-twitter
- The *Managing a river* recipe in this chapter

9
Cluster and Nodes Monitoring

In this chapter we will cover the following topics:

- Controlling cluster health via API
- Controlling cluster state via API
- Getting nodes information via API
- Getting node statistic via API
- Installing and using BigDesk
- Installing and using ElasticSearch-head
- Installing and using SemaText SPM

Introduction

In ElasticSearch ecosystem, it can be immensely useful to monitor nodes and cluster to control and improve their performances and states. There are several scenarios involved in problems at cluster level such as the following:

- Node overheads occur when some nodes can have too many shards allocated and become a bottleneck of all cluster.
- Node shutdown can happen due to a lot of reasons, for example full disk, hardware problem and power problems.
- Shard relocation problems or corruptions in which some shards are unable to become in online status may happen.

Cluster and Nodes Monitoring

- If a shard is too big, the index performance decreases due to Lucene massive segments merging.
- Empty indices and shards only waste memory and storage, but because every shard has a lot of active thread, if there is a huge number of unused indices and shards, the general cluster performance is degraded.

Detecting malfunction or bad performances can be done via API or via some frontend plugins that can be activated in ElasticSearch.

Some of the plugins shown in this chapter allow the readers to have a working web console on their ElasticSearch data and to test query before implementing them in the code.

Controlling cluster health via API

In *Understanding cluster, replication* recipe, *and sharding* in *Chapter 1, Getting Started*, we discussed ElasticSearch cluster and how to manage in the case of red and yellow state.

ElasticSearch provides a convenient way to control the cluster state, which is one of the first things to control in case of problems.

Getting ready

You need a working ElasticSearch cluster.

How to do it...

For controlling the cluster health, we need to perform the following steps:

1. To view the cluster health, the HTTP method is GET and the curl command is as follows:

    ```
    curl -XGET 'http://localhost:9200/_cluster/health'
    ```

2. The result will be:

    ```
    {
      "cluster_name" : "elasticsearch",
      "status" : "green",
      "timed_out" : false,
      "number_of_nodes" : 2,
      "number_of_data_nodes" : 2,
      "active_primary_shards" : 5,
      "active_shards" : 10,
      "relocating_shards" : 0,
      "initializing_shards" : 0,
      "unassigned_shards" : 0
    }
    ```

How it works...

Every ElasticSearch node keeps the cluster status. The status can be of three types:

- **Green**: This means everything is ok.
- **Yellow**: This means some nodes or shards are missing, but they don't compromise the cluster functionality. Mainly some replicas are missing, but there is at least one copy of every shard active. Everything is working fine.
- **Red**: This indicates some shards are missing. You cannot write in the cluster and results can be partial. You need to restart the node that is down and possibly create some replicas.

 The yellow state could be transient if some nodes are in recovery mode.

But, the cluster health has a lot of more information, a few of which are listed as follows:

- `cluster.name`: This is the name of the cluster.
- `timeout`: This is a Boolean value indicating whether the REST API has hit the timeout.
- `number_of_nodes`: This indicates the number of nodes that are present in the cluster.
- `number_of_data_nodes`: This shows the number of nodes that can store data. (refer to *Chapter 2, Downloading and Setting Up ElasticSearch*, for different types of nodes.)
- `active_primary_shards`: This shows the number of active primary shards. The primary shards are the master for writing operations.
- `active_shards`: This shows the number of active shards. These shards can be used for search.
- `relocating_shards`: This shows the number of shards that are relocating, that is, migrating from a node to another one. This is mainly due to cluster node balancing.
- `initializing_shards`: This shows the number of shards that are in initializing status. The initializing process is done at shard startup. It's a transient state before becoming active and it's composed from several steps. The most important ones are as follows:
  - Shard data is copied if the shard is a replica of another one.
  - Performing Lucene indices checks.
  - Transaction log processing is done if required.
- `unassigned_shards`: This shows the number of shards that are not assigned to a node, mainly due to having set a replica number bigger than the number of nodes. During startup, shards not already initialized or initializing will be counted here.

Cluster and Nodes Monitoring

There's more...

The API call is very useful; it's possible to execute it against one or more indices to obtain their health in the cluster. This approach allows isolating indices with problems. The API call to execute this function is as follows:

```
curl -XGET
    'http://localhost:9200/_cluster/health/index1,index2,indexN'
```

The previously mentioned calls also have additional request parameters to control the health of the cluster. These parameters are as follows:

- `level`: This controls the level of the health information returned. This parameter accepts only cluster, index, and shards.
- `timeout`: This is the waiting time of a `wait_for_*` parameter (default 30 seconds).
- `wait_for_status`: This allows the server to wait for the provided status (green, yellow, or red) until timeout.
- `wait_for_relocating_shards`: This allows the server to wait for reaching the provided number of relocating shards or the timeout period. This parameter is very useful for waiting until all the relocations are done.
- `wait_for_nodes`: This waits until the defined number of node is available in the cluster. The value for this parameter can be also an expression such as `>N`, `>=N`, `<N`, `<=N`, `ge(N)`, `gt(N)`, `le(N)`, and `lt(N)`.

See also

- The *Understanding cluster, replication, and sharding* recipe in *Chapter 1, Getting Started*
- The *Setting up different node types (advanced)* recipe in *Chapter 2, Downloading and Setting Up ElasticSearch*

Controlling cluster state via API

The previous recipe returns information only about the health of the cluster. If you need more details on your cluster, you need to query its state.

Getting ready

You need a working ElasticSearch cluster.

How to do it...

For controlling the cluster state, we need to perform the following steps:

1. To view the cluster state, the HTTP method is GET and the curl command is:
   ```
   curl -XGET 'http://localhost:9200/_cluster/state'
   ```

2. The result will be:
   ```
   {
     "cluster_name" : "elasticsearch",
     "master_node" : "pyGyXwh1ScqmnDw5etNS0w",
     "blocks" : { },
     "nodes" : {
       "pyGyXwh1ScqmnDw5etNS0w" : {
         "name" : "Wonder Man",
         "transport_address" : "inet[/192.168.1.5:9300]",
         "attributes" : { }
       },
       "wOIonUlFTwec0DCgf3aOjA" : {
         "name" : "Enigma",
         "transport_address" : "inet[/192.168.1.14:9300]",
         "attributes" : { }
       }
     },
     "metadata" : {
       "templates" : { },
       "indices" : {
         "test" : {
           "state" : "open",
           "settings" : {
             "index.number_of_replicas" : "1",
             "index.number_of_shards" : "5",
             "index.version.created" : "900399"
           },
           "mappings" : {...},
           "aliases" : [..]
         }, .....
       }
     },
   ```

```
            "routing_table" : {
              "indices" : {
                "test" : {
                  "shards" : {
                    "0" : [ {
                      "state" : "STARTED",
                      "primary" : false,
                      "node" : "wOIonUlFTwec0DCgf3aOjA",
                      "relocating_node" : null,
                      "shard" : 0,
                      "index" : "test"
                    }, {
                      "state" : "STARTED",
                      "primary" : true,
                      "node" : "pyGyXwh1ScqmnDw5etNS0w",
                      "relocating_node" : null,
                      "shard" : 0,
                      "index" : "test"
                    } ],….
                  }
                }
              }
            },
            "routing_nodes" : {
              "unassigned" : [ ],
              "nodes" : {
                "pyGyXwh1ScqmnDw5etNS0w" : [ {
                  "state" : "STARTED",
                  "primary" : true,
                  "node" : "pyGyXwh1ScqmnDw5etNS0w",
                  "relocating_node" : null,
                  "shard" : 0,
                  "index" : "test"
                }, …
              }
            },
            "allocations" : [ ]
          }
```

It should be noted that the response gets trimmed by redundant sections.

How it works...

The cluster state contains the information of the whole cluster; it's normal that its output is very large.

The call output is divided into common fields, which are:

- `cluster.name`: This is the name of the cluster.
- `master_node`: This is the identifier of the master node. The master node is the primary node for cluster management.

The output is also divided into the following sections:

- `blocks`: This shows the active blocks in a cluster.
- `nodes`: This shows the list of nodes of the cluster. For every node we have the following:
    - `id`: This is the hash used to identify the node in ElasticSearch (for example, pyGyXwh1ScqmnDw5etNS0w).
    - `name`: This is the name of the node.
    - `transport_address`: This is the IP and port used to connect to the particular node.
    - `attributes`: These are the additional node attributes.
- `metadata`: This defines the indices and the related mappings.
- `routing_table`: These are the indices'/shards' routing tables, which are used to select primary and secondary shards and their nodes.
- `routing_nodes`: This is the routing for the nodes.

The metadata section is the most used one, because it contains all the information related to the indices and their mappings. This is a convenient way to gather all the indices mappings in one shot; otherwise you need to call the get mapping for every type.

The metadata section is composed with several sections that are as follows:

- `templates`: These are indices templates that control the dynamic mapping for created indices.
- `indices`: These are the indices defined in the cluster. The indices subsection returns a full representation of all the metadata description for every index. It contains the following types:
    - `state` (open/closed): This returns a value if an index is open (can be searched and can index data) or closed (refer to the *Opening/closing an index* recipe in *Chapter 4, Standard Operations*).

- ❏ `settings`: These are the index settings listed as follows:

    `index.number_of_replicas`: This defines the number of replicas for the index. It can be changed with an update index settings call.

    `index.number_of_shards`: This defines the number of shards of this index.

    `index.version.created`: This defines the index version.

- ▶ `mappings`: These are defined in the index. This section is similar to the get mapping response (refer to the *Getting a mapping* recipe in *Chapter 4, Standard Operations*).

- ▶ `alias`: This is a list of the index alias.

The routing records for index and shards have similar fields and they are as follows:

- ▶ `state`: This shows the state of the shard or index such as `UNASSIGNED`, `INITIALIZING`, `STARTED`, and `RELOCATING`
- ▶ `primary(true/false)`: This shows whether the shard or node is primary
- ▶ `node`: This shows the code of the node
- ▶ `relocating_node`: This field, if validated, shows the node `id` in which the shard is relocated
- ▶ `shard`: This shows the number of the shard
- ▶ `index`: This shows the name of the shard in which the shard is contained

There's more...

The cluster state call returns a lot of information and it's possible to filter out the different section parts. The parameters are as follows:

- ▶ `filter_blocks(true/false)`: This is used to filter out the blocks part of the response.
- ▶ `filter_nodes(true/false)`: This is used to filter out the node part of the response.
- ▶ `filter_metadata(true/false)`: This is used to filter out the metadata part of the response
- ▶ `filter_routing_table(true/false)`: This is used to filter out the routing_table part of the response.
- ▶ `filter_indices`: This is a list of index names to include in the in metadata.
- ▶ `filter_index_templates(true/false)`: This is used to filter out the templates part of index metadata response.

See also

- The *Understanding cluster, replication, and sharding* recipe in *Chapter 1, Getting Started*
- The *Opening/closing an index* recipe in *Chapter 4, Standard Operations*
- The *Getting a mapping* recipe in *Chapter 4, Standard Operations*

Getting nodes information via API

The previous recipes allow the return of information to the cluster level; ElasticSearch provides calls to gather information to the node level.

Getting ready

You need a working ElasticSearch cluster.

How to do it...

For getting nodes information, we will perform the steps given as follows:

1. To retrieve the node information, the HTTP method is GET and the curl command is as follows:

    ```
    curl -XGET 'http://localhost:9200/_nodes?all=true'
    curl -XGET
      'http://localhost:9200/_nodes/<nodeId1>,<nodeId2>?all=true'
    ```

2. The result will be as follows:

    ```
    {
        "cluster_name": "elasticsearch",
        "nodes": {
    "pyGyXwh1ScqmnDw5etNS0w": {
            "hostname": "andrea",
            "http": {
                "bound_address": "inet[/0:0:0:0:0:0:0:0%0:9200]",
                "max_content_length": "100mb",
                "max_content_length_in_bytes": 104857600,
                "publish_address":
    "inet[/192.168.1.5:9200]"
            },
    ```

```
            "http_address": "inet[/192.168.1.5:9200]",
            "jvm": {
                "mem": {
                    "direct_max": "990.7mb",
                    "direct_max_in_bytes": 1038876672,
                    "heap_init": "256mb",
                    "heap_init_in_bytes": 268435456,
                    "heap_max": "990.7mb",
                    "heap_max_in_bytes": 1038876672,
                    "non_heap_init": "23.1mb",
                    "non_heap_init_in_bytes": 24313856,
                    "non_heap_max": "130mb",
                    "non_heap_max_in_bytes": 136314880
                },
                "pid": 4044,
                "start_time": 1377352221667,
                "version": "1.7.0_25",
                "vm_name": "Java HotSpot(TM) 64-Bit Server VM",
                "vm_vendor": "Oracle Corporation",
                "vm_version": "23.25-b01"
            },
            "name": "Wonder Man",
            "network": {
                "primary_interface": {
                    "address": "192.168.1.5",
                    "mac_address": "00:01:2E:4C:D9:EA",
                    "name": "p4p1"
                },
                "refresh_interval": 5000
            },
            "os": {
                ...
            },
            "plugins": [
                {
                    "description": "Exports elasticsearch REST APIs over thrift",
                    "jvm": true,
                    "name": "transport-thrift",
                    "site": false
                },
                ...
            ],
            "process": {
                "id": 4044,
                "max_file_descriptors": 999999,
                "refresh_interval": 1000
            },
```

```
            "settings": {
                "cluster.name": "elasticsearch",
                "foreground": "yes",
                "name": "Wonder Man",
                "path.home":
    "/opt/elasticsearch/elasticsearch",
                "path.logs": "/opt/elasticsearch/elasticsearch/
    logs"
            },
            "thread_pool": {
                "bulk": {
                    "max": 4,
                    "min": 4,
                    "queue_type": "linked",
                    "reject_policy": "abort",
                    "type": "fixed"
                },...
            },
            "thrift_address": "/192.168.1.5:9500",
            "transport": {
                "bound_address":
    "inet[/0:0:0:0:0:0:0:0%0:9300]",
                "publish_address":
    "inet[/192.168.1.5:9300]"
            },
            "transport_address": "inet[/192.168.1.5:9300]",
            "version": "0.90.3"
        }
    },
    "ok": true
}
```

It should be noted that the response gets trimmed by the redundant sections.

How it works...

The nodes information call provides an overview of the node configuration covering several sections given as follows:

- `hostname`: This is the name of the host.
- `http`: This section gives information about HTTP configuration, such as the following:
    - `bound_address`: This is the address bound by ElasticSearch.
    - `max_content_length` (default 100 MB): This is the maximum size of a HTTP content that ElasticSearch allows to receive. HTTP payloads bigger than this size are rejected.

> The default 100 MB HTTP limit that can be changed in `elasticsearch.yml` can cause malfunction due to big payload (often in conjunction with attachment mapper plugin). So, it's important to keep in mind this limit, when doing bulk actions or working with attachment.

  - `publish_address`: This is the address used to publish the ElasticSearch node.
- `http_address`: This is the address exposed for using HTTP REST API.
- `jvm`: This section contains information about the node JVM namely version, vendor, name, pid and memory (heap and non-heap).
- `network`: This section contains information about the network interfaces used by the node such as address, MAC address and name.
- `os`: This section provides operative system information about the node that is running ElasticSearch namely processor information, mem and swap.
- `plugins`: This section lists every plugin installed in the node, providing information about the following:
  - `name`: This is the plugin name.
  - `description`: This is the plugin description.
  - `jvm`: This ensures whether the plugin is a jar one.
  - `site`: This ensures whether the plugin is a site one.
- `process`: This section contains information about the current running ElasticSearch process. Few of which are given as follows:
  - `id`: This gives the pid ID of the process.
  - `max_file_descriptors`: This gives max file descriptor number.
- `settings`: This section contains information about current cluster and path of ElasticSearch node. The most important fields are as follows:
  - `cluster.name`: This is the name of the cluster.
  - `name`: This is the name of the node.
  - `path.*`: This is configured path of this ElasticSearch instance.
- `thread_pool`: This section contains information about several types of thread pool running in a node.
- `thrift_address`: This is the address of thrift protocol (it is available only if the thrift plugin is installed).

- transport: This section contains information about the transport protocol. The transport protocol is used for intra-cluster communication or by the native client to communicate with a cluster. The response format is similar to the HTTP one:
  - bound_address: if a specific IP is not set into the configuration, ElasticSearch bounds all the interfaces.
  - publish_address: This is the address used for publishing the native transport protocol.
- transport_address: This is the address of the transport protocol.
- version: This is the current ElasticSearch version.

There's more...

The API call allows filtering the section that must be returned. In the next example we have used all=true to return all the section. Otherwise we can select one or more of the following sections:

- http
- jvm
- network
- os
- process
- plugin
- settings
- thread_pool
- transport

For example, if you need only the os and plugin information the call will be as follows:

```
curl -XGET 'http://localhost:9200/_nodes?os=true&plugin=true'
```

See also

- The *Using the Native protocol, Using the HTTP protocol*, and *Using the Thrift protocol* recipes in *Chapter 1, Getting Started*
- The *Networking setup* recipe in *Chapter 2, Downloading and Setting Up ElasticSearch*

Cluster and Nodes Monitoring

Getting node statistic via API

The node statistic call API is used to collect real-time behaviors of your node, for example memory usage, threads usage, number of index, search, and so on.

Getting ready

You need a working ElasticSearch cluster.

How to do it...

For getting nodes statistic, we will perform the steps given as follows:

1. To retrieve the node statistic, the HTTP method is `GET` and the curl command is as follows:

   ```
   curl -XGET 'http://localhost:9200/_nodes/stats?all=true'
   curl -XGET
     'http://localhost:9200/_nodes/<nodeId1>,<nodeId2>/stats?
     all=true'
   ```

2. The result will be a long description of all the node statistics. The result is composed of the following:

   - A header describing the `cluster` name and a `nodes` section:

   ```
   {
     "cluster_name": "elasticsearch",
     "nodes": {
       "pyGyXwh1ScqmnDw5etNS0w": {
   ```

   - Node filesystem statistics:

   ```
   "fs": {
     "data": [
       {
         "available": "24.6gb",...
         "dev": "/dev/sda1",..
         "disk_read_size": "1gb",..
         "disk_reads": 72991,
         "disk_service_time": "0.5",
         "disk_write_size": "36.8gb",...
         "disk_writes": 2554382,
         "free": "29.8gb",
         "free_in_bytes": 32066658304,
         "mount": "/",
         "path":"/opt/elasticsearch/elasticsearch/data/
   elasticsearch/nodes/0",
         "total": "101.7gb"...
   ```

            }
        ],
        "timestamp": 1378673086792
},

- The host name:

"hostname": "andrea",

- Current HTTP connection status:

```
"http": {
    "current_open": 1,
    "total_opened": 53
},
```

- Statistics-related indices:

```
"indices": {
    "docs": {
        "count": 5726,
        "deleted": 0
    },
    "fielddata": {
        "evictions": 0,
        "memory_size": "0b",
        "memory_size_in_bytes": 0
    }, …
},
```

- Statistics-related jvm:

```
"jvm": {
    "buffer_pools": {
        "direct": {
            "count": 124,
            "total_capacity": "17.5mb",
            "total_capacity_in_bytes": 18449860,
            "used": "17.5mb",
            "used_in_bytes": 18449860
        },
        "mapped": {
            "count": 0,
            "total_capacity": "0b",
            "total_capacity_in_bytes": 0,
            "used": "0b",
            "used_in_bytes": 0
        }
    },
```

```
        "gc": ...
    },
    "mem": ...,
    "threads": {
        "count": 68,
        "peak_count": 80
    },
    "timestamp": 1378673086791,
    "uptime": "366 hours, 54 minutes, 25 seconds
  and 124 milliseconds",
    "uptime_in_millis": 1320865124
},
```

- The node name:

```
"name": "Wonder Man",
```

- Networking statistics:

```
"network": {
    "tcp": {
        "active_opens": 2995,
        "attempt_fails": 831,
        "curr_estab": 22,
        "estab_resets": 122,
        "in_errs": 12,
        "in_segs": 7851955,
        "out_rsts": 527,
        "out_segs": 6606565,
        "passive_opens": 28494,
        "retrans_segs": 5236
    }
},
```

- Operative system statistics:

```
"os": {
    "cpu": {
        "idle": 97,
        "stolen": 0,
        "sys": 0,
        "user": 1
    },
    "load_average": [
        0.06,
        0.1,
        0.09
    ],
    "mem": {
        "actual_free": "13.5gb",...
        "actual_used": "1.8gb",...
        "free": "4.5gb",...
```

```
            "free_percent": 87,
            "used": "10.8gb",…
            "used_percent": 12
        },
        "swap": {
            "free": "15.7gb",….
            "used": "0b",…
        },
        "timestamp": 1378673086790,
        "uptime": "986 hours, 58 minutes and 42 seconds",
        "uptime_in_millis": 3553122000
},
```

- Status of the current ElasticSearch process:

```
"process": {
    "cpu": {
        "percent": 0,
        "sys": "38 minutes, 36 seconds and 760 milliseconds",…
                    "total": "1 hour, 38 minutes,
    47 seconds and 460 milliseconds",…
        "user": "1 hour, 10 seconds and 700 milliseconds",…
    },
    "mem": {
        "resident": "260.6mb",
        "resident_in_bytes": 273289216,
        "share": "14.7mb",
        "share_in_bytes": 15482880,
        "total_virtual": "3.2gb",
        "total_virtual_in_bytes": 3503607808
    },
    "open_file_descriptors": 282,
    "timestamp": 1378673086791
},
```

- Statistics-related the thread pools:

```
            "thread_pool": …,
```

- Statistics-related ElasticSearch transport:

```
"transport": {
    "rx_count": 54213,
    "rx_size": "6mb",
    "rx_size_in_bytes": 6357880,
    "server_open": 10,
    "tx_count": 54145,
    "tx_size": "8.9mb",…
},
"transport_address": "inet[/192.168.1.5:9300]"
```

It should be noted that the response gets trimmed by redundant sections.

How it works...

Every ElasticSearch node, during execution, collects statistics about several aspects of node management. These statistics are accessible via stats API call.

In the upcoming recipes we will see some examples of monitor applications that use this information for providing real-time status of a node or a cluster behavior.

The main statistics collected by this API are as follows:

- **Files system data**: This section contains statistics about the data occupation on disk such as free space on devices, mount points, reads, and writes.
- `http`: This gives the number of current open sockets and their maximum number.
- `indices`: This section contains statistics of several indexing aspects given as follows:
    - Memory usage for fields and caches.
    - Statistics about operations such as get, indexing, flush, merges, refresh and warmer.
- `jvm`: This section provides statistics about buffer, pools, garbage collector (creation/destruction of objects and their memory management), memory (used memory, heap, and pools), threads and uptime.
- `network`: This section provides statistics about TCP traffic such as open connection, close connections and data I/O.
- `os`: This sections collects statistics about the operative system such as:
    - CPU usage
    - Node load
    - Memory and Swap
    - Uptime
- `process`: This section contains statistics about CPU used by ElasticSearch, memory and open file descriptors.

> It's very important to monitor the open file descriptors because if you run out of them, the indices may be corrupted.

- `thread_pool`: This section monitors all the thread pools available in ElasticSearch. In case there are pools of low performance that have an excessive overhead, it becomes important to control them. Some of them can be configured to a new max value.
- `transport`: This section contains statistics about the transport layer, mainly bytes read and transmitted.

There's more...

The response related to this recipe is very large. It's possible to limit it by selecting only the needed parts. To do this, you need to pass to the API call some query parameter describing the required sections that are listed as follows:

- `fs`
- `http`
- `indices`
- `jvm`
- `network`
- `os`
- `thread_pool`
- `transport`

For example, to opt for only `os` and `http` statistics the call should be as follows:

```
curl -XGET 'http://localhost:9200/_nodes/stats?os=true&http=true'
```

See also

- The *Using the Native protocol, Using the HTTP protocol*, and *Using the Thrift protocol* recipes in *Chapter 1, Getting Started*
- The *Networking setup* recipe in *Chapter 2, Downloading and Setting Up ElasticSearch*

Installing and using BigDesk

BigDesk is a wonderful web app developed by *Lukáš Vlček*, installable as an ElasticSearch plugin, which allows monitoring and analyzing real-time cluster status.

With this application, it's possible to monitor both cluster and nodes in which ElasticSearch is running.

It's a modern HTML5 application, which requires only a modern browser.

Getting ready

You need a working ElasticSearch cluster.

Cluster and Nodes Monitoring

How to do it...

For installing BigDesk plugin, we will perform the steps given as follows:

1. The BigDesk plugin is a site plugin, an ElasticSearch composed only by HTML, CSS, images and JavaScript. It can be installed as usual by using the following code snippet:

   ```
   bin/plugin -install lukas-vlcek/bigdesk
   ```

2. After a node restart, if it's all right, it should compare in the site list:

   ```
   [INFO ][node] [Cassidy, Theresa] version[0.90.3], pid[37214], build[5c38d60/2013-08-06T13:18:31Z]
   [INFO ][node] [Cassidy, Theresa] initializing ...
   [INFO ][plugins] [Cassidy, Theresa] loaded [], sites [bigdesk]
   [INFO ][node] [Cassidy, Theresa] initialized
   [INFO ][node] [Cassidy, Theresa] starting ...
   ```

3. Now to see the interface you need to navigate with your browser at the address:

   ```
   http://es_address:9200/_plugin/bigdesk/
   ```

If you don't see the cluster statistics, put your node address on the left-hand side and click on **Connect**.

How it works...

When the browser points to the plugin address, the web interface of BigDesk is loaded.

It's composed of three main blocks:

- **BigDesk Endpoint settings bar**: In this, the user sets the server address, the refresh time, the history size, and the connect/disconnect button.
- **The Node or Cluster view**: In this, the user chooses either monitoring nodes or cluster data view.
- **The main view**: This contains data and graphics about the node status.

The node view is the main and the most important one, because it allows monitoring of all the node aspects.

Because the page is very long, it's split into three parts.

Chapter 9

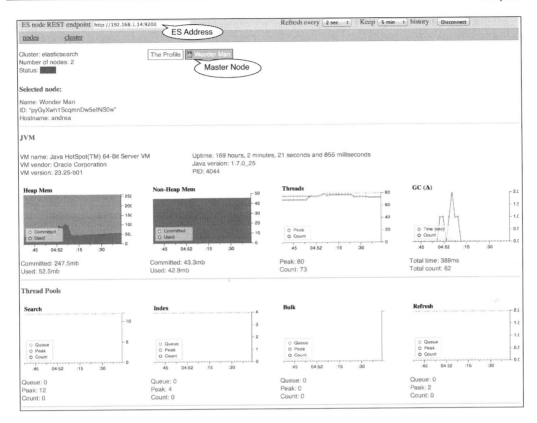

In this first part of the view, we can have a quick look at the following points:

- The name of the nodes in which the master one is marked with a medal. Clicking on a node name switches the interface to monitor the node statistics.
- The JVM information is composed of the following factors:
    - Information about the JVM itself, the name, vendor, version, and uptime.
    - The **Heap Mem** used is a parameter that must be monitored. If a JVM ends the heap memory, it usually core dumps and shuts itself down because it is no longer able to allocate objects.
    - In **Non-Heap Mem**, other memory is used, but not heap.
    - In **Threads**, a JVM is not able to use a high number of threads. If the number of threads is too high, the application stales or exists with some errors.
    - The garbage collector (**GC**) allows monitoring how often objects are created, destructed and the memory released.

Cluster and Nodes Monitoring

- Thread pools section is the one in which you can monitor the following threads:
    - **Search**: This monitors the number of threads used in search.
    - **Index**: This monitors the number of threads used in indexing.
    - **Bulk**: This monitors the number of thread used in bulk actions.
    - **Refresh**: This monitors the number of threads used for refreshing the Lucene index. They allow updating the searchers to work on new indexed data.

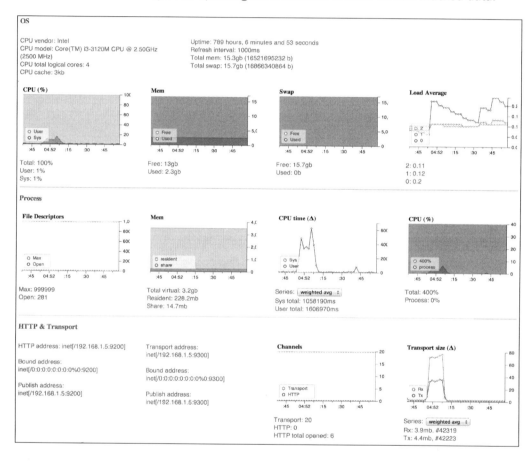

In the second fragment of the page view, we can see the following details:

- Operative system (**OS**) Information:
    - It gives the type of CPU hardware, uptime and memory being used.
    - It shows real-time CPU usage.
    - It gives real-time memory usage. If your node uses all the memory, you need to increment it or add a new cluster node to balance the load.

- It gives real-time swap usage. If you are using the swap memory, it means your server needs more main memory. If you are using swap memory, the system cannot be responsive.
- It gives the real-time load average (that is, the load on the server). If all the values are near one, your server is in high load. In this case, try to put a new node in the cluster to reduce the workload.

▶ The **Process** block has information about the ElasticSearch process:
- **File Descriptors**: This shows the number of open files in the process. When ElasticSearch ends them, Lucene indices may be corrupted and you may lose your data.
- **Memo**: This gives memory used by the ElasticSearch process.
- **CPU (%)**: This gives usage by ElasticSearch process.

▶ The **HTTP & Transport** layer information block contains the following:
- This section gives information about IP and port of several protocols.
- The **Channels** monitor allows controlling the number of HTTP connections. If the number of HTTP connections is too high due to a bad client configuration, connections could be dropped and your applications will have random errors due to lack of connection.
- **Transport size** allows monitoring the bytes received and sent by ElasticSearch.

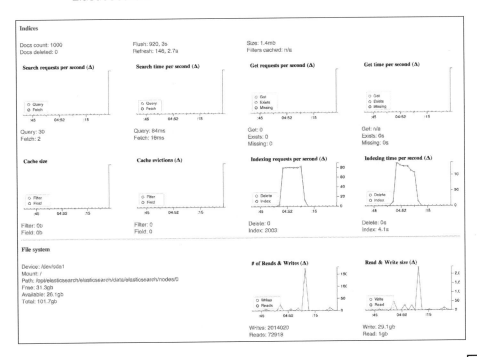

Cluster and Nodes Monitoring

In the third fragment, there are two blocks related to the following factors:

- Index/search performances with details on the following points:
    - Documents present/deleted.
    - Flush and refresh of indices.
    - Search/time in terms of seconds.
    - Get/time in terms of seconds.
    - Cached filters.
    - Cache size and hits.
    - Index request for second and indexing time for seconds.
- Disk I/O in which the main parameters to consider are as follows:
    - Free space.
    - Read and write size. If these values hit the maximum disk I/O operation for seconds, you need to add more nodes to balance the I/O.

There's more...

BigDesk gives a big help in understanding how your cluster is working and to monitor indicators that can reduce your ElasticSearch cluster performances.

BigDesk also provides a cluster view, which is experimental, that can help you to graphically understand which shard is bigger than another and which one uses more disk space.

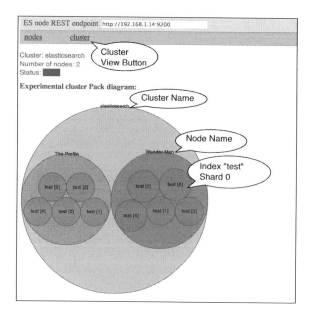

Installing and using ElasticSerach-head

The previous plugin allows monitoring all cluster/node statistics; ElasticSearch-head by *Ben Birch* mainly focuses on data management in your cluster.

It allows iterating with your data via a nice web interface. It speeds up a lot of operations that otherwise require you to write long curl commands.

Getting ready

You need a working ElasticSearch cluster and a modern HTML5 browser.

How to do it...

For installing the Head plugin, we will perform the steps given as follows:

1. The plugin is a site plugin: an ElasticSearch composed only by HTML, CSS, images and JavaScript. It can be installed as usual by means of the following code snippet:

   ```
   bin/plugin -install mobz/elasticsearch-head
   ```

2. After a node restarts, if it's all right, it should compare the following values in site list:

   ```
   [INFO ][node] [Cassidy, Theresa] version[0.90.3], pid[37214], build[5c38d60/2013-08-08T12:28:31Z]
   [INFO ][node] [Cassidy, Theresa] initializing ...
   [INFO ][plugins] [Cassidy, Theresa] loaded [], sites [head]
   [INFO ][node] [Cassidy, Theresa] initialized
   [INFO ][node] [Cassidy, Theresa] starting ...
   ```

3. Now to see the interface, you need to navigate to your browser at the address `http://es_address:9200/_plugin/head/`.

If you don't see the cluster statistics, enter your node address on the left-hand side and click on the **Connect** button.

How it works...

ElasticSearch-head has a multitab interface. Every tab has special purpose, listed as follows:

- **Overview**: This tab shows the topology of your cluster and allows you to perform index and node level operations.
- **Browser**: This tab allows you to navigate your data by index, type or simple field match.
- **Structured Query [+]**: This tab gives you a query builder to search.

Cluster and Nodes Monitoring

- **Any Request [+]**: This tab allows executing custom requests.

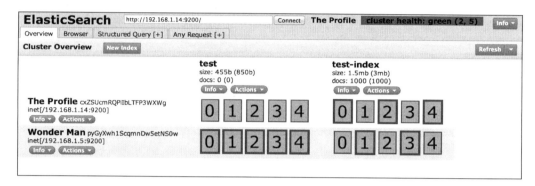

Before looking at the tabs, after connecting to a cluster, a lot of information and actions are available, listed as follows:

- Cluster name and status (shown in the screenshot in green).
- Information about the cluster (the dropdown button on the left-hand side) which allows us to view the following factors:
    - Information about the ElasticSearch server version
    - Status of indices
    - Nodes statistics
    - Cluster nodes
    - Cluster status
    - Cluster health

The **Overview** tab allows executing a lot of cluster, node, and index operations. It's a grid layout with nodes on the left and the indices in columns. Suddenly, in the index columns, the shards distribution shows where the shards are located; if they are primary or secondary and by clicking on it the information about the selected shard is shown.

Under the node name there are two buttons listed as follows:

- **Info**: This option allows you to get information about the running node.
- **Actions**: This option allows executing command on node such as shutdown.

Under the index name there are the following details:

- The index size gives you information about hard disk occupation. The number in the middle of parenthesis gives you the size considering the replicas.
- In this section, the number of documents that are in the index can be seen. In parenthesis, there is the exact number of records including also the deleted ones.

Chapter 9

 Deleted document are purged or based indices merging policies or after an optimize command.

- You can also see information about status and metadata.
- The **Actions** button collects several operations that can be executed on an index, listed as follows:
    - **New Alias**: This allows to add an alias to the current index.
    - **Refresh**: This calls the refresh API.
    - **Flush**: This calls the flush API.
    - **Gateway Snapshot**: This allows to dump the index content on a gateway.
    - **Test Analyzer**: This allows to analyze an analyzer produced tokens.
    - **Open/Close**: This allows to open or close an index.
    - **Delete**: This option allows dropping an index and delete both mappings and data.

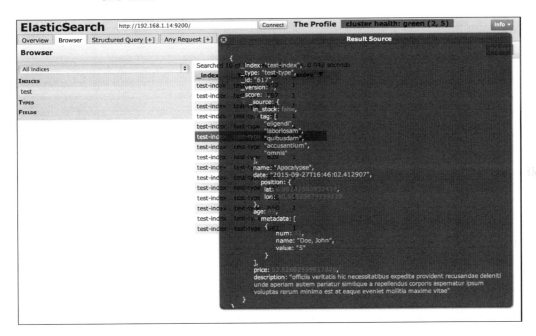

The **Browser** tab is very handy to analyze the data in your cluster. On the left-hand side you can filter your choice by indices and types. If some data is indexed, you can also put values in the fields and the records are filtered by these values.

Cluster and Nodes Monitoring

The results are represented in a table, but if you click on a result, you can see the original JSON record (if the source ID was active during index time). These views are very useful to analyze the record available in your index and to check if the record is correctly saved.

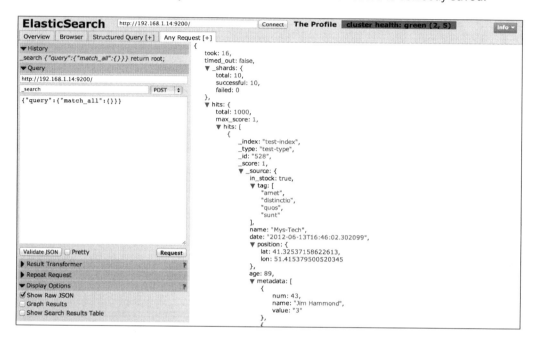

The **Any Request [+]** tab allows executing custom query. On the left-hand side there are the following options:

- History of the executed commands.
- Query to be executed is divided into the following types:
    - URL
    - Rest entry point
    - REST method (for example, GET, POST, PUT, DELETE)
    - Body to be sent
    - The **Validate** button to check if the body is a valid JSON code
    - Pretty check to pretty print the JSON
    - The **Request** button to execute the query
- **Result Transformer** allows to define JavaScript code to post-process the results.
- **Repeat Request** allows iterating the request on the scheduled time.

- **Display Options** provide the following checkboxes:
  - **Show Raw JSON**: This is the default JSON returned by ElasticSearch.
  - **Graph Results**: This shows a graph of results (the results must be a list).
  - **Show Search Results Table**: This shows the results as table as in the **Browser** tab.

There's more...

The Head plugin allows both monitoring of shards distribution and data manipulation via a simple web interface. A lot of action can be done via web interface, without requiring executing curl shell commands.

Similarly to the Head there are other good ElasticSearch GUIs available mainly on GitHub. The most famous ones are as follows:

- ElasticSearch HQ available at `http://www.elastichq.org/`.
- Sense available at `https://chrome.google.com/webstore/detail/sense/doinijnbnggojdlcjifpdckfokbbfpbo` is a chrome plugin that allows only JSON manipulation and query execution, but it doesn't have monitoring capabilities.

The choice of the GUI depends on the taste of the user and on his preferred patterns.

Installing and using SemaText SPM

The plugins that we have seen previously allow real-time monitoring. If you need to monitor your cluster for a long time you need tools that collect your logs and allow running analytics on them.

The SemaText company offers a paid service, which allows remote collecting and processing of your ElasticSearch activities.

Getting ready

You need a working ElasticSearch cluster and a modern HTML5 browser.

Cluster and Nodes Monitoring

How to do it...

For installing SemaText SPM plugin, we will perform the steps given as follows:

1. To use the SPM monitor, you need to register an account to SemaText available at https://apps.sematext.com/users-web/register.do to have a trial period. For every account an application key is generated and this key is required to download and install the client application.

2. The SPM monitor is composed of a client application that must be installed on your server and a web frontend managed by SemaText Cloud.

   SemaText provides native installers for:
   - Centos
   - Amazon Linux
   - RedHat
   - Suse
   - Debian
   - Ubuntu
   - Binaries for other Intel - Linux 64

3. For common Linux distributions, the installation process is very simple: it's enough to add binary repository and use the standard tool to install the application (for example, yum install, rpm -i, apt-get install and so on).

How it works...

After having installed and started the client on the server, this application sends to SemaText cloud your nodes and cluster activities.

The SemaText Cloud stores your activities to provide you with analytics over time: depending on the support plan, it allows you to monitor and compare behaviors for a time range of a year.

The output is given in a similar interface in the following screenshot:

Chapter 9

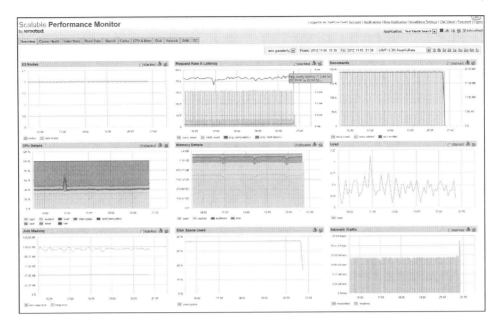

 Because SPM uses the node.name properties to identify the nodes, it is good practice to fix the node names in elasticsearch.yml to uniquely identify nodes in logs.

The SPM from SemaText provides a practical commercial solution to monitor ElasticSearch performances during long usages without requiring to create an infrastructure for collecting, storing and monitoring.

An alternative to the similar service is to set up a Nagios server (available at http://www.nagios.org/) and use the Nagios plugin for ElasticSearch (available at https://github.com/saj/nagios-plugin-elasticsearch).

See also

- Visit http://sematext.com/spm/elasticsearch-performance-monitoring/index.html for **SPM** details
- Also visit the Nagios plugin at https://github.com/saj/nagios-plugin-elasticsearch

10
Java Integration

In this chapter, we will cover the following topics:

- Creating an HTTP client
- Creating a native client
- Managing indices with the native client
- Managing mappings
- Managing documents
- Managing bulk action
- Creating a query
- Executing a standard search
- Executing a facet search
- Executing a scroll/scan search

Introduction

ElasticSearch functionalities can be easily integrated in every Java application in several ways, both via REST API then native ones.

With the use of Java, it's easy to call a REST HTTP interface with one of the many libraries available, such as Apache HTTPComponents Client (http://hc.apache.org/). In this field, there is no library which is used the most; typically developers choose the library that best suits their taste or that they know very well.

Java Integration

Every JVM language can also use the Native protocol to integrate ElasticSearch in their products. The Native protocol, discussed in *Chapter 1, Getting Started*, is one of the fastest protocols available to communicate with ElasticSearch due to many factors, such as its binary nature, the fast native serializer/deserializer of the data, the asynchronous approach for communicating and the hop reduction (native client is able to communicate directly with the node that contains the data without executing a double hop needed in REST calls).

The main disadvantage of using Native protocol is that it evolves during the life of ElasticSearch and there is no guarantee of compatibility between versions. For example, if a field of a request or a response changes, their binary serialization changes, generating incompatibilities between client and server with different versions.

The ElasticSearch community tries not to change often, but in every version, some parts of ElasticSearch are improved and these changes often modify the native API call signature, thus breaking the applications.

In this chapter, we will see how to initialize different clients and how to execute the commands that we have seen in the previous chapters. We will not go in to depth of every call as we have already described for the REST ones.

ElasticSearch uses the Native protocol and API internally, so these are the most tested ones compared to REST calls due to unit and integration tests available in ElasticSearch code base. The official documentation for the native Java API is available at http://www.elasticsearch.org/guide/en/elasticsearch/client/java-api/current/, but it doesn't cover all the API calls.

If you want a complete suite of examples, they are available in the src/test directory of the source code base of ElasticSearch.

As we have already discussed in *Chapter 1, Getting Started*, the ElasticSearch community recommends using the REST when integrating with ElasticSearch as they are more stable between versions and well documented.

All the code presented in these recipes is available in the book's code repository available on Packt's website and can be built with Maven.

Creating an HTTP client

An HTTP Client is one of the easiest clients to create. It's very handy because it allows calling not only the internal methods as the Native protocol does, but also the third-party calls implemented in plugins that can be called only via HTTP.

Getting ready

You need a working ElasticSearch cluster and Maven installed. The code of this recipe is in the *chapter_10/http_client* directory present in the code bundle available on Packt's website.

How to do it...

For creating an HTTP client, we will perform the steps given as follows:

1. For these examples, we have chosen the Apache HttpComponents that is one of the most famous libraries to execute HTTP calls. This library is available in the main Maven repository `search.Maven.org`. To enable the compilation in your Maven `pom.xml` project, just add:

    ```xml
    <dependency>
      <groupId>org.apache.httpcomponents</groupId>
      <artifactId>httpclient</artifactId>
      <version>4.3</version>
    </dependency>
    ```

2. If we want to instantiate a client and fetch a document with a `get` method, the code will look like this:

    ```java
    import org.apache.http.*;
    import org.apache.http.client.methods.CloseableHttpResponse;
    import org.apache.http.client.methods.HttpGet;
    import org.apache.http.impl.client.CloseableHttpClient;
    import org.apache.http.impl.client.HttpClients;
    import org.apache.http.util.EntityUtils;

    import java.io.*;

    public class App {

      private static String wsUrl = "http://127.0.0.1:9200";

      public static void main(String[] args) {
        CloseableHttpClient client = HttpClients.custom()
          .setRetryHandler(new MyRequestRetryHandler()).build();

        HttpGet method = new HttpGet(wsUrl+"/test-index/test-type/1");
        // Execute the method.
    ```

```java
            try {
              CloseableHttpResponse response =
                client.execute(method);

              if (response.getStatusLine().getStatusCode() !=
                HttpStatus.SC_OK) {
                System.err.println("Method failed: " +
                  response.getStatusLine());
              }else{
                HttpEntity entity = response.getEntity();
                String responseBody = EntityUtils.toString(entity);
                System.out.println(responseBody);
              }

            } catch (IOException e) {
              System.err.println("Fatal transport error: " +
                e.getMessage());
              e.printStackTrace();
            } finally {
              // Release the connection.
              method.releaseConnection();
            }

        }
```

3. The result, if the document is available, will be:

   ```
   {"_index":"test-index","_type":"test-
       type","_id":"1","_version":1,"exists":true, "_source" :
       {...}}
   ```

How it works...

We will perform the previous steps to create and use an HTTP client.

The first step is to initialize the HTTP client object. In the previous code, this is done via the following code:

```
CloseableHttpClient client = HttpClients.custom()
    .setRetryHandler(new MyRequestRetryHandler()).build();
```

Before using the client, it is a good practice to tweak it: in general, the client can be modified to provide extra functionalities, such as retry support. Retry support is very important for designing robust applications: the IP network protocol is never 100 percent reliable, so to automatically retry an action if something goes bad (for example, HTTP connection is lost, server overhead, and so on) is good practice.

Chapter 10

In the previous code, we have defined an `HttpRequestRetryHandler` method that monitors the execution and repeats it for three times before raising an error.

After having set up the client, we can define the method call. In the previous example, we want to execute the GET REST call. The used method will be for `HttpGet` and the `Url` method will be item index/type/id (similar to the curl example in the *Getting a document* recipe in *Chapter 4, Standard Operations*). To initialize the method, the code is as follows:

```
HttpGet method = new HttpGet(wsUrl+"/test-index/test-type/1");
```

To improve the quality of our REST call, it's good practice to add an extra management to the method, such as authentication and custom headers.

ElasticSearch server for default doesn't require authentication, so we need to provide some security layer at the top of our architecture. A typical scenario is using your HTTP client with the Jetty plugin (https://github.com/sonian/elasticsearch-jetty) that allows extending ElasticSearch REST with authentication and SSL. The plugin is installed and configured on the server. The following code adds a host entry that allows providing credential only if context calls are targeting that host. The authentication is simply a "basic auth", but works very well for non-complex deployment.

```
HttpHost targetHost = new HttpHost("localhost", 9200, "http");
CredentialsProvider credsProvider = new
  BasicCredentialsProvider();
credsProvider.setCredentials(
new AuthScope(targetHost.getHostName(), targetHost.getPort()),
new UsernamePasswordCredentials("username", "password"));

// Create AuthCache instance
AuthCache authCache = new BasicAuthCache();
// Generate BASIC scheme object and add it to the local auth cache
BasicScheme basicAuth = new BasicScheme();
authCache.put(targetHost, basicAuth);

// Add AuthCache to the execution context
HttpClientContext context = HttpClientContext.create();
context.setCredentialsProvider(credsProvider);
```

The create context must be used in executing the call:

```
response = client.execute(method, context);
```

Java Integration

Custom headers allow passing extra information to the server for executing a call. Some examples could be API key or hints about supported formats. A typical example is using gzip data compression over HTTP to reduce bandwidth usage: to do that, we can add a custom header to the call, informing the server that our client "Accept-Encoding" uses gzip.

```
request.addHeader("Accept-Encoding", "gzip");
```

After having configured the call with all the parameters, we can fire up the request.

```
response = client.execute(method, context);
```

Every response object must be validated on its return status: if the call is OK, the return status should be 200. In the preceding code, the check is done in the `if` statement:

```
if (response.getStatusLine().getStatusCode() != HttpStatus.SC_OK) …
```

If the call was ok—the status code of the response is 200—we can read the answer:

```
HttpEntity entity = response.getEntity();
String responseBody = EntityUtils.toString(entity);
```

The response is wrapped in `HttpEntity`, which is a stream. HTTP client library provides a helper method `EntityUtils.toString` that reads all the content of `HttpEntity` as a string. Otherwise, we need to create some code to read from the string and build the string.

Obviously, all the read part of the call is wrapped in a `try/catch` block to collect all the possible errors due to networking.

There's more...

Apache HttpComponents is one of the most used in the Java world to write REST API client. It provides a lot of advanced features out of the box, without requiring dependence on other libraries for cookie, authentication, and transport layer.

Java provides a lot of libraries for executing the same functionalities of HttpComponents, so it depends on the user to choose their preferred one.

> Now there is not a recommended client for HTTP REST calls in the ElasticSearch community. One of the Java libraries written to resolve this problem is Jest (https://github.com/searchbox-io/Jest), but at the time of writing this book, it doesn't cover all the ElasticSearch features.

See also

- The Apache HttpComponents on `http://hc.apache.org/`
- The Jetty Plugin to provide authenticated ElasticSearch access on `https://github.com/sonian/elasticsearch-jetty`
- Jest on `https://github.com/searchbox-io/Jest`
- The *Using the HTTP protocol* recipe in *Chapter 1, Getting Started*
- The *Getting a document* recipe in *Chapter 4, Standard Operations*

Creating a native client

To create a native client to communicate with an ElasticSearch server, there are two ways:

- Creating an embedded node (a node that doesn't contain data, but it works as arbiter) and getting the client from it. This node will appear in the cluster state nodes and it's able to use discovery capabilities of ElasticSearch to join the cluster (so no node address is required to connect to a cluster). This client is able to reduce the node routing due to knowledge of cluster topology.
- Creating a transport client, which is a standard client that requires the address and port of nodes to connect.

In this recipe, we will see how to create these clients.

Getting ready

You need a working ElasticSearch cluster and a working copy of Maven.

The code of this recipe is in *chapter_10/nativeclient* in the code bundle of this book provided on Packt's website.

How to do it...

To create a native client, we will perform the steps given as follows:

1. Before starting, we must be sure that Maven loads the ElasticSearch jar adding to the code lines to `pom.xml`:

   ```
   <dependency>
     <groupId>org.elasticsearch</groupId>
     <artifactId>elasticsearch</artifactId>
     <version>0.90.5</version>
   </dependency>
   ```

Java Integration

I always suggest using the latest release of ElasticSearch available or in case of connection to a specific cluster, the same version of ElasticSearch of the cluster.

 Native clients only work if the client and the server have the same ElasticSearch version.

2. Now, to create a client, we have two ways:

   - Retrieving the client by a node:

   ```
   import static org.elasticsearch.node.NodeBuilder.*;

   // on startup
   Node node = nodeBuilder().clusterName("elasticsearch").
   client(true).node();
   Client client = node.client();

   // on shutdown
   node.close();
   ```

   - Using the transport protocol:

   ```
   final Settings settings = ImmutableSettings.settingsBuilder()
               .put("client.transport.sniff", true)
               .put("cluster.name", "elasticsearch").build();

   Client client = new TransportClient(settings)
               .addTransportAddress(new
   InetSocketTransportAddress("127.0.0.1", 9300));
   ```

How it works...

The first needed action is to create a node: we set it as client one and we retrieve the client from it. The steps are:

- Importing the `NodeBuilder` class:

   ```
   import static org.elasticsearch.node.NodeBuilder.*;
   ```

- Initializing an ElasticSearch node passing `cluster.name` and indicating that it's a client one (otherwise, it can be considered as a standard node and after joining the cluster, it fetches shards to balance the cluster)

   ```
   Node node = nodeBuilder().clusterName("elasticsearch").
   client(true).node();
   ```

- We can now retrieve a client from the node

   ```
   Client client = node.client();
   ```

If the client is retrieved from an embedded node before closing the application, we need to free the resource needed by the node; this can be done by calling the `close()` method on the node:

```
node.close();
```

The second way to create a native client is to create a transport client.

The steps to create a transport client are:

- Create the settings required to configure the client. Typically, they hold the cluster name and some other options which we'll discuss later.

  ```
  final Settings settings = ImmutableSettings.settingsBuilder()
      .put("client.transport.sniff", true)
      .put("cluster.name", "elasticsearch").build();
  ```

- Now we can create the client passing it settings, addresses, and port of our cluster:

  ```
  new TransportClient(settings)
      .addTransportAddress(new
          InetSocketTransportAddress("127.0.0.1", 9300));
  ```

The `addTransportAddress` method can be iterated several times until all the required addresses and ports are set.

Using one of these approaches gives the same result: a working client that allows the execution of native calls on an ElasticSearch server.

During both steps, it is important to correctly define the name of the cluster, otherwise problems arise in node joining or the transport client gives you warning of invalid names.

The embedded node is a complete ElasticSearch node. So pay attention while defining it that it must be considered as a client one.

There's more...

There are several settings that can be passed when creating a transport client. They are:

- `client.transport.sniff`: This is by default `false`. If activated, the client retrieves the other node address after the first connection, reading it by the cluster state and reconstructing the cluster topology.
- `client.transport.ignore_cluster_name`: This is by default `false`. If you set it to `true`, cluster name validation of connected nodes is ignored. This prevents printing a warning if the client's cluster name is different than the connected cluster name.

Java Integration

- `client.transport.ping_timeout`: This is by default 5s. Every client pings the node for checking its state. This value defines by how much time the client should wait before a timeout.
- `client.transport.nodes_sampler_interval`: This is by default 5s. This interval defines how often to sample/ping the nodes listed and connected. These pings reduce the failures in case of node down and allow balancing the requests with the available node.

See also

- The *Setting up ElasticSearch for Linux systems* recipe in *Chapter 2, Downloading and Setting up ElasticSearch*
- The *Using the Native protocol* recipe in *Chapter 1, Getting Started*

Managing indices with the native client

In the previous recipe we have seen how to initialize a client to send calls to an ElasticSearch cluster. In this recipe, we will see how to manage indices via client calls.

Getting ready

You need a working ElasticSearch cluster and a working copy of Maven.

The code of this recipe is in *chapter_10/nativeclient* in the code bundle, which can be downloaded from Packt's website, and the referred class is `IndicesOperations`.

How to do it...

ElasticSearch client maps all indices operations under the `admin.indices` object of the client. Here, there are all the indices operation (create, delete, exists, open, close, optimize, and so on). In the following example, we will only see the most used calls on indices.

The following code retrieves a client and executes the main operation on indices:

```
import
  org.elasticsearch.action.admin.indices.exists.indices
    .IndicesExistsResponse;
import org.elasticsearch.client.Client;

public class IndicesOperations {
  private final Client client;
```

```java
    public IndicesOperations(Client client) {
      this.client = client;
    }

    public boolean checkIndexExists(String name){
      IndicesExistsResponse
        response=client.admin().indices().prepareExists(name)
        .execute().actionGet();
      return response.isExists();
    }

    public void createIndex(String name){
      client.admin().indices().prepareCreate(name)
        .execute().actionGet();
    }

    public void deleteIndex(String name){
      client.admin().indices().prepareDelete(name)
        .execute().actionGet();
    }

    public void closeIndex(String name){
      client.admin().indices().prepareClose(name)
        .execute().actionGet();
    }

    public void openIndex(String name){
      client.admin().indices().prepareOpen(name)
        .execute().actionGet();
    }

    public static void main( String[] args ) throws
      InterruptedException {
      Client client =NativeClient.createTransportClient();
      IndicesOperations io=new IndicesOperations(client);
      String myIndex = "test";
      if(io.checkIndexExists(myIndex))
      io.deleteIndex(myIndex);
      io.createIndex(myIndex);
      Thread.sleep(1000);
      io.closeIndex(myIndex);
      io.openIndex(myIndex);
      io.deleteIndex(myIndex);
    }
}
```

Java Integration

How it works...

Before executing every index operation, a client must be available (we have seen how to create one in the previous recipe). The client has a lot of methods grouped by functionalities:

- In the root (`client.***`), we have record operations, such as index, delete of records, search, and update
- Under `admin.indices.***`, we have indices related methods, such as create index, and delete index
- Under `admin.cluster.***`, we have cluster related methods, such as state and health

The client methods usually follow some conventions:

- Methods starting from `prepare*` (that is,. `prepareCreate`) returns a request builder that can be executed with the "`execute`" method
- Methods that starts with verb (that is, `create`) require a build request and some optional action listener

After having built the request, it can be executed with an `actionGet` method that can receive an optional timeout, and a response is returned.

In the previous example, we have several indices calls:

- Checking the existence, the method call is `prepareExists` and returns a `IndicesExistsResponse` object which contains the information if the index exists or not.
    ```
    IndicesExistsResponse
        response=client.admin().indices().prepareExists(name).
        execute().actionGet();
    return response.isExists();
    ```
- Creating an index with the `prepareCreate` call:
    ```
    client.admin().indices().prepareCreate(name).execute().
        actionGet();
    ```
- Closing an index with the `prepareClose` call:
    ```
    client.admin().indices().prepareClose(name).execute().
        actionGet();
    ```
- Opening an index with the `prepareOpen` call:
    ```
    client.admin().indices().prepareOpen(name).execute().
        actionGet();
    ```
- Deleting an index with the `prepareDelete` call:
    ```
    client.admin().indices().prepareDelete(name).execute().
        actionGet();
    ```

Chapter 10

 In the code, we have put a delay of 1 second (`Thread.wait(1000)`) to prevent the fast actions on indices, because their shard allocations are asynchronous and they require some milliseconds to be ready.

See also

- The *Creating an index* recipe in *Chapter 4*, *Standard Operations*
- The *Deleting an index* recipe in *Chapter 4*, *Standard Operations*
- The *Opening/closing an index* recipe in *Chapter 4*, *Standard Operations*

Managing mappings

After creating an Index the next step is to add some mapping to it. We have already seen how to put a mapping via REST API in *Chapter 4*, *Standard Operations*. In this recipe, we will see how to manage mappings via native client.

Getting ready

You need a working ElasticSearch cluster and a working copy of Maven.

The code of this recipe is in `chapter_10/nativeclient` in the code bundle of this book, available on Packt's website, and the referred class is `MappingsOperations`.

How to do it...

In the following code, we add a `mytype` mapping to a `myindex` via native client:

```
import
   org.elasticsearch.action.admin.indices.mapping.put.
   PutMappingResponse;
import org.elasticsearch.client.Client;
import org.elasticsearch.common.xcontent.XContentBuilder;

import java.io.IOException;

import static
   org.elasticsearch.common.xcontent.XContentFactory.jsonBuilder;

public class MappingOperations {

    public static void main( String[] args )
```

295

Java Integration

```java
{
  String index="mytest";
  String type="mytype";
  Client client =NativeClient.createTransportClient();
  IndicesOperations io=new IndicesOperations(client);
  if(io.checkIndexExists(index))
  io.deleteIndex(index);
  io.createIndex(index);

  XContentBuilder builder = null;
  try {
    builder = jsonBuilder().
    startObject().
    field("type1").
    startObject().
    field("properties").
    startObject().
    field("nested1").
    startObject().
    field("type").
    value("nested").
    endObject().endObject().endObject().
    endObject();
//put the mapping
    PutMappingResponse
       response=client.admin().indices().
       preparePutMapping(index).setType(type).
       setSource(builder).execute().actionGet();
    if(!response.isAcknowledged()){
    System.out.println("Something strange happens");
    }
  } catch (IOException e) {
    System.out.println("Unable to create mapping");
  }

//delete the mapping      client.admin().indices().
prepareDeleteMapping(index).setType(type).execute().actionGet();

  io.deleteIndex(index);
  }
}
```

How it works...

Before executing every mapping operation, a client must be available and the index must be created. In the previous example, if the index exists, it's deleted and a new one is recreated, so we are sure to start a scratch.

```
Client client =NativeClient.createTransportClient();
IndicesOperations io=new IndicesOperations(client);
if(io.checkIndexExists(index)) io.deleteIndex(index);
io.createIndex(index);
```

Now that we have a fresh index to put the mapping, we need to create it. The mapping, as every standard object in ElasticSearch, is a JSON object. ElasticSearch provides a convenient way to create JSON programmatically via `XContentBuilder/jsonBuilder`. For using them, you need to add these imports to your Java file:

```
import org.elasticsearch.common.xcontent.XContentBuilder;
import static
   org.elasticsearch.common.xcontent.XContentFactory.jsonBuilder;
```

The `jsonBuilder` method allows building JSON programmatically, as it is a Swiss-knife of JSON generation in ElasticSearch due its ability to be chained; it has a lot of methods. These methods always return a builder, so they can be easily chained. The most important one are:

- The `startObject()` and `startObject(name)` builders where name is the name of the JSON object. It starts with the definition of a JSON object. The object must be closed with an `endObject()`.

- The `field(name)` or `field(name, value)` builders where the name must always be a string, the value must be a valid value that can be converted to JSON. It's used to define a field in a JSON object.

- The `value(value)` builder where the value must be a valid value that can be converted to JSON. It defines a single value in a field.

- The `startArray()` and `startArrayt(name)` builders where name is the name of the JSON array. It starts with the definition of a JSON array that must end with `endArrayt()`.

Generally in ElasticSearch, every method that accepts a JSON object as parameter also accepts a JSON builder.

Now that we have the mapping in the builder, we need to call the Put Mapping API. This API is in the `client.admin().indices()` namespace and you need to define the index, the type, and the mapping to execute this call:

```
PutMappingResponse
   response=client.admin().indices().preparePutMapping(index).
   setType(type).setSource(builder).execute().actionGet();
```

Java Integration

If everything is fine, you can check the status in the `response.isAcknowledged()` instance that must be `true` (Boolean). Otherwise, an error is raised.

If you need to update a mapping, you need to execute the same call, but in the mapping put only the fields that you need to add. To delete a mapping, you need to call the Delete Mapping API. It requires the index and the type to be deleted. In the previous example, the mapping created is deleted with:

```
client.admin().indices().prepareDeleteMapping(index).setType(type)
   .execute().actionGet();
```

There's more...

There is another important call used in managing the mapping: the Get Mapping API. The call is similar to the delete and returns `GetMappingResponse`.

```
GetMappingResponse
   response=client.admin().indices().prepareGetMapping(index)
   .setType(type).execute().actionGet();
```

The response contains the mapping information. The data returned is structured as in an index map that contains mapping mapped as name and `MappingMetaData`.

The `MappingMetaData` is an object that contains all the mapping information and contains all the sections that we discussed in *Chapter 4, Standard Operations*.

See also

- The *Putting a mapping in an index* recipe in *Chapter 4, Standard Operations*
- The *Getting a mapping* recipe in *Chapter 4, Standard Operations*
- The *Deleting a mapping* recipe in *Chapter 4, Standard Operations*

Managing documents

The native APIs for managing document (index, delete, and update) are the most important after the search ones. In this recipe, we will see how to use them. In the next one we will evolve in executing bulk actions to improve performances.

Getting ready

You need a working ElasticSearch cluster and a working copy of Maven.

The code of this recipe is in *chapter_10/nativeclient* in the code bundle of this book available on Packt's website, and the referred class is `DocumentOperations`.

How to do it...

For managing documents, we will perform the steps given as follows:

1. We'll execute all the document with CRUD operations (CReate, Update, Delete) via native client:

```java
import org.elasticsearch.action.delete.DeleteResponse;
import org.elasticsearch.action.get.GetResponse;
import org.elasticsearch.action.index.IndexResponse;
import org.elasticsearch.action.update.UpdateResponse;
import org.elasticsearch.client.Client;
import org.elasticsearch.common.xcontent.XContentFactory;

import java.io.IOException;

public class DocumentOperations {


  public static void main( String[] args )
  {
    String index="mytest";
    String type="mytype";
    Client client =NativeClient.createTransportClient();
    IndicesOperations io=new IndicesOperations(client);
    if(io.checkIndexExists(index))
      io.deleteIndex(index);

    try {
      client.admin().indices().prepareCreate(index)
      .addMapping(type, XContentFactory.jsonBuilder()
      .startObject()
      .startObject(type)
      .startObject("_timestamp").field("enabled",
        true).field("store", "yes").endObject()
      .startObject("_ttl").field("enabled",
        true).field("store", "yes").endObject()
      .endObject()
      .endObject())
      .execute().actionGet();
    } catch (IOException e) {
      System.out.println("Unable to create mapping");
    }
```

```java
        // We index a document
        IndexResponse ir=client.prepareIndex("test", "type",
            "2").setSource("text",
            "value").execute().actionGet();
        System.out.println("Version: "+ir.getVersion());
        // We get a document
        GetResponse gr=client.prepareGet("test", "type",
            "2").execute().actionGet();
        System.out.println("Version: "+gr.getVersion());
        // We update a document
        UpdateResponse ur = client.prepareUpdate("test",
            "type", "2").setScript("ctx._source.text =
            'v2'").execute().actionGet();
        System.out.println("Version: "+ur.getVersion());
        // We delete a document
        DeleteResponse dr = client.prepareDelete("test",
            "type", "2").execute().actionGet();
        io.deleteIndex("test");
    }
}
```

2. The result will be:

```
Sep 24, 2013 10:58:20 PM org.elasticsearch.plugins
INFO: [Masked Rose] loaded [], sites []
Version: 1
Version: 1
Version: 2
```

The document version, after an update action and if the document is re-indexed with new changes, is always incremented by one.

How it works...

Before executing every document action, a client must be available and the index and document mapping must be created (the mapping is optional).

To index a document via native client, the method `prepareIndex` is created. It requires the index and the type as arguments. If an ID is provided, it will be used; otherwise a new one will be created. In the previous example, we have put the source in the form of a key value, but many forms are available to pass as source. They are:

- A JSON string: `"{"field": "value"}"`
- A string and a value (from one to four couples): `field1`, `value1`, `field2`, `value2`, `field3`, `value3`, `field4`, and `value4`

- A builder: `jsonBuilder().startObject().field(field,value).endObject()`
- A byte arrays

Obviously it's possible to add all the parameters that we saw in the *Indexing a document* recipe in *Chapter 4, Standard Operations*, such as parent, and routing. In the previous example, the call was:

```
IndexResponse ir=client.prepareIndex("test", "type",
    "2").setSource("text", "value").execute().actionGet();
```

The return value (`IndexReponse`) can be used in several ways:

- Checking if the index was successful
- Getting the ID of the indexed document, if it was not provided during index action
- Retrieving the document version

To retrieve a document, knowing the index/type/ID, the client method is `prepareGet`. It requires the usual triple (index, type, and ID), but a lot of other methods are available to control the routing (such as souring and parent) or fields as we have seen in the *Getting a document* in *Chapter 4, Standard Operations*. In the previous example, the call is:

```
GetResponse gr=client.prepareGet("test", "type",
    "2").execute().actionGet();
```

The return type (`GetResponse`) contains all the requests (if the document exists) and document information (source, version, index, type, and ID).

To update a document, it's required to know the index/type/ID and provide a script or a document to be used for the update. The client method is `prepareUpdate`. In the previous example, there is:

```
UpdateResponse ur = client.prepareUpdate("test", "type",
    "2").setScript("ctx._source.text = 'v2'" )
    .execute().actionGet();
```

The script code must be a string. If the script language is not defined, the default ("MVEL") is used. The returned response contains information about the execution and the new version value to manage concurrency.

To delete a document (without the need to execute a query), we must know the index/type/ID triple and we can use the client method `prepareDelete` to create or delete request. In the previous code, we used:

```
DeleteResponse dr = client.prepareDelete("test", "type",
    "2").execute().actionGet();
```

The delete request allows passing to it all the parameters we saw in the *Deleting a document* recipe in *Chapter 4, Standard Operations*, to control routing and version.

Java Integration

See also

- The *Indexing a document* recipe in *Chapter 4, Standard Operations*
- The *Getting a document* recipe in *Chapter 4, Standard Operations*
- The *Deleting a document* recipe in *Chapter 4, Standard Operations*
- The *Updating a document* recipe in *Chapter 4, Standard Operations*

Managing bulk action

Executing atomic operation on items via single call is often a bottleneck if you need to index or delete thousands/millions of records: the best practice in this case is to execute a bulk action. We discussed bulk action via REST API in the *Speeding up atomic operations (bulk)* recipe in *Chapter 4, Standard Operations*.

Getting ready

You need a working ElasticSearch cluster and a working copy of Maven.

The code of this recipe is in *chapter_10/nativeclient* in the code bundle of this book available on Packt's website and the referred class is `BulkOperations`.

How to do it...

For managing a bulk action, we will perform the steps given as follows:

1. We'll execute a bulk action adding 1000 elements, updating them and deleting them:

```java
import org.elasticsearch.action.bulk.BulkRequestBuilder;
import org.elasticsearch.client.Client;
import org.elasticsearch.common.xcontent.XContentFactory;

import java.io.IOException;

public class BulkOperations {
  public static void main( String[] args )
  {
    String index="mytest";
    String type="mytype";
    Client client =NativeClient.createTransportClient();
    IndicesOperations io=new IndicesOperations(client);
    if(io.checkIndexExists(index))
      io.deleteIndex(index);
```

```java
try {
  client.admin().indices().prepareCreate(index)
  .addMapping(type, XContentFactory.jsonBuilder()
  .startObject()
  .startObject(type)
  .startObject("_timestamp").field("enabled",
    true).field("store", "yes").endObject()
  .startObject("_ttl").field("enabled",
    true).field("store", "yes").endObject()
  .endObject()
  .endObject())
  .execute().actionGet();
} catch (IOException e) {
  System.out.println("Unable to create mapping");
}

BulkRequestBuilder bulker=client.prepareBulk();
for (Integer i=1; i<=1000; i++){
  bulker.add(client.prepareIndex("test", "type",
    i.toString()).setSource("text", i.toString()));
}
System.out.println("Number of action: " +
  bulker.numberOfActions());
bulker.execute().actionGet();


System.out.println("Number of actions for index: " +
  bulker.numberOfActions());
bulker.execute().actionGet();

bulker=client.prepareBulk();
for (Integer i=1; i<=1000; i++){
  bulker.add(client.prepareUpdate(index, type, i.
    toString()).setScript("ctx._source.text += 2"));
}
System.out.println("Number of actions for udpate: " +
  bulker.numberOfActions());
bulker.execute().actionGet();

bulker=client.prepareBulk();
for (Integer i=1; i<=1000; i++){
  bulker.add(client.prepareDelete(index, type,
    i.toString()));
}
```

Java Integration

```
        System.out.println("Number of actions  for delete: " +
          bulker.numberOfActions());
        bulker.execute().actionGet();

        io.deleteIndex(index);
    }
  }
```

2. The result will be:

```
Number of actions for index: 1000
Number of actions for udpate: 1000
Number of actions for delete: 1000
```

How it works...

Before executing these bulk actions, a client must be available and the index and document mapping must be created (the mapping is optional).

We can consider the `bulkBuilder` method as a collector of different actions:

- `IndexRequest` or `IndexRequestBuilder`
- `UpdateRequest` or `UpdateRequestBuilder`
- `DeleteRequest` or `DeleteRequestBuilder`
- a bulk formatted array of bytes.

Generally, when used in code, we can consider it as an "`ArrayList`" in which we add actions of the supported types.

To initialize a `bulkBuilder` method, we use:

```
BulkRequestBuilder bulker=client.prepareBulk();
```

In the previous example, we have added `1000` index actions (the `IndexBuilder` method is similar to the previous recipe):

```
for (Integer i=1; i<=1000; i++){
  bulker.add(client.prepareIndex("test", "type",
    i.toString()).setSource("text", i.toString()));
}
```

After having added all the actions, we can print, for example, the number of actions and then execute them.

```
System.out.println("Number of action: " +
  bulker.numberOfActions());
bulker.execute().actionGet();
```

After having executed the bulk builder, the bulker is empty. We have populated the bulk with 1000 update actions:

```
for (Integer i=1; i<=1000; i++){
  bulker.add(client.prepareUpdate("test", "type",
    i.toString()).setScript("ctx._source.text += 2"));
}
```

After having added all the update actions, we can execute them in bulk:

```
bulker.execute().actionGet();
```

After that, the same step is done with the delete action:

```
for (Integer i=1; i<=1000; i++){
  bulker.add(client.prepareDelete("test", "type", i.toString()));
}
```

To commit the delete action, we need to execute the bulk. In this example, to simplify it, I have created bulk with the same type of actions, but as described previously, you can put the same bulk in every supported type of action.

See also

- The *Speeding up atomic operations (bulk)* recipe in *Chapter 4, Standard Operations*

Creating a query

Before search, a query must be built: ElasticSearch provides several ways to build these queries. In this recipe, will see how to create a query object via `QueryBuilder` and via simple strings.

Getting ready

You need a working ElasticSearch cluster and a working copy of Maven. The code of this recipe is in *chapter_10/nativeclient* in the code bundle of this book available on Packt's website and the referred class is `QueryCreation`.

Java Integration

How to do it...

For creating a query, we will perform the steps given as follows:

1. There are several ways to define a query in ElasticSearch; they are interoperable. Generally a query can be defined as a:

    - QueryBuilder: This is a helper to build a query.
    - XContentBuilder: This is a helper to create JSON code. We discussed it in the *Managing mapping* recipe in this chapter. The JSON code to be generated is similar to the previous REST, but converted in programmatic code.
    - Array of bytes or string: In this case, it's usually the JSON to be executed as we have seen in REST calls.
    - Map: This contains query and value of the query.

2. We'll create a query using QueryBuilder and execute a search (the search via native API will be discussed in the next recipes):

    ```
    ….
    import org.elasticsearch.common.xcontent.XContentFactory;
    import org.elasticsearch.index.query.BoolQueryBuilder;
    import org.elasticsearch.index.query.QueryBuilder;
    import org.elasticsearch.index.query.RangeQueryBuilder;
    import org.elasticsearch.index.query.TermFilterBuilder;

    import java.io.IOException;
    import static org.elasticsearch.index.query.QueryBuilders.*;
    import static org.elasticsearch.index.query.FilterBuilders.*;

    public class QueryCreation {

      public static void main( String[] args )
      {
        String index="mytest";
        ...

        BulkRequestBuilder bulker=client.prepareBulk();
        for (Integer i=1; i<1000; i++){
          bulker.add(client.prepareIndex(index, type, i.
            toString()).setSource("text", i.toString(),
            "number1", i+1, "number2", i%2));
        }
        bulker.execute().actionGet();

        client.admin().indices().prepareRefresh(index).
    ```

```
            execute().actionGet();

        TermFilterBuilder filter = termFilter("number2", 1);
        RangeQueryBuilder range =
            rangeQuery("number1").gt(500);
        BoolQueryBuilder bool = boolQuery().must(range);

        QueryBuilder query = filteredQuery(bool, filter);

        SearchResponse response=client.prepareSearch(index).
            setTypes(type).setQuery(query).execute().actionGet();
        System.out.println("Matched records of elements: " +
            response.getHits().getTotalHits());

        io.deleteIndex(index);        }
}
```

I removed the redundant parts that are similar to the example of the previous recipe.

3. The result will be:

```
Matched records of elements: 250
```

How it works...

In the previous example, we have created a query via `QueryBuilder`. The first step is to import the query builder from the namespace:

```
import static org.elasticsearch.index.query.QueryBuilders.*;
```

Because we need the field builders, we also need to import them:

```
import static org.elasticsearch.index.query.FilterBuilders.*;
```

The query of the example is a filtered query composed of a Boolean query and a term filter. The goal of the example is to show how to mix several query/filter types for creating a complex query.

The Boolean query contains a must clause with a range query. We start to create the range query:

```
RangeQueryBuilder range = rangeQuery("number1").gte(500);
```

This range query matches, in the `"number1"` field, all the values bigger than (`"gte"`) 500. After having created the range query, we can add it to a Boolean query in the must block:

```
BoolQueryBuilder bool = boolQuery().must(range);
```

Java Integration

In real-world complex queries, you can have a lot of nested queries in a Boolean query or filter.

To build our filtered query, we need to define a filter. In this case, we have used a term filter, which is one of the most used:

```
TermFilterBuilder filter = termFilter("number2", 1);
```

The `termFilter` instance accepts a field and a value, which must be a valid ElasticSearch type. The previous code is similar to the JSON REST `{"term": {"number2":1}`.

Now, we can build the final filtered query that we can execute in the search:

```
QueryBuilder query = filteredQuery(bool, filter);
```

> Before executing a query and to be sure not to miss any results, the index must be refreshed. In the example, it's done with `client.admin().indices().prepareRefresh(index).execute().actionGet();`.

There's more...

The possible native queries/filters are same as the REST ones and have the same parameters: the only difference is that they are exposed via builder methods.

The most common query builders are:

- `matchAllQuery`: This allows matching all the documents.
- `matchQuery` and `matchPhraseQuery`: This is used to match against the text string.
- `termQuery` and `termsQuery`: This is used to match a value/s.
- `boolQuery`: This is used to aggregate other queries.
- `idsQuery`: This is used to match a list of IDs.
- `fieldQuery`: This is used to match a field with a text.
- `wildcardQuery`: This is used to match terms with wildcards (*?.).
- `regexpQuery`: This is used to match terms via a regular expression.
- `spanTermsQuery`, `spanTermQuery`, `spanORQuery`, `spanNotQuery`, `spanFirstQuery`, `span`, and so on: These are a few examples from the span query family. These are used in building span query.
- `filteredQuery`: In this, the query is composed of a query and a filter.
- `constantScoreQuery`: This accepts a query or a filter and all the matched documents are set with the same score.
- `moreLikeThisQuery` and `fuzzyLikeThisQuery`: These are used to retrieve similar documents.
- `hasChildQuery`, `hasParentQuery`, and `nestedQuery`: These are used in manage related documents.

The previous list is not complete, because it is evolving during the life of ElasticSearch. New query types are added to cover new search cases or they are seldom renamed, such as text query in match query.

Similar to the query builders, there are a lot of query filters:

- `matchAllFilter`: This matches all the documents
- `termFilter` and `termsFilter`: These are used to filter a given value/s
- `idsFilter`: This is used to filter a list of IDs
- `typeFilter`: This is used to filter all the documents of a type
- `andFilter`, `orFilter`, and `notFilter`: These are used to build Boolean filters
- `wildcardFilter`: This is used to filter terms with wildcards (*?.)
- `regexpFilter`: This is used to filter terms via a regular expression
- `rangeFilter`: This is used to filter using a range
- `scriptFilter`: This is used to filter documents using the scripting engine
- `geoDistanceFilter`, `geoBoundingBoxFilter`, and other geo filter: These provide geo filtering of documents
- `boolFilter`: This is used to create a Boolean filter which aggregates other filters

See also

- Query/filter-related recipes in *Chapter 5, Search, Queries, and Filters*

Executing a standard search

In the previous recipe, we saw how to build queries. In this recipe, we can execute this query to retrieve some documents.

Getting ready

You need a working ElasticSearch cluster and a working copy of Maven.

The code of this recipe is in *chapter_10/nativeclient* in the code bundle of this book available on Packt's website and the referred class is `QueryExample`.

Java Integration

How to do it...

For executing a standard query, we will perform the steps given as follows:

1. After having created a query, to execute it is enough using the prepareQuery call and pass to it your query object. Here, there is a complete example:

    ```java
    import org.elasticsearch.action.search.SearchResponse;
    import org.elasticsearch.client.Client;
    import org.elasticsearch.index.query.QueryBuilder;
    import org.elasticsearch.search.SearchHit;
    import static org.elasticsearch.index.query.FilterBuilders.*;
    import static org.elasticsearch.
      index.query.QueryBuilders.*;

    public class QueryExample {
      public static void main(String[] args) {
        String index = "mytest";
        String type = "mytype";
        QueryHelper qh = new QueryHelper();
        qh.populateData(index, type);
        Client client=qh.getClient();

        QueryBuilder query =
          filteredQuery(boolQuery().must(rangeQuery("number1")
            .gte(500)), termFilter("number2", 1));

        SearchResponse response = client.prepareSearch(index)
          .setTypes(type)
        .setQuery(query).addHighlightedField("name")
        .execute().actionGet();
        if(response.status().getStatus()==200){
          System.out.println("Matched number of documents: " +
        response.getHits().totalHits());
        System.out.println("Maximum score: " +
          response.getHits().maxScore());

        for(SearchHit hit: response.getHits().getHits()){
          System.out.println("hit:
            "+hit.getIndex()+":"+hit.getType()+":
            "+hit.getId());
        }
        }
        qh.dropIndex(index);
      }
    }
    ```

2. The result should be similar to this one:

   ```
   Matched number of documents: 251
   Maximum score: 1.0
   hit: mytest:mytype:505
   hit: mytest:mytype:517
   hit: mytest:mytype:529
   hit: mytest:mytype:531
   hit: mytest:mytype:543
   hit: mytest:mytype:555
   hit: mytest:mytype:567
   hit: mytest:mytype:579
   hit: mytest:mytype:581
   hit: mytest:mytype:593
   ```

How it works...

The call to execute a search is the `prepareSearch` call and it returns a `SearchResponse`.

```
import org.elasticsearch.action.search.SearchResponse;
....
SearchResponse response =
  client.prepareSearch(index).setTypes(type).
  setQuery(query).execute().actionGet();
```

The `search` call has a lot of methods to allow the setting of all the parameters that we have already seen in the searching recipes in *Chapter 5, Search, Queries, and Filters*. The most used are:

- `setIndices`: This allows defining the indices to be used.
- `setTypes`: This allows defining the document types to be used.
- `setQuery`: This allows setting the query to be executed.
- `addField(s)`: This allows setting fields to be returned (used to reduce the bandwidth by returning only the required fields).
- `addFacet`: This allows adding facets to be computed.
- `addHighlighting`: This allows adding highlighting to be returned. The simple case is of highlighting a field `"name"`:

  ```
  .addHighlightedField("name")
  ```

Java Integration

- `addScriptField`: This allows returning scripted field. A scripted field is a field computed by a server-side scripting using one of the available scripting languages. For example, it can be:

  ```
  Map<String, Object> params = MapBuilder.<String,
     Object>newMapBuilder().put("factor", 2.0).map();
  .addScriptField("sNum1", "doc['num1'].value * factor",
     params)
  ```

After having executed a search, a response object is returned.

It's good practice to check if the search is successful by checking the returned status and optionally the number of hits. If the search was executed correctly, the return status is 200.

```
if(response.status().getStatus()==200){
```

The response object contains a lot of sections that we analyzed in the *Executing a search* and *Sorting a search* recipes in *Chapter 5, Search, Queries, and Filters*. The most important one is the "hits" section that contains our results. The main methods of this section are:

- `totalHits`: This allows obtaining the total number of results.

  ```
  System.out.println("Matched number of documents: " +
     response.getHits().totalHits());
  ```

- `maxScore`: This gives the maximum score of the documents. It is the same score value of the first `SearchHit`.

  ```
  System.out.println("Maximum score: " +
     response.getHits().maxScore());
  ```

- `hits`: This is an array of `SearchHit`, which contains the results, if available.

The `SearchHit` object is the result object. It has a lot of methods. The most important ones are:

- `index()`: This is the index which contains the document.
- `type()`: This is the type of the document.
- `id()`: This is the ID of the document.
- `score()`: This is, if available, the query score of the document.
- `version()`: This is, if available, the version of the document.
- `source()`, `sourceAsString()`, `sourceAsMap()`, and so on: These return the source of the document in different forms, if available.
- `explanation()`: This, if available (required in the search), contains the query explanation.

Chapter 10

- `fields` and `field(String name)`: These return the fields requested if passed by fields to search object.
- `sortValues()`: This is the value/values used to sort the record. It's only available if sort is specified during search phase.
- `shard()`: This is the shard of the search hit. This value is very important in case of custom routing.

In the following example, we have printed only the index, type, and ID of every hit:

```
for(SearchHit hit: response.getHits().getHits()){
  System.out.println("hit:
    "+hit.getIndex()+":"+hit.getType()+":"+hit.getId());
}
```

> The number of returned hits, if not defined, is limited to 10. To retrieve more hits, you need to define a bigger value in the `size` method or paginate using the `from` method.

See also

- The *Executing a search* recipe in *Chapter 5*, *Search, Queries, and Filters*

Executing a facet search

The previous recipe can be extended to support facet and to retrieve analytics on indexed data.

Getting ready

You need a working ElasticSearch cluster and a working copy of Maven.

The code of this recipe is in *chapter_10/nativeclient* in the code bundle of this book available on Packt's website and the referred class is `FacetExample`.

How to do it...

For executing a facet search, we will perform the steps given as follows:

1. We'll calculate two different facets (term and statistical):

    ```
    import org.elasticsearch.action.search.SearchResponse;
    import org.elasticsearch.client.Client;
    import org.elasticsearch.search.facet.FacetBuilder;
    ```

Java Integration

```java
import
  org.elasticsearch.search.facet.statistical
  .StatisticalFacet;
import org.elasticsearch.search.facet.terms.TermsFacet;

import static
  org.elasticsearch.index.query.QueryBuilders.*;
import static org.elasticsearch.search.facet.FacetBuilders.*;

public class FacetExample {
  public static void main(String[] args) {
    ...
    Client client=qh.getClient();
    FacetBuilder
      facetBuilder=termsFacet("tag").field("tag");
    FacetBuilder
      facetBuilder2=statisticalFacet("number1")
      .field("number1");

    SearchResponse response = client.prepareSearch(index)
      .setTypes(type)
    .setQuery(matchAllQuery()).addFacet(facetBuilder)
    .addFacet(facetBuilder2)
    .execute().actionGet();
    if(response.status().getStatus()==200){
      System.out.println("Matched number of documents: " +
        response.getHits().totalHits());
      TermsFacet facet = response.getFacets().facet("tag");
      System.out.println("Facet name: " + facet.getName());
      System.out.println("Facet total: " +
        facet.getTotalCount());
      System.out.println("Facet missing: " +
        facet.getMissingCount());
      System.out.println("Facet other: " +
        facet.getOtherCount());
      for (TermsFacet.Entry entry:facet.getEntries()){
        System.out.println(" - " + entry.getCount()+"
          "+entry.getTerm());
      }

      StatisticalFacet facet2 =
        response.getFacets().facet("number1");
      System.out.println("Facet name: " +
        facet2.getName());
      System.out.println("Count: " + facet2.getCount());
      System.out.println("Min: " + facet2.getMin());
```

```
            System.out.println("Max: " + facet2.getMax());
            System.out.println("Mean: " + facet2.getMean());
            System.out.println("Standard Deviation: " +
               facet2.getStdDeviation());
            System.out.println("Sum of Squares: " +
               facet2.getSumOfSquares());
            System.out.println("Variance: " +
               facet2.getVariance());
            System.out.println("Total: " + facet2.getTotal());

      }
      qh.dropIndex(index);
   }
}
```

2. The result should be similar to this one:

```
Matched number of documents: 1000
Facet name: tag
Facet total: 1000
Facet missing: 0
Facet other: 0
 - 260 amazing
 - 251 bad
 - 249 nice
 - 240 cool
Facet name: number1
Count: 1000
Min: 2.0
Max: 1001.0
Mean: 501.5
Standard Deviation: 288.6749902572095
Sum of Squares: 3.348355E8
Variance: 83333.25
Total: 501500.0
```

How it works...

The search part is similar to the previous example. In this case, we have used a `matchAllQuery`, which matches all the documents.

To execute a facet, you need to create it. There are three ways to do so:

- Using a string that maps a JSON object
- Using an `XContentBuilder` which will be used to produce a JSON
- Using a `FacetBuilder`

The first two ways are trivial; the third one requires that the builders are imported:

```
import static org.elasticsearch.search.facet.FacetBuilders.*;
```

There are several types of facet. The first one, which we have created with the FacetBuilder, is a Term one, which counts all terms occurrences.

```
FacetBuilder facetBuilder=termsFacet("tag").field("tag");
```

The required value for every facet is the name, passed in the builder constructor. In the case of a term facet, the field is required to be able to process the request. (There are a lot of other parameters, see the *Executing terms facets* recipe in *Chapter 6, Facets*, for full details).

The second facetBuilder, that we have created, is a statistical one based on the "number1" numeric field.

```
FacetBuilder
   facetBuilder2=statisticalFacet("number1").field("number1");
```

Now that we have created the facetBuilder, we can add them on a search method via the addFacet method.

```
SearchResponse response = client.prepareSearch(index).setTypes(type)
   .setQuery(matchAllQuery())
   .addFacet(facetBuilder).addFacet(facetBuilder2)
   .execute().actionGet();
```

Now the response holds information about our facets. To access them, we need to process the getFacets section of the response. The facets results are contained in a hash-like structure and you can retrieve them with the names that you have defined previously in the request.

To retrieve the first facet results, we need to get it and cast it to the correct type:

```
TermsFacet facet = response.getFacets().facet("tag");
```

Now that we have a facet result of type TermsFacet (see the *Executing terms facets* recipe in *Chapter 6, Facets*), we can get the facet properties and iterate on entries:

```
System.out.println("Facet name: " + facet.getName());
System.out.println("Facet total: " + facet.getTotalCount());
System.out.println("Facet missing: " + facet.getMissingCount());
System.out.println("Facet other: " + facet.getOtherCount());
for (TermsFacet.Entry entry:facet.getEntries()){
  System.out.println(" - " + entry.getCount()+"
     "+entry.getTerm());
}
```

To retrieve the second facet results, because the result is of type `StatisticalFacet`, you need to cast to it:

```
StatisticalFacet facet2 = response.getFacets().facet("number1");
```

Now you can access the result properties of this kind of facet:

```
System.out.println("Facet name: " + facet2.getName());
System.out.println("Count: " + facet2.getCount());
System.out.println("Min: " + facet2.getMin());
System.out.println("Max: " + facet2.getMax());
System.out.println("Mean: " + facet2.getMean());
System.out.println("Standard Deviation: " +
   facet2.getStdDeviation());
System.out.println("Sum of Squares: " + facet2.getSumOfSquares());
System.out.println("Variance: " + facet2.getVariance());
System.out.println("Total: " + facet2.getTotal());
```

Using facets with native client is quite easy. You only need to pay attention to returned facet type to execute correct type cast to access your results.

See also

- The *Executing terms facets* recipe in *Chapter 6, Facets*
- The *Executing statistical facets* recipe in *Chapter 6, Facets*

Executing a scroll/scan search

The standard query works very well if you need to provide results in which documents do not change too often. Otherwise, doing pagination with live data brings a strange behavior to the returned results. To bypass this problem, ElasticSearch provides an extra parameter in the query: the scroll.

Getting ready

You need a working ElasticSearch cluster and a working copy of Maven.

The code of this recipe is in *chapter_10/nativeclient* in the code bundle of this book available on Packt's website and the referred class is `ScrollScanQueryExample`.

Java Integration

How to do it...

The search is done as in the previous recipe. The big difference is a `setScroll` timeout, which allows storing in memory the resultant IDs for a query for a defined timeout.

We can change the code of the previous recipe by using scroll in the following way:

```java
import org.elasticsearch.action.search.SearchResponse;
import org.elasticsearch.action.search.SearchType;
import org.elasticsearch.client.Client;
import org.elasticsearch.common.unit.TimeValue;
import org.elasticsearch.index.query.QueryBuilder;

import static
  org.elasticsearch.index.query.FilterBuilders.termFilter;
import static org.elasticsearch.index.query.QueryBuilders.*;

public class ScrollScanQueryExample {
  public static void main(String[] args) {
    String index = "mytest";
    String type = "mytype";
    QueryHelper qh = new QueryHelper();
    qh.populateData(index, type);
    Client client=qh.getClient();

    QueryBuilder query =
      filteredQuery(boolQuery().must(rangeQuery("number1")
      .gte(500)), termFilter("number2", 1));

    SearchResponse response =
      client.prepareSearch(index).setTypes(type)
    .setQuery(query).setScroll(TimeValue.timeValueMinutes(2))
    .execute().actionGet();

    // do something with searchResponse.getHits()
    while(response.getHits().hits().length!=0){
      // do something with searchResponse.getHits()
      //your code here
      //next scroll
      response =
        client.prepareSearchScroll(response.getScrollId())
        .setScroll(TimeValue.timeValueMinutes(2))
        .execute().actionGet();
    }
```

```
        SearchResponse searchResponse = client.prepareSearch()
          .setSearchType(SearchType.SCAN)
          .setQuery(matchAllQuery())
          .setSize(100)
          .setScroll(TimeValue.timeValueMinutes(2))
          .execute().actionGet();

         while (true) {
           searchResponse =
             client.prepareSearchScroll(searchResponse.getScrollId())
               .setScroll(TimeValue.timeValueMinutes(2)).execute()
               .actionGet();
           // do something with searchResponse.getHits() if any

           if (searchResponse.getHits().hits().length == 0) {
             break;
           }
         }

         qh.dropIndex(index);
       }
     }
```

How it works...

To use the result, scrolling is enough to add the `setScroll` method with a timeout to the method call.

When using scrolling, some behaviors must be considered:

- The timeout defines the time slice that an ElasticSearch server keeps for the results. Asking a scroll, after the timeout, the server returns an error. So pay attention to very small timeouts.
- The scroll consumes memory until the scroll ends or a timeout is raised. Setting too large a timeout without consuming the data results in large memory occupation. Using a large number of open scroller consumes a lot of memory, which is proportional to the number of IDs and their related data (score, order, and so on) in the results.
- With scrolling, it's not possible to paginate the documents, as there is no `"start"`. The scrolling is designed to fetch consecutive results.

So, a standard search is changed in a scroll in the following way:

```
SearchResponse response =
    client.prepareSearch(index).setTypes(type).setQuery(query)
      .setScroll(TimeValue.timeValueMinutes(2)).execute().actionGet();
```

Java Integration

The response contains the results as the standard search plus a scroll ID that is required to fetch the next results.

To execute the scroll, you need to call the `prepareSearchScroll` client method with a scroll ID and a new timeout. In the following example, we process all the result documents:

```
while(response.getHits().hits().length!=0){
  // do something with searchResponse.getHits()
  //your code here
  //next scroll
  response =
    client.prepareSearchScroll(response.getScrollId())
    .setScroll(TimeValue.timeValueMinutes(2)).execute()
    .actionGet();
}
```

To understand that we are at the end of the scroll, we can check that no results are returned.

There are a lot of scenarios in which scroll is very important: working on big data solutions, when the results number is very huge, it's very easy to hit the timeout. In these scenarios, it is important to have a good architecture in which you fetch the results as fast as possible and you don't process the results in the loop, but you defer the result manipulation in a distributed way.

There's more...

The scroll call is used in conjunction with the scan query (see the *Executing a scan query* recipe in *Chapter 5, Search, Queries, and Filters*). The scan query allows executing a query and providing results in a scroller for fast performances.

The scan query consumes less memory than a standard scroll query because:

- It doesn't compute score and doesn't return it
- It doesn't allow sorting, so it doesn't keep in memory the order value(s)
- It doesn't allow computing facets
- It doesn't allow to be executed with child query or nested query, to reduce memory usage

The scan method collects the results and iterates over them. It's very useful to "scan" in a big data way, all the documents that match a query.

To execute the scan query, the search type value must be passed to the search call.

```
SearchResponse searchResponse = client.prepareSearch()
  .setSearchType(SearchType.SCAN)
  .setQuery(matchAllQuery())
  .setSize(100)
  .setScroll(TimeValue.timeValueMinutes(2))
  .execute().actionGet();
```

A big difference from the scroll is that the first call doesn't return hits but only the scroll ID. So to gather the first results, you need to execute a new scroll query.

In the previous code, the loop iterates until no results are available:

```
while (true) {
  searchResponse =
    client.prepareSearchScroll(searchResponse.getScrollId())
    .setScroll(TimeValue.timeValueMinutes(2))
    .execute().actionGet();
  // do something with searchResponse.getHits() if any
  if (searchResponse.getHits().hits().length == 0) {
  break;
  }
}
```

See also

- The *Executing a scan query* recipe in *Chapter 5, Search, Queries, and Filters*

11
Python Integration

In this chapter, we will cover the following topics:

- Creating a client
- Managing indices
- Managing mappings
- Managing documents
- Executing a standard search
- Executing a facet search

Introduction

In the previous chapter, we saw how it is possible to use a native client for accessing the ElasticSearch server via Java. This chapter is dedicated to Python language and how to manage common tasks via its clients.

As well as Java, ElasticSearch team supports official clients for Perl, PHP, Python, and Ruby (refer to the announcement post on ElasticSearch blog at `http://www.elasticsearch.org/blog/unleash-the-clients-ruby-python-php-perl/`). They are pretty new as their initial public release was in September 2013. These clients have the following advantages against other implementations:

- They are strongly tied to the ElasticSearch API. ElasticSearch team says *These clients are direct translations of the native ElasticSearch REST interface.*
- They handle dynamic node detection and failover. They are built with a strong networking base for communicating with the cluster.
- They have a full coverage of the REST API.

Python Integration

- They share the same application approach for every language in which they are available, so it's faster switching from one language to another.
- They provide transport abstraction, so that a user can plug different backends.
- They are easily extendable.

The Python client plays very well with other Python frameworks such as Django, web2py, and Pyramid. It allows very fast access to documents, indices, and clusters.

Other than the standard ElasticSearch client in this chapter, it's presented with the PyES client developed by me and other contributors since 2010. PyES extends the standard client with a lot of functionalities and helpers such as:

- Automatic management of common conversion between types.
- Object-oriented approach to common ElasticSearch elements. The standard client only considers the use of Python dictionary as the standard element.
- Helpers on search such as advanced iterators on results and Django-like query set.

In this chapter, I'll try to describe the most important functionalities of ElasticSearch's official Python client and PyES. For additional examples and for deep reference I suggest you have a look at the online GitHub repository https://github.com/elasticsearch/elasticsearch-py and documentation.

Creating a client

The official ElasticSearch clients are designed to use several transport layers. They allow using the HTTP, thrift or memcached protocol without changing your application code.

The thrift and memcached protocols are binary ones and due to their structures they are generally a bit faster than the HTTP one. They wrap the REST API and share the same behavior so that switching between protocols is very easy.

In this recipe, we'll see how to instantiate a client with different protocols.

Getting ready

You need a working ElasticSearch cluster and plugins for extra protocols. The full code of this recipe is in the `chapter_11/client_creation.py` file.

How to do it...

For creating a client, we need to perform the following steps:

1. Before using the Python client, it is required to install it (possibly in a Python virtual environment). The client is officially hosted on PyPi (http://pypi.python.org/) and it's easy to install with the following `pip` command:

   ```
   pip install elasticsearch
   ```

   This standard installation only provides the HTTP protocol.

2. To install the thrift protocol, you need to install the plugin on the ElasticSearch server as follows:

   ```
   bin/plugin -install elasticsearch/elasticsearch-transport-thrift/1.6.0
   ```

3. On the client side we need to install thrift support for Python available in the thrift package (https://pypi.python.org/pypi/thrift/), installable via `pip`:

   ```
   pip install thrift
   ```

4. To install the memcached protocol, you need to install the plugin on the ElasticSearch server as follows:

   ```
   bin/plugin -install elasticsearch/elasticsearch-transport-memcached/1.6.0
   ```

5. On the client side we need to install memchached support for Python provided by the `pylibmc` package, installable via `pip`:

   ```
   pip install pylibmc
   ```

   For compiling this library if not installed, `libmemcache` must be installed. On Mac OS X, you can install it via "brew install libmemcached", on Linux via the `libmemcache-dev` package.

6. After having installed the server and the required libraries to use the protocol, we can instantiate the client. It resides in Python's `elasticsearch` package and it must be imported to call the client as follows:

   ```
   import elasticsearch
   ```

   If you don't pass arguments to the `elasticsearch.ElasticSearch` class, it instantiates a client that connects to localhost and port 9200 (the default ElasticSearch HTTP one).

   ```
   es = elasticsearch.Elasticsearch()
   ```

Python Integration

7. If your cluster is composed by more than one node, you can pass the list of nodes to the round-robin connect between them and distribute the HTTP load.

   ```
   es = elasticsearch.Elasticsearch(["search1:9200", "search2:9200"])
   ```

8. Often the complete topology of the cluster is unknown. If you know at least one node's IP address, you can use the `sniff_on_start=True` option. This option activates the client ability to detect other nodes in the cluster.

   ```
   es = elasticsearch.Elasticsearch(["search1:9200"], sniff_on_start=True)
   ```

9. If you want to use the HTTP requests transport, you need to override the `connection_class` parameter passing a RequestsHttpConnection object as follows:

   ```
   from elasticsearch.connection import RequestsHttpConnection

   es = elasticsearch.Elasticsearch( sniff_on_start=True, connection_class= RequestsHttpConnection)
   ```

10. If you want to use thrift as the transport layer, you should import the `ThriftConnection` and pass it to the client as follows:

    ```
    from elasticsearch.connection import ThriftConnection

    es = elasticsearch.Elasticsearch(["search1:9500"], sniff_on_start=True, connection_class= ThriftConnection)
    ```

11. If you want to use memcached as the transport layer, you should import the `MemcachedConnection` class and pass it to the client as follows:

    ```
    from elasticsearch import Elasticsearch, MemcachedConnection

    es = elasticsearch.Elasticsearch(["search1:11211"], sniff_on_start=True, connection_class=MemcachedConnection)
    ```

How it works...

To communicate with an ElasticSearch cluster, a client is required.

The client manages all communication layers from your application to an ElasticSearch server, using a defined protocol. The standard protocol for REST calls is the HTTP one.

The ElasticSearch Python client allows using one of the following protocols:

- **HTTP**: This provides two implementations, one based on requests (https://pypi.python.org/pypi/requests) and the other one based on urllib3 (https://pypi.python.org/pypi/urllib3).

- **Thrift**: This is one of the fastest protocols available. To use it, both server and client thrift libraries must be installed.
- **Memcached**: This allows communicating to ElasticSearch, as if it was a memcached server. To use it, both server and client memcache libraries must be installed.

For general usage, HTTP protocol is very good and it's the standard de facto. The other protocols work very well if you are able to reuse the client, so that you don't have to reinstantiate the connections too often.

The ElasticSearch Python client requires a server to connect to: if not defined, it tries to use one in the local machine (localhost). If you have more than a node, you can pass a list of servers to connect to.

> The client automatically tries to balance the operations on all cluster nodes. This is a very powerful functionality provided by the ElasticSearch client.

To improve the list of available nodes, it is possible to set the client to autodiscover new nodes. I suggest using this feature because it is common to have a cluster with a lot of nodes and you need to shut down some of them for maintenance. The options that can be passed to the client to control discovery are as follows:

- `sniff_on_start` (default `False`): This allows obtaining the list of nodes from the cluser at startup time
- `sniffer_timeout` (default `None`): This is the number of seconds between automatic sniff of the cluster nodes
- `sniff_on_connection_fail` (default `False`): This controls if a connection failure triggers a sniff of cluster nodes

The default client configuration uses HTTP protocol via urllib3 library. If you want to use other transport protocol, you need to pass the type of the transport class to the `transport_class` variable. The current implemented classes are as follows:

- `Urllib3HttpConnection` (default): This uses HTTP (usually on port 9200)
- `RequestsHttpConnection`: This is an alternative to Urllib3HttpConnection based on requests library
- `ThriftConnection`: This uses the thrift protocol (usually on port 9500)
- `MemcachedConnection`: This uses the memcached protocol (usually on port 11211)

Python Integration

There's more...

If you need more high-level functionalities than the official client, PyES gives you a more pythonic and object-oriented approach to work with ElasticSearch. PyES is easy installable via `pip` (the more recent version is available on GitHub):

```
pip install pyes
```

To initialize a client, you need to import the ES object and instantiate it as follows:

```
from pyes import ES
es = ES()
```

The protocol is inferred by the URL of servers list passed to the constructor. If no server parameter is passed to the constructor, the localhost on port 9200 is used.

PyES client offers the same connection functionalities of the official client described previously as it internally uses the official ElasticSearch client.

See also

- PyES on GitHub at `https://github.com/aparo/pyes` and on PyPi at `https://pypi.python.org/pypi/pyes`
- PyES online documentation at `http://pythonhosted.org/pyes/`
- Python thrift library at `https://pypi.python.org/pypi/thrift/`
- ElasticSearch thrift plugin at `https://github.com/elasticsearch/elasticsearch-transport-thrift`
- Python thrift library at `https://pypi.python.org/pypi/thrift/`
- ElasticSearch transport memcached at `https://github.com/elasticsearch/elasticsearch-transport-memcached`
- Python memcached library at `http://pypi.python.org/pypi/pylibmc/1.2.3`

Managing indices

In the previous recipe we saw how to initialize a client to send calls to an ElasticSearch cluster. In this recipe, we will see how to manage indices via client calls.

Getting ready

You need a working ElasticSearch cluster and required packages of the *Creating a client* recipe of this chapter.

The full code of this recipe is in the `chapter_11/indices_management.py` file.

How to do it...

In Python, managing the lifecycle of your indices is very easy, we need to perform the following steps:

1. We initialize a client as follows:

   ```
   import elasticsearch
   es = elasticsearch.Elasticsearch()
   index_name = "my_index"
   ```

2. All the indices methods are available in the `client.indices` namespace. We can create and wait for the creation of an index as follows:

   ```
   es.indices.create(index_name)
   es.cluster.health(wait_for_status="yellow")
   ```

3. We can close/open an index as follows:

   ```
   es.indices.close(index_name)

   es.indices.open(index_name)
   es.cluster.health(wait_for_status="yellow")
   ```

4. We can optimize an index as follows:

   ```
   es.indices.optimize(index_name)
   ```

5. We can delete an index as follows:

   ```
   es.indices.delete(index_name)
   ```

How it works...

ElasticSearch Python client has two special managers one for indices (`<client>.indices`) and one for cluster (`<client>.cluster`).

For every operation that needs to work with indices, the first value is generally the name of the index. If you need to execute an action on several indices in one shot, the indices must be concatenated with a comma , (that is, `index1,index2,indexN`).

In PyES, the concatenation is automatically managed.

To create an index, the call requires the `index_name` parameter and other optional parameters such as index settings and mapping (we'll see this advanced feature in the next recipe).

```
es.indices.create(index_name)
```

Python Integration

The index creation can take a lot of time (from a few milliseconds to seconds). It is an asynchronous operation and it depends on the complexity of the cluster, the speed of the disk, the network congestion, and so on. To be sure that this action is completed, we need to check that the cluster heath becomes `yellow` or `green`, with the following command:

```
es.cluster.health(wait_for_status="yellow")
```

> It's good practice to wait for the cluster status `yellow` (at least) after operations that involve indices creation and opening, because these actions are asynchronous and they can bring concurrency problems if actions are taken on them before these operations are completed.

To close an index, the method is `<client>.indices.close` giving the name of the index to close.

```
es.indices.close(index_name)
```

To open an index, the method is `<client>.indices.open` giving the name of index to open.

```
es.indices.open(index_name)
es.cluster.health(wait_for_status="yellow")
```

Similar to index creation, after an index is opened, it is a good practice to wait until the index is fully opened (all the shards are activated) before executing the operation on the index. This action is done by checking the cluster health.

To improve the performance of an index, ElasticSearch allows optimizing it by removing the deleted documents (documents are marked deleted, but not purged from the segments index for performance reasons) and reducing the number of segments. To optimize an index, the `<client>.indices.optimize` method must be called on the index to be optimized.

```
es.indices.optimize(index_name)
```

Finally, if we want to remove the index, we can call the `<client>.indices.delete` method giving the name of the index to be removed. Remember that deleting an index removes everything related to it and this action cannot be reverted.

PyES indices management is similar to the official client one.

See also

- The *Creating an index* recipe in *Chapter 4, Standard Operations*
- The *Deleting an index* recipe in *Chapter 4, Standard Operations*
- The *Opening/closing an index* recipe in *Chapter 4, Standard Operations*

Managing mappings

After creating an index, the next step is to add some mapping to it. We have already seen how to put a mapping via REST API in *Chapter 4, Standard Operations*. In this recipe, we will see how to manage mappings via official Python client and PyES.

Getting ready

You need a working ElasticSearch cluster and required packages of the *Creating a client* recipe of this chapter.

The code of this recipe is in `chapter_11/mapping_management.py` and `chapter_11/mapping_management_pyes.py`.

How to do it...

After having initialized a client and created an index, the steps required for managing the indices are as follows:

- Create a mapping
- Retrieve a mapping
- Delete a mapping

These steps are easily managed with code as follows:

1. We initialize the client as follows:

   ```
   import elasticsearch
   
   es = elasticsearch.Elasticsearch()
   ```

2. We create an index as follows:

   ```
   index_name = "my_index"
   type_name = "my_type"
   es.indices.create(index_name)
   es.cluster.health(wait_for_status="yellow")
   ```

3. We put the mapping as follows:

   ```
   es.indices.put_mapping(index_name, type_name, {"_type": {"store": "yes"}, "type": "object", "properties": {
       "uuid": {"index": "not_analyzed", "type": "string", "store": "yes"},
   ```

```
        "title": {"index": "analyzed", "type": "string", "store":
"yes", "term_vector": "with_positions_offsets"},
        "parsedtext": {"index": "analyzed", "type": "string", "store":
"yes", "term_vector": "with_positions_offsets"},
    ... truncated...}}})
```

4. We retrieve the mapping as follows:

   ```
   mappings = es.indices.get_mapping(index_name, type_name)
   ```

5. We delete the mapping as follows:

   ```
   es.indices.delete_mapping(index_name, type_name)
   ```

6. We delete the index as follows:

   ```
   es.indices.delete(index_name)
   ```

How it works...

We already saw the initialization of the client and the index creation in the previous recipe. For creating a mapping, the method call is `<client>.indices.create_mapping` giving the index name, the type name, and the mapping. The building of the mapping is fully covered in *Chapter 3, Managing Mapping*. In Python it is easy to convert the standard Python types in JSON and vice versa.

```
es.indices.put_mapping(index_name, type_name, {…})
```

If an error is generated in mapping processing, an exception is raised. The `put_mapping` API has two behaviors: creating and updating.

> In ElasticSearch, you cannot remove a property from a mapping. The schema manipulation allows only entering new properties with the Put Mapping call.

To retrieve a mapping the Get Mapping API uses `<client>.indices.get_mapping` method providing `index_name` and `type_name` as follows:

```
mappings = es.indices.get_mapping(index_name, type_name)
```

The return type is obviously the dictionary describing the mapping.

To remove a mapping the method is `<client>.indices.delete_mapping` and it requires the `index_name` and the `type_name` parameters.

```
es.indices.delete_mapping(index_name, type_name)
```

> Deleting a mapping is a destructive operation. It removes the mapping and all the data contained in it.

There's more...

Creating a mapping using the official ElasticSearch client requires a lot of attention in building the dictionary that defines the mapping.

PyES provides also an object-oriented approach for mapping creation, reducing the probability of errors in defining the mapping, and adding the typed field with useful presets. The previous mapping can be converted in PyES, in the following way:

```
from pyes.mappings import *
docmapping = DocumentObjectField(name=mapping_name)
    docmapping.add_property(
        StringField(name="parsedtext", store=True, term_vector="with_positions_offsets", index="analyzed"))
    docmapping.add_property(
        StringField(name="name", store=True, term_vector="with_positions_offsets", index="analyzed"))
    docmapping.add_property(
        StringField(name="title", store=True, term_vector="with_positions_offsets", index="analyzed"))
    docmapping.add_property(IntegerField(name="position", store=True))
    docmapping.add_property(DateField(name="date", store=True))
    docmapping.add_property(StringField(name="uuid", store=True, index="not_analyzed"))
    nested_object = NestedObject(name="nested")
    nested_object.add_property(StringField(name="name", store=True))
    nested_object.add_property(StringField(name="value", store=True))
    nested_object.add_property(IntegerField(name="num", store=True))
    docmapping.add_property(nested_object)
```

The main fields are as follows:

- `DocumentObjectField`: This is a document mapping that contains the properties
- `StringField`, `DateField`, `IntegerField`, `LongField`, `BooleanField`: These map to the respective type fields
- `ObjectField`: This allows mapping an embedded object field
- `NestedObject`: This allows mapping a nested object
- `AttachmentField`: This maps the attachment field
- `IPField`: This maps the IP field

The object definition of the mapping enforces that if the types are correctly defined, all the mapping properties are valid.

The PyES Get Mapping API does not return a Python dictionary, but a `DocumentObjectField` of the required mapping, automatically managing the transformation from dictionary to objects for easily parsing and editing.

See also

- The *Putting a mapping in an index* recipe in *Chapter 4, Standard Operations*
- The *Getting a mapping* recipe in *Chapter 4, Standard Operations*
- The *Deleting a mapping* recipe in *Chapter 4, Standard Operations*

Managing documents

The APIs for managing the documents (index, update, and delete) are the most important ones after the search ones. In this recipe, we will see how to use them in a standard way and in bulk actions to improve the performance.

Getting ready

You need a working ElasticSearch cluster and required packages of the *Creating a client* recipe of this chapter.

The full code of this recipe is in the `chapter_11/document_management.py` and `chapter_11/document_management_pyes.py` files.

How to do it...

The main operations to manage documents are as follows:

- `index`: This stores a document in ElasticSearch. It is mapped on the Index API call.
- `update`: This allows updating some values in a document. This operation is composed internally (via the Lucene nature) by deleting the previous document and reindexing of the document with the new values. It is mapped on the Update API call.
- `delete`: This deletes a document from the index. It is mapped on the Delete API call.

With the ElasticSearch Python client, the following operations can be done with the following steps.

1. We initialize a client and create an index with the mapping as follows:
   ```
   import elasticsearch
   from datetime import datetime
   es = elasticsearch.Elasticsearch()
   
   index_name = "my_index"
   type_name = "my_type"
   
   from utils import create_and_add_mapping
   create_and_add_mapping(es, index_name, type_name)
   ```

2. We index a document as follows:

   ```
   es.index(index=index_name, doc_type=type_name, id=1,
            body={"name": "Joe Tester", "parsedtext": "Joe Testere
   nice guy", "uuid": "11111", "position": 1,
            "date": datetime(2013, 12, 8)})
   ```
   ...

3. We update a document as follows:

   ```
   es.update(index=index_name, doc_type=type_name, id=2,
   body={"script": 'ctx._source.position += 1'})
   ```

4. We delete a document as follows:

   ```
   es.delete(index=index_name, doc_type=type_name, id=3)
   ```

5. We insert some documents in bulk as follows:

   ```
   from elasticsearch.helpers import bulk_index
   bulk_index(es, [{"name": "Joe Tester", "parsedtext": "Joe Testere
   nice guy", "uuid": "11111", "position": 1,
            "date": datetime(2013, 12, 8), "_index":index_name,
   "_type":type_name, "_id":"1"},
   ...
   ])
   ```

6. We remove the index as follows:

   ```
   es.indices.delete(index_name)
   ```

How it works...

To simplify the example, after having instantiated the client, a function of the `utils` package, which sets up the index and puts the mapping, is called as follows:

```
from utils import create_and_add_mapping
create_and_add_mapping(es, index_name, type_name)
```

This function contains the code for creating the mapping of the previous recipe.

To index a document, the method is `<client>.index` and it requires the name of the index, the type of the document, and the body of the document, as given in the following code:

```
es.index(index=index_name, doc_type=type_name, id=1,
         body={"name": "Joe Tester", "parsedtext": "Joe Testere
nice guy", "uuid": "11111", "position": 1,
         "date": datetime(2013, 12, 8)})
```

Python Integration

It also accepts all the parameters that we have seen in the REST Index API call in the *Indexing a document* recipe in *Chapter 4, Standard Operations*. The most common parameters passed to this function are as follows:

- `id`: This provides an ID to be used to index the document
- `routing`: This provides a shard routing to index the document in the specified shard
- `parent`: This provide a parent ID to be used to put the child document in the correct shard

To update a document, the method is `<client>.update` and it requires the following parameters:

- Index name
- Type name
- ID of the document
- Script or document to update the document

The following code includes these parameters:

```
es.update(index=index_name, doc_type=type_name, id=2, body={"script": 'ctx._source.position += 1'})
```

Obviously the call accepts all the parameters that we have discussed in the *Updating a document* recipe in *Chapter 4, Standard Operations*.

To delete a document, the method is `<client>.delete` and it requires the following parameters:

- Index name
- Type name
- ID of the document

The following code includes these parameters:

```
es.delete(index=index_name, doc_type=type_name, id=3)
```

> Remember that all the ElasticSearch document actions that work on a document are never seen instantly on searching. If you want to search without having to wait for the automatic refresh (every 1s), you need to manually call the Refresh API on the index.

To execute bulk indexing, the ElasticSearch client provides a helper function, which accepts a connection, an iterable (list) of documents and the bulk size. The bulk size (default 500) defines the number of actions to send via a single bulk call. The parameters that must be passed to correctly control the indexing of the document, are placed in the document with the _ prefix. These special fields are generally:

- `_index`: This is the name of the index that must be used to store the document
- `_type`: This is the document type
- `_id`: This is the ID of the document

These parameters are given in the following code:

```
from elasticsearch.helpers import bulk_index
bulk_index(es, [{"name": "Joe Tester", "parsedtext": "Joe Testere nice guy", "uuid": "11111", "position": 1,
        "date": datetime(2013, 12, 8), "_index":index_name, "_type":type_name, "_id":"1"},
...
])
```

There's more...

The previous code can be executed in PyES as follows:

```
from pyes import ES

es = ES()

index_name = "my_index"
type_name = "my_type"

from utils_pyes import create_and_add_mapping

create_and_add_mapping(es, index_name, type_name)

es.index(doc={"name": "Joe Tester", "parsedtext": "Joe Testere nice guy", "uuid": "11111", "position": 1},
        index=index_name, doc_type=type_name, id=1)
es.index(doc={"name": "data1", "value": "value1"}, index=index_name, doc_type=type_name + "2", id=1, parent=1)
es.index(doc={"name": "Bill Baloney", "parsedtext": "Bill Testere nice guy", "uuid": "22222", "position": 2},
        index=index_name, doc_type=type_name, id=2, bulk=True)
...
```

Python Integration

```
es.force_bulk()

es.update(index=index_name, doc_type=type_name, id=2, script='ctx._source.position += 1')
es.update(index=index_name, doc_type=type_name, id=2, script='ctx._source.position += 1', bulk=True)

es.delete(index=index_name, doc_type=type_name, id=1, bulk=True)
es.delete(index=index_name, doc_type=type_name, id=3)

es.force_bulk()
es.indices.refresh(index_name)

es.indices.delete_index(index_name)
```

The PyES index/update/delete methods are similar to the ElasticSearch official client, with the exception that the document must be inserted in the `doc` variable.

In PyES, to execute an action as bulk, the `bulk=True` parameter must be passed to the index/update/create method. Activating the bulk parameter, the body of the action is stored in a `ListBulker` object that collects elements until it is full. When the bulk "basket" is full (the size is defined during the ES client initialization), the actions are sent to the server and the basket is empty, ready to accept new documents.

To force the bulk (even it is not full), you can call the `<client>.force_bulk` method or you can execute a refresh or flush index action.

See also

- The *Indexing a document* recipe in *Chapter 4, Standard Operations*
- The *Getting a document* recipe in *Chapter 4, Standard Operations*
- The *Deleting a document* recipe in *Chapter 4, Standard Operations*
- The *Updating a document* recipe in *Chapter 4, Standard Operations*
- The *Speeding up atomic operations (bulk)* recipe in *Chapter 4, Standard Operations*

Executing a standard search

After having inserted documents, the most common executed action in ElasticSearch is the search. The official ElasticSearch client APIs for searching are similar to the REST one.

Getting ready

You need a working ElasticSearch cluster and required packages of the *Creating a client* recipe of this chapter.

The code of this recipe is in the `chapter_11/searching.py` and `chapter_11/searching_pyes.py` files.

How to do it...

To execute a standard query, the client search method must be called passing the query parameters as we saw in *Chapter 5, Search, Queries, and Filters*. The required parameters are at least the index name, the type name, and the query DSL. In the following example I'll show how to call a match all query, a term query and a filter query. We need to perform the following steps:

1. We will initialize the client and populate the index as follows:

   ```
   import elasticsearch
   from pprint import pprint

   es = elasticsearch.Elasticsearch()
   index_name = "my_index"
   type_name = "my_type"

   from utils import create_and_add_mapping, populate

   create_and_add_mapping(es, index_name, type_name)

   populate(es, index_name, type_name)
   ```

2. We will execute a search with a `match_all` query and print the results as follows:

   ```
   results = es.search(index_name, type_name, {"query": {"match_all": {}}})
   pprint(results)
   ```

3. We will execute a search with a term query and print the results as follows:

   ```
   results = es.search(index_name, type_name, {
       "query": {
           "query": {
               "term": {"name": {"boost": 3.0, "value": "joe"}}}
       }})
   pprint(results)
   ```

4. We will execute a search with a filtered query and print the results as follows:

   ```
   results = es.search(index_name, type_name, {"query": {
       "filtered": {
           "filter": {
               "or": [
                   {"term": {"position": 1}},
                   {"term": {"position": 2}}]
           },
           "query": {"match_all": {}}}}})
   pprint(results)
   ```

5. We will remove the index as follows:

   ```
   es.indices.delete(index_name)
   ```

How it works...

The idea behind the ElasticSearch official clients is that they should offer a common API more similar to REST calls. In Python it is very easy to use the vanilla query DSL as it provides an easy mapping from the Python dictionary to JSON objects and vice versa.

In the preceding example, before calling the search, we need to initialize the index and put some data in it. This is done using the two helpers available in the `utils` package of the chapter's sample directory.

The two methods available are as follows:

- `create_and_add_mapping(es, index_name, type_name)`: This initializes the index and puts the correct mapping to perform correct search. The code of this function is taken from the *Managing mappings* recipe of this chapter.
- `populate(es, index_name, type_name)`: This populates the index with data. The code of this function is taken from the previous recipe.

After having initialized some data, we can execute queries against it. To execute a search, the method that must be called is the search on the client. This method accepts all parameters described for REST calls in searching discussed *Chapter 5, Search, Queries, and Filters*.

Chapter 11

The actual method signature for the search method is as follows:

```
@query_params('analyze_wildcard', 'analyzer', 'default_operator',
'df', 'explain', 'fields', 'ignore_indices', 'indices_boost',
'lenient', 'lowercase_expanded_terms', 'offset', 'preference', 'q',
'routing', 'scroll', 'search_type', 'size', 'sort', 'source', 'stats',
'suggest_field', 'suggest_mode', 'suggest_size', 'suggest_text',
'timeout', 'version')
    def search(self, index=None, doc_type=None, body=None,
params=None):
```

The `index` value can be as follows:

- An index name or an alias name
- A list of index (or alias) names as a string separated by comma (that is, `index1,index2,indexN`)
- `_all`: This is the special keyword that indicates all the indexes

The `type` value can be as follows:

- A type name
- A list of type names as a string separated by comma (that is, `type1,type2,typeN`)
- `None`: This is used to indicate all the types

The body is the Search DSL as we have seen in *Chapter 5, Search, Queries, and Filters*. In the preceding example we have:

- A `match_all` query (refer to the *Matching all the documents* recipe of *Chapter 5, Search, Queries, and Filters*) to match all the index type documents, looks as follows:
  ```
  results = es.search(index_name, type_name, {"query":{"match_all":
  {}}})
  ```

- A `term` query that matches a name term `joe` with `boost` of `3.0` (for further details, refer to the *Querying/filtering for term* recipe in *Chapter 5, Search, Queries, and Filters*) looks as follows:
  ```
  results = es.search(index_name, type_name, {
      "query": {
          "query": {
              "term": {"name": {"boost": 3.0, "value": "joe"}}
          }
  }})
  ```

Python Integration

- A `filtered` query between a query (`match_all`) and an `or` filter between two term filters matching positions 1 and 2 looks as follows:

```
results = es.search(index_name, type_name, {"query": {
    "filtered": {
        "filter": {
            "or": [
                {"term": {"position": 1}},
                {"term": {"position": 2}}]
        },
        "query": {"match_all": {}}}}})
```

The returned result is a JSON dictionary that we analyzed in *Chapter 5, Search, Queries, and Filters*.

If some hits are matched, they are returned in the hits field. The standard number of results returned is 10. To return more results, you need to paginate the results with the `from` and `start` parameters.

In *Chapter 5, Search, Queries, and Filters* there is a definition of all the parameters used in search.

There's more...

By using PyES, you can execute the previous code in a more object-oriented way using query and filter objects. These objects wrap the lower-level code normally used to process a query, generating the JSON and validating it during generation. The previous example can be rewritten in PyES with the following code:

```
...
from.query import *
from pyes.filters import *

results = es.search(index_name, type_name, MatchAllQuery())

print "total:", results.total
for r in results:
    print r

print "first element: ", results[0]
print "slice elements: ", results[1:4]

results = es.search(index_name, type_name, TermQuery("name", "joe", 3), scan=True)

...
```

To have access to query objects, you need to import the `query` and `filters` namespaces as follows:

```
from pyes.query import *
from pyes.filters import *
```

To execute a `MatchAllQuery`, the client method is search with the same parameters of the ElasticSearch's official client. The main difference is that the `body` parameter is mapped as `query` in PyES as follows:

```
results = es.search(index_name, type_name, MatchAllQuery())
```

The PyES search method accepts as query the following values:

- A dictionary as the official client
- A query object or a derived class
- A search object that wraps a query and adds additional functionalities related to search such as highlighting, suggest, facet, and explain

The main difference of the PyES search method from the official ElasticSearch client is that the returned result is a special `ResultSet` object that can be iterated. The `ResultSet` object is a useful helper because of the following reasons:

- It's lazy, so the query is fired only when the results need to be evaluated/iterated.
- It's iterable, so you can traverse all the records automatically fetching new ones when required (otherwise you need to manually manage the pagination). If the size is not defined, you can traverse all the results. If you define the size, you can traverse only through the size of the object.
- It automatically manages scroll and scan queries without thinking to manage the scroller.
- It tries to cache a fetch range, to reduce the server usage.
- It can process extra results manipulation such as automatic conversion from String to date time.

For further details on query/filter objects, I suggest you refer to the online documentation at `http://pythonhosted.org/pyes/`.

See also

- The *Executing a search* recipe in *Chapter 5, Search, Queries, and Filters*
- The *Matching all the documents* recipe in *Chapter 5, Search, Queries, and Filters*
- Refer to the PyES online documentation at `http://pythonhosted.org/pyes/`

Python Integration

Executing a facet search

Searching for results is obviously the main activity of a search engine, thus facet is very important because it often helps to complete the results.

Faceting is executed along the search doing analytics on searched results.

Getting ready

You need a working ElasticSearch cluster and required packages of the *Creating a client* recipe of this chapter.

The code of this recipe is in the `chapter_11/faceting.py` and `chapter_11/faceting_pyes.py` files.

How to do it...

To extend a query with the facet part, you need to define a facet section as we have already seen in *Chapter 6*, *Facets*. In the case of the official ElasticSearch client, you can add the facet DSL to the search dictionary to provide facets. We need to perform the following steps:

1. We need to initialize the client and populate the index as follows:

    ```
    import elasticsearch
    from pprint import pprint

    es = elasticsearch.Elasticsearch()
    index_name = "my_index"
    type_name = "my_type"

    from utils import create_and_add_mapping, populate

    create_and_add_mapping(es, index_name, type_name)
    populate(es, index_name, type_name)
    ```

2. We can execute a search with a `terms` facet as follows:

    ```
    results = es.search(index_name, type_name,
                {
                    "query": {"match_all": {}},
                    "facets": {
                        "tag": {"terms": {"field": "tag",
    "size": 10}}
                    }
                })
    pprint(results)
    ```

3. We can execute a search with a `date_histogram` facet as follows:

```
results = es.search(index_name, type_name,
                    {
                        "query": {"match_all": {}},
                        "facets": {
                            "date_facet": {"date_histogram":
{"field": "date", "interval": "month"}}
                        }
                    })
pprint(results)

es.indices.delete(index_name) \
```

How it works...

As described in *Chapter 6, Facets*, the facets are calculated during search in a distributed way. When you send a query to ElasticSearch with facets defined, it adds a new step in the processing of the query, allowing facet computation.

In the preceding example there were two kinds of facets: the `term` facet and the `date_histogram` facet. The first one is used to count terms and it's often seen in sites that provide lateral filtering on term facets of results such as producers and geographic locations.

```
results = es.search(index_name, type_name,
                    {
                        "query": {"match_all": {}},
                        "facets": {
                            "tag": {"terms": {"field": "tag", "size": 10}}
                        }
                    })
```

The `terms` facet requires a field to count on. The default number of facets for field returned is 10, this value can be changed by defining the `size` parameter.

The second kind of facet calculated is `date_histogram`, which provides hits based on a date time field. This facet requires at least two parameters, the date time field to be used as the source and the interval to be used for computation.

```
results = es.search(index_name, type_name,
                    {
                        "query": {"match_all": {}},
                        "facets": {
                            "date_facet": {"date_histogram": {"field": "date", "interval": "month"}}
                        }
                    })
```

Python Integration

The search results are standard search responses that we have already seen in Chapter 6, *Facets*.

There's more...

The preceding code can be rewritten in PyES in the following way:

```
...
from pyes.query import *

q = MatchAllQuery()
search = q.search()
search.facet.add_term_facet('tag')

results = es.search(index_name, type_name, q)

from pyes.facets import *
q = MatchAllQuery()
q = q.search()
q.facet.add(DateHistogramFacet('date_facet',
    field='date',
    interval='month'))

results = es.search(index_name, type_name, q)
...
```

In this case the code is much more readable. Similar to queries and filters classes, PyES provides facet objects that are available in the `pyes.facets` namespace.

Because facet is a search property and not a query (remember that queries can be used also for delete and count calls), we need to define the facet in a `Search` object.

Every query can be converted in a `Search` object using the `.search()` method as follows:

```
q = MatchAllQuery()
search = q.search()
```

The `Search` object provides the following helpers to improve the search experience:

- `FacetFactory`: This helper is accessible via the `facet` property, to easily build facets
- `Highlighter`: This helper is accessible via the `highlight` property, to easily build highlight fields
- `Sorted`: This helper is accessible via the `sort` property, to add sorts field to search
- `ScriptFields`: This helper is accessible via the `script_fields` property, to add script fields

Chapter 11

The `FacetFactory` is a helper to easily define the following types of facets:

- `add_term_facet`: This defines a term facet. For example in the preceding code we have used the `add_term_facet`.
- `search.facet.add_term_facet('tag')`
- `add_date_facet`: This defines a `date_histogram` facet.
- `add_geo_facet`: This defines a `geo_distance` facet.
- `add`: This allows to add every facet object to the facet definition as follows:

    ```
    q.facet.add(DateHistogramFacet('date_facet',
        field='date',
        interval='month'))
    ```

After having executed the query, in the `ResultSet` object there is the calculated facet contained in the `facets` field (that is, `results.facets`).

> The `ResultSet` object also provides an additional method `fix_facets` that, if called, converts the entries in `date_histogram` to date time objects. Generally, the entries in `date_histogram` are returned as integer values and must be converted to datetime objects to be easily used and displayed.

See also

- The *Executing terms facets* in *Chapter 6, Facets*
- The *Executing statistical facets* recipe in *Chapter 6, Facets*

12
Plugin Development

In this chapter, we will cover the following topics::

- Creating a site plugin
- Creating a simple plugin
- Creating a REST plugin
- Creating a cluster action
- Creating an analyzer plugin
- Creating a river plugin

Introduction

ElasticSearch is designed to be extended with plugins to improve its capabilities. In the previous chapters, we installed and used a lot of them (Transport, River, and Scripting plugins).

The plugins are application extensions that can cover a lot of aspects of ElasticSearch. They can have the following usages:

- Adding new transport layer (thrift and memcached plugins are examples of this type)
- Adding new language scripting (that is, Python and JavaScript plugins)
- Extending Lucene supported analyzers and tokenizers
- Using the native scripting for speeding up computation of scores, filters, and field manipulations
- Extending node capabilities, for example, creating a Node plugin that can execute your logic
- Adding a new river to support new sources
- Monitoring and administering the cluster

Plugin Development

ElasticSearch plugins are of two different kinds: site and jar plugins.

The site plugin is generally a standard HTML5 web application. The jar-native one is a standard Java JAR file with some extra resources to define the plugin entry point.

In this chapter, the Java language will be used for the JAR developing a plugin, but it is possible to use any JVM language that generates the JAR files.

Creating a site plugin

The site plugins do not add internal functionalities to ElasticSearch. They mainly are HTML web applications that work at the top of ElasticSearch. They generally provide high-level functionalities such as monitoring and administration. In *Chapter 9*, *Cluster and Nodes Monitoring* we already saw several kinds of site plugin: ElasticSearch-head and BigDesk.

Getting ready

You need a working ElasticSearch node, a web browser, and your preferred HTML editor.

How to do it...

For creating a site plugin, we need to perform the following steps:

1. The site plugin is one of the easiest ones to develop. It is mainly a standard web application composed by only HTML, JavaScript, and images. The easiest one is composed by the following `index.html` page:

   ```
   <!DOCTYPE html>
   <html>
     <head>
       <title>Simle site plugin</title>
       <meta name="viewport" content="width=device-width, initial-scale=1.0">
         <link href="http://netdna.bootstrapcdn.com/twitter-bootstrap/2.3.0/css/bootstrap-combined.min.css" rel="stylesheet">
     </head>
     <body>
       <h1>Hello, from the site plugin!</h1>

       <script src="http://code.jquery.com/jquery.js"></script>
       <script src="http://netdna.bootstrapcdn.com/twitter-bootstrap/2.3.0/js/bootstrap.min.js"></script>
     </body>
   </html>
   ```

2. The HTML file and the resources must be placed in the `_site` directory under the `plugin` one.

Chapter 12

How it works...

When ElasticSearch starts, it analyzes the plugin directory. If a `_site` directory is present in the `plugin` folder, it loads the plugin as the first site; otherwise the plugin is considered native.

The site plugin contains static contents. When the browser is pointed to the server address of the plugin (that is, `http://localhost:9200/_plugins/<plugin_name>/`), ElasticSearch serves the resources as traditional web applications. It generally searches for an `index.html` file and serves it and its related resources.

> While writing a plugin to prevent error in resource loading (that is, images, JavaScript, and CSS), every resource must be relative to the `index.html` file or have an absolute URL.

You need to pay attention to the plugin URLs that must be relative to `index.html`.

The site plugins work very well to package small web applications that execute the following focused tasks:

- Information display such as status, data aggregation, and quick view of some important aspects of your ElasticSearch cluster or indices.
- Administration, sending commands via a web interface is easier than via CURL commands or programming API. A user can aggregate his administrative pipeline (index creation, data manipulation, custom commands) and use it to manage his custom data.

> To easily develop your plugin, I suggest you to develop it outside ElasticSearch and pack it in a ZIP file for delivery.

The site plugins allow using every HTML5 web application framework available for client site development. It's quite normal that the current available site plugins use different JavaScript framework such as: jQuery (+ Bootstrap), Angular.js, and ember.js.

There's more...

Many of the interfaces used to manage an ElasticSearch cluster are generally developed as site plugins. The most famous ones are as follows:

- The BigDesk plugin
- The ElasticSearch-head plugin
- ElasticSearch HQ

We have already seen a lot of them in *Chapter 9, Cluster and Nodes Monitoring*

Plugin Development

See also

- Refer to the ElasticSearch plugin page at `http://www.elasticsearch.org/guide/en/elasticsearch/reference/current/modules-plugins.html#_plugins`

Creating a simple plugin

In the previous recipe we saw the site plugin, but ElasticSearch allows creating a most powerful type of plugin, the native JAR ones.

Native plugins allow extending several aspects of the ElasticSearch server, but they require good Java knowledge. Because they are compiled in native JVM, they are generally very fast.

In this recipe we will see how to set up a system to develop native plugins.

Getting ready

You need a working ElasticSearch node, a Maven built tool, and an optional Java IDE. The code of this recipe is available in the `chapter12/simple_plugin` directory.

How to do it...

Generally ElasticSearch plugins are developed in Java using the Maven built tool and deployed as a ZIP file.

For creating a simple JAR plugin, we need to perform the following steps:

1. To correctly build and serve a plugin, the following files must be defined:
   - `pom.xml`: This is used to define the build configuration for Maven.
   - `es-plugin.properties`: This defines the namespace of the plugin class that must be loaded.
   - `<name>Plugin.java`: This is the main plugin class, which is loaded at start up and initializes the plugin actions.
   - `plugin.xml`: These are the assemblies that define how to execute the assembly steps of Maven. It is used to build the ZIP file to deliver the plugin.

2. A standard `pom.xml` file for creating a plugin contains the following code:

   ❑ The `maven pom.xml` header is as follows:

   ```
   <?xml version="1.0" encoding="UTF-8"?>
   <project xmlns="http://maven.apache.org/POM/4.0.0"
           xmlns:xsi="http://www.w3.org/2001/XMLSchema-instance"
           xsi:schemaLocation="http://maven.apache.org/POM/4.0.0
   http://maven.apache.org/xsd/maven-4.0.0.xsd">
       <name>elasticsearch-simple-plugin</name>
       <modelVersion>4.0.0</modelVersion>
       <groupId>com.packtpub</groupId>
       <artifactId>simple-plugin</artifactId>
       <version>0.0.1-SNAPSHOT</version>
       <packaging>jar</packaging>
       <description>A simple plugin for ElasticSearch</description>
       <inceptionYear>2013</inceptionYear>
       <licenses>…   </licenses>
   ```

   ❑ The `parent pom.xml` file used to derive common properties or settings is as follows:

   ```
   <parent>
       <groupId>org.sonatype.oss</groupId>
       <artifactId>oss-parent</artifactId>
       <version>7</version>
   </parent>
   ```

   ❑ Some properties mainly used to simplify the dependencies are defined as follows:

   ```
   <properties>
       <elasticsearch.version>0.90.5</elasticsearch.version>
   </properties>
   ```

   ❑ A list of jar dependencies is as follows:

   ```
   <dependencies>
       <dependency>
           <groupId>org.elasticsearch</groupId>
           <artifactId>elasticsearch</artifactId>
           <version>${elasticsearch.version}</version>
           <scope>compile</scope>
       </dependency>

       <dependency>
           <groupId>log4j</groupId>
           <artifactId>log4j</artifactId>
   ```

Plugin Development

```xml
            <version>1.2.17</version>
            <scope>runtime</scope>
        </dependency>
        <!--test dependencies -->
</dependencies>
```

- A list of Maven plugins required to build and deploy the artifact is as follows:

```xml
<build>
    <plugins>
        <plugin>
            <groupId>org.apache.maven.plugins</groupId>
            <artifactId>maven-compiler-plugin</artifactId>
            <version>2.3.2</version>
            <configuration>
                <source>1.6</source>
                <target>1.6</target>
            </configuration>
        </plugin>
        <plugin>
            <groupId>org.apache.maven.plugins</groupId>
            <artifactId>maven-surefire-plugin</artifactId>
            <version>2.12.3</version>
            <configuration>
                <includes>
                    <include>**/*Tests.java</include>
                </includes>
            </configuration>
        </plugin>
        <plugin>
            <groupId>org.apache.maven.plugins</groupId>
            <artifactId>maven-source-plugin</artifactId>
            <version>2.1.2</version>
            <executions>
                <execution>
                    <id>attach-sources</id>
                    <goals>
                        <goal>jar</goal>
                    </goals>
                </execution>
            </executions>
        </plugin>
        <plugin>
            <artifactId>maven-assembly-plugin</artifactId>
            <version>2.3</version>
```

```xml
            <configuration>
                <appendAssemblyId>false</appendAssemblyId>
<outputDirectory>${project.build.directory}/releases/</outputDirectory>
                <descriptors>
<descriptor>${basedir}/src/main/assemblies/plugin.xml</descriptor>
                </descriptors>
            </configuration>
            <executions>
                <execution>
                    <phase>package</phase>
                    <goals><goal>single</goal></goals>
                </execution>
            </executions>
        </plugin>
     </plugins>
  </build>
</project>
```

3. In the JAR file, there must be an `es-plugin.properties` file, which defines the entry point class that must be loaded during plugin initialization. It generally contains a single line of code. For example:

   ```
   plugin=org.elasticsearch.plugin.simple.SimplePlugin
   ```

4. The `SimplePlugin.java` class is an example of the base minimum required code to be compiled for executing a plugin and its definition is as follows:

   ```java
   package org.elasticsearch.plugin.simple;
   import org.elasticsearch.plugins.AbstractPlugin;
   public class SimplePlugin extends AbstractPlugin {

       @Override
       public String name() {
           return "simple-plugin";
       }

       @Override
       public String description() {
           return "A simple plugin implementation";
       }
   }
   ```

Plugin Development

5. To complete the compile and deploy workflow, we need to define a `plugin.xml` file used in Maven assembly step as follows:

```xml
<?xml version="1.0"?>
<assembly>
    <id>plugin</id>
    <formats>
        <format>zip</format>
    </formats>
    <includeBaseDirectory>false</includeBaseDirectory>
    <dependencySets>
        <dependencySet>
            <outputDirectory>/</outputDirectory>
            <useProjectArtifact>true</useProjectArtifact>
<useTransitiveFiltering>true</useTransitiveFiltering>
            <excludes>
<exclude>org.elasticsearch:elasticsearch</exclude>
            </excludes>
        </dependencySet>
        <dependencySet>
            <outputDirectory>/</outputDirectory>
            <useProjectArtifact>true</useProjectArtifact>
          <useTransitiveFiltering>true</useTransitiveFiltering>
            <includes></includes>
        </dependencySet>
    </dependencySets>
</assembly>
```

This file defines the resources that must be packaged into the final ZIP archive.

How it works...

Several parts compose the development lifecycle of a plugin, such as designing, coding, building, and deploying. To speed up the building and deploying parts, which are always common to every plugin, we need to create a Maven `pom.xml` file.

The preceding `pom.xml` file is a standard one to develop ElasticSearch plugins.
This file is composed by:

- Several section entries used to set up the current Maven project. In detail, we have:
    - The name of the plugin (that is, `elasticsearch-simple-plugin`)

    `<name>elasticsearch-simple-plugin</name>`

- The `groupId` and `artifactId` tags are used to define the plugin artifact name as follows:

```
<groupId>com.packtpub</groupId>
<artifactId>simple-plugin</artifactId>
```

- The plugin version using the `version` tag:

```
<version>0.0.1-SNAPSHOT</version>
```

- The type of packaging using the `packaging` tag:

```
<packaging>jar</packaging>
```

- A project description with the starting year as follows:

```
<description>A simple plugin for ElasticSearch</description>
<inceptionYear>2013</inceptionYear>
```

▶ An optional license section, in which we can define the license for the plugin. For the standard Apache one, the code should look as follows:

```
<licenses>
    <license>
        <name>The Apache Software License, Version 2.0</name>
        <url>http://www.apache.org/licenses/LICENSE-2.0.txt</url>
        <distribution>repo</distribution>
    </license>
</licenses>
```

▶ A parent pom is used to inherit common properties. Generally for plugins, it is useful to inherit from Sonatype base pom.

```
<parent>
    <groupId>org.sonatype.oss</groupId>
    <artifactId>oss-parent</artifactId>
    <version>7</version>
</parent>
```

▶ Global variables set for all the builds. Typically in this section the ElasticSearch version and other library versions are set as follows:

```
<properties>
    <elasticsearch.version>0.90.5</elasticsearch.version>
</properties>\
```

It is very important that the Elasticsearch JAR version matches the ElasticSearch cluster one to prevent issues due to changes between releases.

Plugin Development

- For compiling a plugin, the ElasticSearch JAR and the `log4j` library, and the list of dependencies are required in the compiling phase:

```xml
<dependency>
    <groupId>org.elasticsearch</groupId>
    <artifactId>elasticsearch</artifactId>
    <version>${elasticsearch.version}</version>
    <scope>compile</scope>
</dependency>
<dependency>
    <groupId>log4j</groupId>
    <artifactId>log4j</artifactId>
    <version>1.2.17</version>
    <scope>runtime</scope>
</dependency>
```

- The Maven plugin section contains a list of Maven plugins that executes several build steps. We have:

    - The compiler section, which requires a source compilation. The Java version is fixed to 1.6.

```xml
<plugin>
    <groupId>org.apache.maven.plugins</groupId>
    <artifactId>maven-compiler-plugin</artifactId>
    <version>2.3.2</version>
    <configuration>
        <source>1.6</source>
        <target>1.6</target>
    </configuration>
</plugin>
```

    - The source section, which enables the creation of source packages to be released with the binary (useful for debugging) is as follows:

```xml
<plugin>
    <groupId>org.apache.maven.plugins</groupId>
    <artifactId>maven-source-plugin</artifactId>
    <version>2.1.2</version>
    <executions>
        <execution>
            <id>attach-sources</id>
            <goals>
                <goal>jar</goal>
            </goals>
        </execution>
    </executions>
</plugin>
```

- The assembly section, which builds a ZIP file taking a configuration file (`plugin.xml`) and inserting the output in the releases directory is as follows:

```xml
<plugin>
    <artifactId>maven-assembly-plugin</artifactId>
    <version>2.3</version>
    <configuration>
        <appendAssemblyId>false</appendAssemblyId>
<outputDirectory>${project.build.directory}/releases/</outputDirectory>
        <descriptors>
<descriptor>${basedir}/src/main/assemblies/plugin.xml</descriptor>
        </descriptors>
    </configuration>
    <executions>
        <execution>
            <phase>package</phase>
            <goals><goal>single</goal></goals>
        </execution>
    </executions>
</plugin>
```

Related to `pom.xml`, we have the `plugin.xml` file, which describes how to assemble the final ZIP file. This file is usually contained in the `/src/main/assemblies/` directory of the project.

The most important sections of this file are as follows:

- `formats`: In this section the destination format is defined as follows

  ```xml
  <formats><format>zip</format></formats>
  ```

- `excludes sets` in `dependencySet`: This contains the artifacts to be excluded from the package. Generally, we exclude ElasticSearch JAR as it is already provided in the server install.

  ```xml
  <dependencySet>
      <outputDirectory>/</outputDirectory>
      <useProjectArtifact>true</useProjectArtifact>
      <useTransitiveFiltering>true</useTransitiveFiltering>
      <excludes>
          <exclude>org.elasticsearch:elasticsearch</exclude>
      </excludes>
  </dependencySet>
  ```

Plugin Development

- `includes` sets in `dependencySet`: This contains the artifacts to be included into the package. They are mainly the required JARs to run the plugin.

```xml
<dependencySet>
    <outputDirectory>/</outputDirectory>
    <useProjectArtifact>true</useProjectArtifact>
    <useTransitiveFiltering>true</useTransitiveFiltering>
    <includes>...</includes>
</dependencySet>
```

While packaging the plugin, the include and exclude rules are verified and only the files that are allowed to be distributed are put in the ZIP file.

After having configured Maven, we can start to write the main plugin class.

Every plugin class must be derived by the `AbstractPlugin` one and it must be `public` otherwise it cannot be loaded dynamically from the JAR.

```java
import org.elasticsearch.plugins.AbstractPlugin;
public class SimplePlugin extends AbstractPlugin {
```

The `AbstractPlugin` class needs the two methods to be defined: the `name` and `description`.

The `name` method must return a string and it's usually a short name. This value is shown in the plugin loading log as follows:

```java
@Override
public String name() {
    return "simple-plugin";
}
```

The `description` method must return a string too. It is mainly a long description of the plugin.

```java
@Override
public String description() {
    return "A simple plugin implementation";
}
```

After defining all the required files, to generate a ZIP release of our plugin it is enough to invoke the `maven package` command. This command will compile the code and create a ZIP package in the `target/releases` directory of your project.

In this recipe we have configured a working environment to build, deploy, and test plugins. In the next recipes we will re-use this environment to develop several plugin types.

There's more...

Compiling and packaging the plugin is not enough to define a good lifecycle for your plugin, you need to add a test phase.

Testing the plugin functionalities with test cases reduces the number of bugs that can affect the plugin when released.

It's possible to add a test phase in Maven build `pom.xml`.

The ElasticSearch community mainly uses the testNG (http://testng.org/) and the hamcrest (https://code.google.com/p/hamcrest/) libraries. To use them you need to add their dependencies in the `dependency` section of the `pom.xml` file:

```xml
<dependency>
    <groupId>org.testng</groupId>
    <artifactId>testng</artifactId>
    <version>6.8</version>
    <scope>test</scope>
    <exclusions>
        <exclusion>
            <groupId>org.hamcrest</groupId>
            <artifactId>hamcrest-core</artifactId>
        </exclusion>
        <exclusion>
            <groupId>junit</groupId>
            <artifactId>junit</artifactId>
        </exclusion>
    </exclusions>
</dependency>
<dependency>
    <groupId>org.hamcrest</groupId>
    <artifactId>hamcrest-all</artifactId>
    <version>1.3</version>
    <scope>test</scope>
</dependency>
```

These dependencies are not standard, because they are tuned to exclude some unwanted packages. Note that the compiling scope is `test`, which means that these dependencies are only considered during the test phase.

Plugin Development

To complete the `test` part, a Maven plugin which executes the tests, must be defined as follows:

```
<plugin>
    <groupId>org.apache.maven.plugins</groupId>
    <artifactId>maven-surefire-plugin</artifactId>
    <version>2.12.3</version>
    <configuration>
        <includes><include>**/*Tests.java</include></includes>
    </configuration>
</plugin>
```

The include section lists all the possible classes that contains test via glob expression.

Creating a REST plugin

The previous recipe described how to set up an environment and the steps required to build a simple plugins. In this recipe, we will see how to create one of the most common ElasticSearch plugin, the REST one.

These kinds of plugins allow extending the standard REST calls with custom ones to easily improve the capabilities of ElasticSearch.

In this recipe we will see how to define a REST entry point and in the next one how to execute this action distributed in shards.

Getting ready

You need a working ElasticSearch node, a maven built tool, and an optional Java IDE. The code of this recipe is available in the `chapter12/rest_plugin` directory.

How to do it...

To create a REST entry point, we need to create the action and then register it in the plugin. We need to perform the following steps:

1. We create a REST "simple" action (`RestSimpleAction.java`):

    ```
    ...
    public class RestSimpleAction extends BaseRestHandler {
        @Inject
        public RestSimpleAction(Settings settings, Client client,
    RestController controller) {
            super(settings, client);
    ```

```java
            controller.registerHandler(POST, "/_simple", this);
            controller.registerHandler(POST, "/{index}/_simple", 
this);
            controller.registerHandler(POST, "/_simple/{field}", 
this);
            controller.registerHandler(GET, "/_simple", this);
            controller.registerHandler(GET, "/{index}/_simple", this);
            controller.registerHandler(GET, "/_simple/{field}", this);
    }
    @Override
    public void handleRequest(final RestRequest request, final 
RestChannel channel) {
        final SimpleRequest simpleRequest = new 
SimpleRequest(Strings.splitStringByCommaToArray(request.
param("index")));
        simpleRequest.setField(request.param("field"));
        client.execute(SimpleAction.INSTANCE, simpleRequest, new 
ActionListener<SimpleResponse>() {

            @Override
            public void onResponse(SimpleResponse response) {
                try {
                    XContentBuilder builder = RestXContentBuilder.
restContentBuilder(request);
                    builder.startObject();
                    builder.field("ok", true);
                    buildBroadcastShardsHeader(builder, response);
                    builder.array("terms", response.getSimple().
toArray());
                    builder.endObject();
                    channel.sendResponse(new 
XContentRestResponse(request, OK, builder));
                } catch (Exception e) {
                    onFailure(e);
                }
            }

            @Override
            public void onFailure(Throwable e) {
                try {
                    channel.sendResponse(new XContentThrowableRest
Response(request, e));
                } catch (IOException e1) {
                    logger.error("Failed to send failure 
response", e1);
```

Plugin Development

```
                    }
                }
            });
        }
    }
```

2. And we need to register it in the plugin with the following lines:

```
public class RestPlugin extends AbstractPlugin {

    @Override
    public String name() {
        return "simple-plugin";
    }

    @Override
    public String description() {
        return "A simple plugin implementation";
    }

    public void onModule(RestModule module) {
        module.addRestAction(RestSimpleAction.class);
    }
}
```

How it works...

Adding a REST action is very easy, we need to create a `RestXXXAction` class that answers to the calls.

The REST action is derived from the `BaseRestHandler` class and needs to implement the `handleRequest` method.

The constructor is very important and is defined as follows:

```
@Inject
public RestSimpleAction(Settings settings, Client client,
RestController controller)
```

Its signature usually injects via Guice (a lightweight dependency injection framework very common in the Java ecosystem. Refer to the library home page for more details at https://code.google.com/p/google-guice/) for the following parameters:

▶ `Settings`: This parameter can be used to load custom settings for your REST action

- **Client**: This parameter will be used to communicate with the cluster (refer to *Chapter 10, Java Integration*)
- **RestController**: This parameter is used to register the REST action to the controller

In the constructor of the REST action, the list of actions that must be revolved are registered in the `RestController` as follows:

```
controller.registerHandler(POST, "/_simple", this);
...
```

To register an action, the following parameters must be passed to the controller:

- The REST method (GET/POST/PUT/DELETE/HEAD/OPTIONS)
- The URL entry point
- The `RestHandler` class, usually the same class, which must answer the call

After having defined the constructor, if an action is fired, the class method `handleRequest` is called as follows:

```
@Override
    public void handleRequest(final RestRequest request, final RestChannel channel) {
```

This method is the core of the REST action. It processes the request and sends back the result. The parameters passed to the method are as follows:

- **RestRequest**: This is the REST request that hits the ElasticSearch server
- **RestChannel**: This is the channel used to send back the response

A `handleRequest` method is usually composed by the following phases:

- Process the REST request and build an inner ElasticSearch request object
- Call the client with the ElasticSearch request
- If it is OK, process the ElasticSearch response and build the result JSON
- If there are errors, send back the JSON error response

In the preceding example we have created a `SimpleResponse` processing the request as follows:

```
final SimpleRequest simpleRequest = new SimpleRequest(Strings.splitStringByCommaToArray(request.param("index")));
simpleRequest.setField(request.param("field"));
```

We will discuss the `SimpleRequest` class in the next recipe.

Plugin Development

It accepts a list of indices (we split the classic comma-separated list of indices via the `Strings.splitStringByCommaToArray` helper) and we add the `field` parameter if available.

Now that we have `SimpleRequest`, we can send it to the cluster and get back a `SimpleResponse` as follows:

```
client.execute(SimpleAction.INSTANCE, simpleRequest, new ActionListener<SimpleResponse>() {
```

The `client.execute` method accepts an action, a request, and an `ActionListener` class that maps a future response. We can have the following kinds of responses:

- `onResponse`: This is the response if everything is all right
- `onFailure`: This is the response if something goes wrong

The `onFailure` method is usually the propagation of the error via REST:

```
@Override
public void onFailure(Throwable e) {
    try {
        channel.sendResponse(new XContentThrowableRestResponse(request, e));
    } catch (IOException e1) {
        logger.error("Failed to send failure response", e1);
    }
}
```

The `onResponse` receives a `Response` object that must be converted in a JSON result as follows:

```
@Override public void onResponse(SimpleResponse response)
```

To build the JSON response, a builder helper is used, that is inferred by the request as follows:

```
XContentBuilder builder = RestXContentBuilder.restContentBuilder(request);
```

The builder is a standard JSON `XContentBuilder` class that we have already seen in *Chapter 10, Java Integration*

After having processed the cluster response and built the JSON response, it can be sent via `channel` as follows:

```
channel.sendResponse(new XContentRestResponse(request, OK, builder));
```

Obviously if something goes wrong during JSON creation, an exception must be raised as follows:

```
try {/* JSON building*/
} catch (Exception e) {
    onFailure(e);
}
```

There's more...

To test the plugin, you can compile it and assembly with an `mvn` package.

Then you need to deploy the unzipped resulted file in an ElasticSearch server in the `plugins` directory.

After having restarted the server, the name of the plugin should pop up in the list of installed ones as follows:

```
[…] [INFO ] [node    ] [Amalgam] initializing ...
[…] [INFO ] [plugins ] [Amalgam] loaded [river-twitter, transport-thrift, jdbc-river, rest-plugin], sites [HQ]
```

If everything is all right, we can test it as follows:

```
curl -XPOST http://127.0.0.1:9200/_simple
```

And the response will be as follows:

```
{"ok":true,"_shards":{"total":15,"successful":15,"failed":0},"terms":["null_4","null_1","null_0","null_3","null_2"]}
```

Or:

```
curl -XPOST http://127.0.0.1:9200/_simple/goofy
```

And the response will be as follows:

```
{"ok":true,"_shards":{"total":15,"successful":15,"failed":0},"terms":["goofy_1","goofy_2","goofy_3","goofy_4","goofy_0"]}
```

To fully understand the response, the next recipe will show you how the action is executed at cluster level.

See also

- Refer to Google Guice used for dependency injection at https://code.google.com/p/google-guice/

Plugin Development

Creating a cluster action

In the previous recipe, we saw how to create a REST entry point, but to execute the action at cluster level we need to create a cluster action.

An ElasticSearch action is generally executed and distributed in the cluster and in this recipe, we will see how to implement these kinds of actions. The cluster action will be very bare, we will be sending a string with a value for every shard and these strings echo a result string concatenating the string with the shard number.

Getting ready

You need a working ElasticSearch node, a Maven built tool, and an optional Java IDE. The code of this recipe is available in the `chapter12/rest_plugin` directory.

How to do it...

In this recipe, we have seen that a REST call is converted to an internal cluster action.

To execute an internal cluster action, the following classes are required:

- A `Request` and `Response` class to communicate with the cluster.
- A `RequestBuilder` class used to execute a request to the cluster.
- An `Action` class used to register the "action" and bound `Request`, `Response`, and `RequestBuilder`.
- A `Transport*Action` to bind request and response to `ShardRequest` and `ShardResponse`. It manages the "reduce" part of the query.
- A `ShardRequest` and a `ShardResponse` class to manage shard query.

We need to perform the following steps:

1. We need to write a SimpleRequest class as follows:

    ```
    ...
    public class SimpleRequest extends BroadcastOperationRequest<Simpl
    eRequest> {
      private String field;

        SimpleRequest() {}

        public SimpleRequest(String... indices) {
            super(indices);
            operationThreading(BroadcastOperationThreading.THREAD_PER_SHARD);
    ```

```
        }
        public void setField(String field) {this.field = field; }
        public String getField() {return field; }

        @Override
         public void readFrom(StreamInput in) throws IOException {
            super.readFrom(in);
            field = in.readString();
          }

        @Override
         public void writeTo(StreamOutput out) throws IOException {
            super.writeTo(out);
            out.writeString(field);
          }
    }
```

The `SimpleResponse` class is very similar to the `SimpleRequest` class.

2. To bind the request and the response, an action (`SimpleAction`) is required:

```
...
public class SimpleAction extends Action<SimpleRequest,
SimpleResponse, SimpleRequestBuilder> {

      public static final SimpleAction INSTANCE = new
SimpleAction();
      public static final String NAME = "indices/simple";

      private SimpleAction() {
          super(NAME);
      }

      @Override
      public SimpleResponse newResponse() {
          return new SimpleResponse();
      }

      @Override
      public SimpleRequestBuilder newRequestBuilder(Client client) {
          return new SimpleRequestBuilder((InternalGenericClient)
client);
      }
}
```

Plugin Development

3. The `Transport` class is the core of the action. It's quite long so we present only the main important parts.

```
public class TransportSimpleAction extends TransportBroadcastOpe
rationAction<SimpleRequest, SimpleResponse, ShardSimpleRequest,
ShardSimpleResponse> {

...

    @Override
    protected SimpleResponse newResponse(SimpleRequest request,
AtomicReferenceArray shardsResponses, ClusterState clusterState) {
        int successfulShards = 0;
        int failedShards = 0;
        List<ShardOperationFailedException> shardFailures = null;
        Set<String> simple = new HashSet<String>();
        for (int i = 0; i < shardsResponses.length(); i++) {
            Object shardResponse = shardsResponses.get(i);
            if (shardResponse == null) {
                // a non active shard, ignore...
            } else if (shardResponse instanceof
BroadcastShardOperationFailedException) {
                failedShards++;
                if (shardFailures == null) {
                    shardFailures = newArrayList();
                }
                shardFailures.add(new
DefaultShardOperationFailedException
((BroadcastShardOperationFailedException) shardResponse));
            } else {
                successfulShards++;
                if (shardResponse instanceof ShardSimpleResponse)
{
                    ShardSimpleResponse resp =
(ShardSimpleResponse) shardResponse;
                    simple.addAll(resp.getTermList());
                }
            }
        }
        return new SimpleResponse(shardsResponses.length(),
successfulShards, failedShards, shardFailures, simple);
    }

...
```

```
        @Override
        protected ShardSimpleResponse shardOperation(ShardSimpleReque
st request) throws ElasticSearchException {
            synchronized (simpleMutex) {
                InternalIndexShard indexShard = (InternalIndexShard)
indicesService.indexServiceSafe(request.index()).
shardSafe(request.shardId());
                indexShard.store().directory();
                Set<String> set = new HashSet<String>();
                set.add(request.getField() + "_" + request.shardId());
                return new ShardSimpleResponse(request.index(),
request.shardId(), set);
            }
        }
    ...
```

How it works...

As you have seen previously for executing a cluster action the following classes are required:

- A couple of `Request/Response` classes to interact with the cluster
- A task action to cluster level
- A couple of `Request/Response` classes to interact with the shards
- A `Transport` class to manage the map or reduce the shard part that must be invocated by the REST call

These classes must extend one of the supported kinds of action available:

- `BroadcastOperationRequest/Response`: These are used for actions that must be spread across all the clusters
- `MasterNodeOperationRequest`: These are used for actions that must host only the master node (such as index and mapping configuration)
- `NodeOperationRequest`: These are used for actions that must be executed by every node (that is, all the node statistic actions)
- `IndexReplicationOperationRequest`: These are used for actions that must be executed at index level (that is, delete by query)
- `SingleCustomOperationRequest`: These are used for actions that must be executed only by a node (that is, percolate or analyze actions)
- `InstanceShardOperationRequest`: These are used for actions that must be executed on every shard instance (that is, bulk shard operations)
- `SingleShardOperationRequest`: These are used for actions that must be executed only in a shard (that is, the GET action)

Plugin Development

In our example, we have defined an action that will be broadcast to every shard as follows:

```
public class SimpleRequest extends BroadcastOperationRequest<SimpleRequest>
```

All the `Request/Response` classes extend a `Streamable` class, so the two following methods for serializing their content must be provided:

- `readFrom`: This reads from `StreamInput`, a class that encapsulates common input stream operations. This method allows deserializing the data we transmit on the wire. In the preceding example we have read a string, with the following code:

    ```
    @Override
    public void readFrom(StreamInput in) throws IOException {
        super.readFrom(in);
        field = in.readString();
    }
    ```

- `writeTo`: This writes the contents of the class to be sent via network. The `StreamOutput` class provides convenient methods to process the output. In the preceding example, we have serialized a string as follows:

    ```
    @Override
    public void writeTo(StreamOutput out) throws IOException {
        super.writeTo(out);
        out.writeString(field);
    }
    ```

In both the actions, `super` must be called to allow the correct serialization of parent classes.

> Every internal action in ElasticSearch is designed as request/response iteration.

To complete the request/response action, we must define an action that binds the request with the correct response and a builder to construct it. To do so, we need to define an `Action` class as follows:

```
public class SimpleAction extends Action<SimpleRequest,
SimpleResponse, SimpleRequestBuilder>
```

This `Action` object is a singleton object. We obtain it by creating a default static instance and private constructors:

```
public static final SimpleAction INSTANCE = new SimpleAction();
public static final String NAME = "indices/simple";
private SimpleAction() {super(NAME); }
```

The static string, NAME is used to univocally define the action at cluster level.

To complete the Action definition, the following two methods must be defined:

- newResponse: This is used to create a new empty response as follows:

  ```
  @Override public SimpleResponse newResponse() {
      return new SimpleResponse();
  }
  ```

- newRequestBuilder: This is used to return a new request builder for the current action type as follows:

  ```
  @Override
  public SimpleRequestBuilder newRequestBuilder(Client client) {
      return new SimpleRequestBuilder((InternalGenericClient) client);
  }
  ```

When the action is executed, the request and the response are serialized and sent to the cluster. To execute our custom code at cluster level, a transport action is required.

The transport actions are usually defined as map and reduce jobs. The map part consists of executing the action on several shards (via the ShardRequest and ShardResponse classes) and the reduce part consists of collecting all the results from the shards in a response that must be sent back to the requester.

The transport action is a long class with many methods, but the most important ones are the ShardOperation (map part) and newResponse (reduce part).

The original request is converted into a distributed ShardRequest that is processed by the shardOperation method as follows:

```
@Override protected ShardSimpleResponse shardOperation(ShardSimpleRequest request) throws ElasticSearchException {
```

It is good practice to execute the shard operation using a lock to prevent concurrency problems.

```
synchronized (simpleMutex) {...}
```

To obtain the internal shard, we need to ask at the IndexService class to return a shard based on the wanted index.

The shard request contains the index and the ID of the shard that must be used to execute the action.

```
InternalIndexShard indexShard = (InternalIndexShard) indicesService.indexServiceSafe(request.index()).shardSafe(request.shardId());
```

Plugin Development

The `InternalIndexShard` object allows executing every possible shard operation (search, get, index, and many others). In this method, we can execute every data shard manipulation that we want.

> Custom shard action can execute applicative business operation in a distributed and faster way.

In the preceding example, we have created a simple set of values as follows:

```
Set<String> set = new HashSet<String>();
set.add(request.getField() + "_" + request.shardId());
```

The final step of our shard operation is to create a response to send back to the reduce step. While creating the shard response we need to return the result in addition to the information about the index and the shard that executed the action, as given in the following code:

```
return new ShardSimpleResponse(request.index(), request.shardId(),
    set);
```

The distributed shard operations are collected in the reduce step (the `newResponse` method). In this step, we need to aggregate all the shard results and produce the result to send back to the original `Action`.

```
@Override protected SimpleResponse newResponse(SimpleRequest request,
    AtomicReferenceArray shardsResponses, ClusterState clusterState) {
```

Other than the result, we also need to collect the information about the shard execution (if there are failures on them). This information is usually collected in three values: `successfulShards`, `failedShards`, and `shardFailures`.

```
int successfulShards = 0;
int failedShards = 0;
List<ShardOperationFailedException> shardFailures = null;
```

The request result is a set of collected strings.

```
Set<String> simple = new HashSet<String>();
```

To collect the results, we need to iterate on the shard responses as follows:

```
for (int i = 0; i < shardsResponses.length(); i++) {
    Object shardResponse = shardsResponses.get(i);
```

We need to skip the null `shardResponse`, mainly due to inactive shards.

```
if (shardResponse == null) {}
```

If a failure is raised, we also need to collect them to inform the caller.

```
else if (shardResponse instanceof
BroadcastShardOperationFailedException) {
    failedShards++;
    if (shardFailures == null) {
        shardFailures = newArrayList();
    }
    shardFailures.add(new
DefaultShardOperationFailedException
((BroadcastShardOperationFailedException) shardResponse));
```

We can aggregate the valid results as follows:

```
} else {
    successfulShards++;
     if (shardResponse instanceof ShardSimpleResponse) {
         ShardSimpleResponse resp = (ShardSimpleResponse)
shardResponse;
         simple.addAll(resp.getTermList());
     }
}
```

The final step is to create the response collecting the previous result and response status.

```
return new SimpleResponse(shardsResponses.length(), successfulShards,
failedShards, shardFailures, simple);
```

Creating a cluster action is required when there are low-level operations that we want to execute very quickly, such as special facet or complex manipulation that requires the ElasticSearch call to be executed, but that can be easily written as a cluster action.

See also

- The *Creating a REST plugin* recipe in this chapter

Plugin Development

Creating an analyzer plugin

ElasticSearch provides, out of the box, a large set of analyzers and tokenizers to cover general standard needs. Sometimes we need to extend the capabilities of ElasticSearch adding new analyzers.

Typically you need to create an analyzer plugin when you need to add standard Lucene analyzers/tokenizers not provided by ElasticSearch, to integrate third-party analyzers, and to add custom analyzers.

In this recipe we will add a new custom English analyzer similar to the one provided by ElasticSearch.

Getting ready

You need a working ElasticSearch node, a Maven built tool, and an optional Java IDE. The code of this recipe is available in the `chapter12/analysis_plugin` directory.

How to do it...

An analyzer plugin is generally composed by the following classes:

- A plugin class, which registers `BinderProcessor`
- A `BinderProcessor` class, which registers one or more `AnalyzerProviders` classes
- An `AnalyzerProviders` class, which provides an analyzer

For creating an analyzer plugin, we need to perform the following steps:

1. The plugin class is the same as in the previous recipes, only a binder registration method is added as follows:

    ```
    @Override
    public void processModule(Module module) {
        if (module instanceof AnalysisModule) {
            AnalysisModule analysisModule = (AnalysisModule) module;
            analysisModule.addProcessor(new CustomEnglishBinderProcessor());
        }
    }
    ```

2. The `BinderProcessor` registers in the `AnalysisModule` one or more `AnalyzerProvider` as follows:

   ```
   public class CustomEnglishBinderProcessor extends AnalysisModule.AnalysisBinderProcessor {

       @Override public void processAnalyzers(AnalyzersBindings analyzersBindings) {
           analyzersBindings.processAnalyzer(CustomEnglishAnalyzerProvider.NAME, CustomEnglishAnalyzerProvider.class);
       }
   }
   ```

3. The `AnalyzerProvider` class provides the initialization of our analyzer, passing parameters provided by the settings as follows:

   ```
   import org.apache.lucene.analysis.en.EnglishAnalyzer;
   import org.apache.lucene.analysis.util.CharArraySet;
   import org.elasticsearch.common.inject.Inject;
   import org.elasticsearch.common.inject.assistedinject.Assisted;
   import org.elasticsearch.common.settings.Settings;
   import org.elasticsearch.env.Environment;
   import org.elasticsearch.index.Index;
   import org.elasticsearch.index.settings.IndexSettings;

   public class CustomEnglishAnalyzerProvider extends AbstractIndexAnalyzerProvider<EnglishAnalyzer> {
       public static String NAME="custom_english";

       private final EnglishAnalyzer analyzer;

       @Inject
       public CustomEnglishAnalyzerProvider(Index index, @IndexSettings Settings indexSettings, Environment env, @Assisted String name, @Assisted Settings settings) {
           super(index, indexSettings, name, settings);
           analyzer = new EnglishAnalyzer(version,
                   Analysis.parseStopWords(env, settings, EnglishAnalyzer.getDefaultStopSet(), version),
                   Analysis.parseStemExclusion(settings, CharArraySet.EMPTY_SET, version));
       }

       @Override
       public EnglishAnalyzer get() {
           return this.analyzer;
       }
   }
   ```

After having built the plugin and installed it an ElasticSearch server, our analyzer is accessible as every native ElasticSearch analyzer.

How it works...

Creating an analyzer plugin is quite simple. The general workflow is as follows:

- Wrap the analyzer initialization in a provider
- Register the analyzer provider in the binder so that the analyzer is accessible to the `AnalysisModule` level
- Register the binder in the plugin

In the preceding example, we have registered a `CustomEnglishAnalyzerProvider`, which extends the `EnglishAnalyzer`.

```
public class CustomEnglishAnalyzerProvider extends AbstractIndexAnalyzerProvider<EnglishAnalyzer>
```

We need to provide a name to the analyzer by using the following code:

```
public static String NAME="custom_english";
```

We instantiate an inner analyzer to be provided on request with the GET method as follows:

```
    private final EnglishAnalyzer analyzer;
```

The `CustomEnglishAnalyzerProvider` constructor can be injected via Google Guice with settings that can be used to provide cluster defaults, via index settings or `elasticsearch.yml`.

```
    @Inject
    public CustomEnglishAnalyzerProvider(Index index, @IndexSettings
    Settings indexSettings, Environment env, @Assisted String name, @
    Assisted Settings settings) {
```

To correctly work, we need to set up the parent constructor via the `super` call as follows:

```
super(index, indexSettings, name, settings);
```

Now, we can initialize the internal analyzer that must be returned by the GET method as follows:

```
analyzer = new EnglishAnalyzer(version, Analysis.parseStopWords(env,
settings, EnglishAnalyzer.getDefaultStopSet(), version),
        Analysis.parseStemExclusion(settings, CharArraySet.EMPTY_
SET, version));
```

This analyzer accepts:

- The Lucene version
- A list of stopwords that can be loaded by settings or set by the default ones

▶ A list of words that must be excluded by the stemming step

After having created a provider for our analyzer, we need to create another class `CustomEnglishBinderProcessor`, which registers our provider in `AnalysisModule`.

```
public class CustomEnglishBinderProcessor extends AnalysisModule.AnalysisBinderProcessor {
```

To register our analyzer in the binder, we need to override the `processAnalyzers` method and add our analyzer defining the name (used to be referred in the REST calls) and the class of our provider.

```
@Override public void processAnalyzers(AnalyzersBindings analyzersBindings) {
        analyzersBindings.processAnalyzer(CustomEnglishAnalyzerProvider.NAME, CustomEnglishAnalyzerProvider.class);
    }
}
```

Finally we need to register our binding in the plugin hooking with `processModule` checking that the module is an `AnalysisModule`.

```
@Override
public void processModule(Module module) {
    if (module instanceof AnalysisModule) {
```

The `AnalysisModule` allows registering via the `addProcessor` method, one or more bind processors that will be initialized during the `AnalysisModule` service initialization.

```
AnalysisModule analysisModule = (AnalysisModule) module;
analysisModule.addProcessor(new CustomEnglishBinderProcessor());
```

Creating a river plugin

In *Chapter 8, Rivers*, we have seen how powerful the river plugin is. It allows populating an ElasticSearch cluster from different sources (DBMS, NoSQL system, streams, and so on).

Creating a custom river is generally required if you need to add a new NoSQL data source that is not supported by the already existing plugins, add a new stream type, or add a custom business logic for importing data in ElasticSearch such as fields modification, data aggregation, and, in general, data brewery.

In this recipe we will see a simple river that generates documents with a field containing an incremental value.

Plugin Development

Getting ready

You need a working ElasticSearch node, a Maven built tool, and an optional Java IDE. The code of this recipe is available in the `chapter12/river_plugin` directory.

How to do it...

To create a river plugin we need atleast the following classes:

- The plugin that registers a river module
- A river module that registers our river
- The river that executes our business logic

We need to perform the following steps:

1. The part of the plugin class is similar to previous one:

    ```
    ...
    public void onModule(RiversModule module) {
        module.registerRiver("simple", SimpleRiverModule.class);
    }
    ...
    ```

    The common plugin part is omitted as similar to the previous one.

2. The river module registers the `River` class as singleton:

    ```
    public class SimpleRiverModule extends AbstractModule {

        @Override
        protected void configure() {
            bind(River.class).to(SimpleRiver.class).asEagerSingleton();
        }
    }
    ```

3. Now we can write the river core. This code section is very long, so I split it in to several parts:

    - The class definition is as follows:

    ```
    ...
    public class SimpleRiver extends AbstractRiverComponent implements River {
        ...
    ```

    - The constructor definition, in which you set up the river and collect user settings is as follows:

```
@SuppressWarnings({"unchecked"})
@Inject
public SimpleRiver(RiverName riverName, RiverSettings settings, Client client, ThreadPool threadPool) {
    super(riverName, settings);
    this.client = client;

    if (settings.settings().containsKey("simple")) {
        Map<String, Object> simpleSettings = (Map<String, Object>) settings.settings().get("simple");
        simpleNumber = XContentMapValues.nodeIntegerValue(simpleSettings.get("number"), 100);
        fieldName = XContentMapValues.nodeStringValue(simpleSettings.get("field"), "test");
        poll = XContentMapValues.nodeTimeValue(simpleSettings.get("poll"), TimeValue.timeValueMinutes(60));
    }

    logger.info("creating simple stream river for [{} numbers] with field [{}]", simpleNumber, fieldName);

    if (settings.settings().containsKey("index")) {
        Map<String, Object> indexSettings = (Map<String, Object>) settings.settings().get("index");
        indexName = XContentMapValues.nodeStringValue(indexSettings.get("index"), riverName.name());
        typeName = XContentMapValues.nodeStringValue(indexSettings.get("type"), "simple_type");
        bulkSize = XContentMapValues.nodeIntegerValue(indexSettings.get("bulk_size"), 100);
        bulkThreshold = XContentMapValues.nodeIntegerValue(indexSettings.get("bulk_threshold"), 10);
    } else {
        indexName = riverName.name();
        typeName = "simple_type";
        bulkSize = 100;
        bulkThreshold = 10;
    }
}
```

- The `start` function that manages the starting of the river is as follows:

```
@Override
public void start() {
```

Plugin Development

```
        logger.info("starting simple stream");
        currentRequest = client.prepareBulk();
        thread = EsExecutors.daemonThreadFactory(settings.
globalSettings(), "Simple processor").newThread(new
SimpleConnector());
        thread.start();
    }
```

- The `close` function that cleans up internal states before exiting is as follows:

```
@Override
public void close() {
    logger.info("closing simple stream river");
    this.closed = true;
    thread.interrupt();
}
```

- The wait function to reduce throughput is as follows:

```
private void delay() {
    if (poll.millis() > 0L) {
        logger.info("next run waiting for {}", poll);
        try {
            Thread.sleep(poll.millis());
        } catch (InterruptedException e) {
            logger.error("Error during waiting.", e, (Object) null);
        }
    }
}
```

- A helper function that controls if the bulk is required and processes it is as follows

```
private void processBulkIfNeeded() {
        if (currentRequest.numberOfActions() >= bulkSize) {
            // execute the bulk operation
            int currentOnGoingBulks = onGoingBulks.incrementAndGet();
            if (currentOnGoingBulks > bulkThreshold) {
                onGoingBulks.decrementAndGet();
                logger.warn("ongoing bulk, [{}] crossed threshold [{}], waiting", onGoingBulks, bulkThreshold);
                try {
                    synchronized (this) {
                        wait();
                    }
```

```
                } catch (InterruptedException e) {
                    logger.error("Error during wait", e);
                }
            }
        {
            try {
                currentRequest.execute(new
ActionListener<BulkResponse>() {
                    @Override
                    public void onResponse(BulkResponse
bulkResponse) {
                        onGoingBulks.decrementAndGet();
                        notifySimpleRiver();
                    }

                    @Override
                    public void onFailure(Throwable e) {
                        onGoingBulks.decrementAndGet();
                        notifySimpleRiver();
                        logger.warn("failed to execute bulk");
                    }
                });
            } catch (Exception e) {
                onGoingBulks.decrementAndGet();
                notifySimpleRiver();
                logger.warn("failed to process bulk", e);
            }
        }
        currentRequest = client.prepareBulk();
    }
}
```

- The notify function is as follows:

```
private void notifySimpleRiver() {
    synchronized (SimpleRiver.this) {
        SimpleRiver.this.notify();
    }
}
```

- The producer class that yields the item to be executed in bulk is as follows:

```
private class SimpleConnector implements Runnable {
```

Plugin Development

```java
            @Override
            public void run() {
                while (!closed) {
                    try {
                        for(int i=0; i<simpleNumber; i++){
                            XContentBuilder builder = XContentFactory.jsonBuilder();
                            builder.startObject();

                            builder.field(fieldName, i);
                            builder.endObject();
                            currentRequest.add(Requests.indexRequest(indexName).type(typeName).id(UUID.randomUUID().toString()).create(true).source(builder));
                            processBulkIfNeeded();
                        }
                        if(currentRequest.numberOfActions()>0){
                            currentRequest.execute().get();
                            currentRequest = client.prepareBulk();
                        }
                        delay();
                    } catch (Exception e) {
                        logger.error(e.getMessage(), e, (Object)null);
                        closed = true;
                    }
                    if (closed) {
                        return;
                    }
                }
            }
        }
    }
}
```

4. After having deployed our river plugin in an ElasticSearch cluster, we can activate it with the following call:

```
curl -XPUT localhost:9200/_river/simple_river/_meta -d '
{
    "type" : "simple",
    "simple" : {
        "field" : "myfield",
        "number" : 1000
    },
```

```
        "index" : {
            "index" : "simple_data",
            "type" : "simple_type",
            "bulk_size" : 10,
            "bulk_threshold" : 50
        }
    }'
```

How it works...

The river core is quite long but covers a lot of interesting parts that are useful not only for the river, such as processing the settings passed to a river, initializing a thread that populates the data (consumer), and its status management, and executing a "safe" bulk index

A generic custom river class must extend the `AbstractRiverComponent` and implement the interfaces defined in the `River` interface as follows:

```
public class SimpleRiver extends AbstractRiverComponent implements River {
```

The river constructor accepts generally the following parameters:

- The `RiverName` object, that contains the name defined in the call /_river/<river_name>/_meta
- The river settings are the settings that are passed via JSON
- A client to send/receive data, which is the native client of the previous chapter
- A thread pool, to control the thread allocation

These parameters are given in the following code:

```
@Inject
    public SimpleRiver(RiverName riverName, RiverSettings settings, Client client, ThreadPool threadPool) {
```

We need to pass the `riverName` and `settings` parameters to the parent constructor to initialize it as follows:

```
        super(riverName, settings);
```

We store the client for future bulk operations as follows:

```
        this.client = client;
```

Plugin Development

Now we can check if our river settings are available (the `simple` section in the JSON) as follows:

```
if (settings.settings().containsKey("simple")) {
```

We can extract the number of items to be created and the field to be populated as follows:

```
Map<String, Object> simpleSettings = (Map<String, Object>) settings.
settings().get("simple");
simpleNumber = XContentMapValues.nodeIntegerValue(simpleSettings.
get("number"), 100);
fieldName = XContentMapValues.nodeStringValue(simpleSettings.
get("field"), "test");
}
```

ElasticSearch's content parser gives a lot of useful functionalities to pass this kind of data.

Usually some index settings are given to define the index that must be used to store the data, the type that must be used and parameters to control the bulk.

```
if (settings.settings().containsKey("index")) {
    Map<String, Object> indexSettings = (Map<String, Object>) settings.settings().get("index");
    indexName = XContentMapValues.nodeStringValue(indexSettings.get("index"), riverName.name());
    typeName = XContentMapValues.nodeStringValue(indexSettings.get("type"), "simple_type");
    bulkSize = XContentMapValues.nodeIntegerValue(indexSettings.get("bulk_size"), 100);
    bulkThreshold = XContentMapValues.nodeIntegerValue(indexSettings.get("bulk_threshold"), 10);
```

It is good practice to provide default ones if not given, as follows:

```
indexName = riverName.name();
typeName = "simple_type";
bulkSize = 100;
bulkThreshold = 10;
```

A river is internally seen as a service, so we need to provide a `start` and `close` method.

The `start` method initializes an empty bulk request and starts the producer thread `SimpleConnector` as follows:

```
@Override
public void start() {
    logger.info("starting simple stream");
    currentRequest = client.prepareBulk();
    thread = EsExecutors.daemonThreadFactory(settings.
globalSettings(), "Simple processor").newThread(new
SimpleConnector());
    thread.start();
}
```

The `close` method usually sets the status as closed and stops the producer thread as follows:

```
@Override
public void close() {
    logger.info("closing simple stream river");
    this.closed = true;
    thread.interrupt();
}
```

In the code, a `delay` method is present and it is used to delay the producer thread to prevent the overloading of the ElasticSearch cluster.

The plugin is generally composed by a producer thread, which produces data to be indexed and a consumer thread (in this case we have simplified to a single bulker function), which consumes the data in bulk actions. The bulk function is very important and it needs to be tweaked. Too fast bulking can cause your cluster to hang due to too much overhead. Generally, a threshold is set to limit the bulking rate.

In the `processBulkIfNeeded` method, we check first if the bulk is needed to be executed checking the number of actions as follows:

```
if (currentRequest.numberOfActions() >= bulkSize) {
```

Then we check if we have hit `bulkThreshold`, otherwise, we need to wait as follows:

```
int currentOnGoingBulks = onGoingBulks.incrementAndGet();
if (currentOnGoingBulks > bulkThreshold) {
    onGoingBulks.decrementAndGet();
    logger.warn("ongoing bulk, [{}] crossed threshold [{}], waiting",
onGoingBulks, bulkThreshold);
    try {
        synchronized (this) {
            wait();
```

Plugin Development

```
        }
    } catch (InterruptedException e) {
        logger.error("Error during wait", e);
    }
}
```

Now we can execute the bulk action and when it is completed (successfully or with failure) we can decrement the running bulk list using the following code:

```
try {
    currentRequest.execute(new ActionListener<BulkResponse>() {
        @Override
        public void onResponse(BulkResponse bulkResponse) {
            onGoingBulks.decrementAndGet();
            notifySimpleRiver();
        }

        @Override
        public void onFailure(Throwable e) {
            onGoingBulks.decrementAndGet();
            notifySimpleRiver();
            logger.warn("failed to execute bulk");
        }
    });
} catch (Exception e) {
    onGoingBulks.decrementAndGet();
    notifySimpleRiver();
    logger.warn("failed to process bulk", e);
}
```

After having executed a bulk action, we prepare a new empty bulk container to collect new index actions as follows:

```
currentRequest = client.prepareBulk();
```

The core of the river is the producer thread, which generates index actions to be executed in bulk. This object is a thread and implements the methods of the `Runnable` class as given in the following code:

```
private class SimpleConnector implements Runnable {
```

Obviously, the main method of this class is `run` as given in the following code:

```
@Override
public void run() {
```

While executing the run part in the thread, we must check if active or close (stopped) as follows:

```
while (!closed) {
```

The main part of the `run` method generates documents with the builder (as we have seen in the previous chapter) and then it adds them to the bulker. Remember that the `processBulkIfNeeded` method must be called for every element added to the bulk to execute it when full.

After having executed the required actions and exiting from the main loop, we must check if the bulk container contains something. If the bulk container is not empty, we need to flush the bulk, otherwise we will lose elements contained in it.

```
if(currentRequest.numberOfActions()>0){
    currentRequest.execute().get();
    currentRequest = client.prepareBulk();
}
```

There's more...

Creating a river for the first time can be a long and complex process, but the base skeleton is very reusable (it changes very little from river to river). The biggest time of developing a river is spent in designing and parsing the settings and in developing the `run` function of the producer thread. The other parts are often reused in a lot of rivers.

If you want to improve your knowledge in writing rivers, good samples are available on GitHub and we have already seen some of them in *Chapter 8, Rivers*. The most complete and well-structured ones are maintained by the ElasticSearch community and company.

See also

- *Chapter 8, Rivers*

Index

Symbols

_all parameter 54
_analyzer parameter 54
_boost parameter 53
<client>.force_bulk method 338
{dynamic_type} 57
_id field 44, 337
_id option 118
_id parameter 53, 113
_index field 337
_indexed_chars property 71
_index option 118
_index parameter 53, 113
_local parameter 103
{name} 57
_parent parameter 54
_parent property 61, 62
_primary parameter 103
_routing parameter 54
_score option 118
.search() method 346
_shards option 118
_size parameter 54
_source option 118
_source parameter 54
_timestamp parameter 54
_ttl parameter 54
_type field 184, 337
_type option 118
_type parameter 53, 113
_uid parameter 53

A

abs(a) function 217
acknowledge 246
acksql 246
acksqlparams 246
acos(a) function 217, 218
actionGet method 294
Actions button 277
active_primary_shards 253
active_shards 253
add 347
add_date_facet 347
addFacet 311
addField(s) 311
add_geo_facet 347
addHighlighting 311
additional script plugins
  installing 212-214
addProcessor method 379
addScriptField 312
add_term_facet 347
addTransportAddress method 291
admin.indices object 292
alias 258
all_terms parameter 185
analyzer parameter 157
analyzer plugin
  creating 376-379
analyzers
  mapping 73, 74
and filter
  executing 169-171
andFilter 309
and parameter 144

Apache HttpComponents
  URL 289
Apache HTTPComponents client
  URL 283
API
  cluster health, controlling via 252-254
  cluster state, controlling via 254-259
  nodes information, obtaining via 259-263
  node statistic, obtaining via 264-269
arrays
  mapping 48
asin(a) function 217
atan2(y, x) function 217
atan(a) function 217, 218
atomic operations
  speeding up 109-111
attachment field
  mapping 69, 71
AttachmentField 333
autocommit 246

B

base types
  mapping 44-47
BigDesk
  installing 269-274
  using 269-274
blocks 257
Boolean filter
  using 148-150
Boolean query
  using 148-150
boolFilter 309
bool parameter 144
boolQuery 308
boost option 47
boost parameter 144, 167
BroadcastOperationRequest/Response 371
bulk action
  managing 302-305
bulkBuilder method 304
bulk_size parameter 235, 246
bulk_timeout parameter 235

C

cbrt(a) function 217
ceil(a) function 217
child document
  managing 60-62
client
  creating 324-328
client.admin().indices() 297
client.execute method 366
Client parameter 365
client.transport.ignore_cluster_name 291
client.transport.nodes_sampler_interval 292
client.transport.ping_timeout 292
client.transport.sniff 291
close function 382
close() method 291, 386, 387
cluster 8-12
cluster action
  creating 368-375
cluster health
  controlling, via API 252-254
cluster.name 253, 257
cluster state
  controlling, via API 254-259
config directory 26
connection_class parameter 326
consistency parameter 110
consistency value 100
constantScoreQuery 308
consumer thread 232
correct query
  suggesting 131-133
cos(a) function 217
cosh(x) function 218
CouchDB river
  URL 235
  using 233-235
count field 202
counting query
  executing 134, 135
CRUD (Create-Read-Update-Delete) 76
ctx.op 225
ctx._source 225
ctx._timestamp 225

custom parameter 103
cutoff_frequency parameter 157
cyclic
  using 231

D

data
  managing 10-12
date_detection option 56
date histogram facets
  executing 194-197
db parameter 234
delay method 387
delete 334
delete by query
  executing 135-137
description method 360
digesting 246
disable_coord parameter 144
Distance parameter 175
distance_type parameter 176
distance_type (plane/arc/factor) parameter 126
document
  deleting 104, 105
  indexing 97-100
  managing 298-338
  mapping 51, 54
  matching 137-139
  obtaining 101-103
  updating 106-108
document mapping
  dynamic templates, using 55-57
DocumentObjectField 333
driver 245
dynamic_date_formats option 56
dynamic templates
  using, in document mapping 55-57

E

ElasticSearch
  communicating with 15
  directories 26
  downloading 24-26
  installing 24-26
  operations 11
  setting up, for Linux systems 31, 32
  URL 24
ElasticSearch blog
  URL 323
ElasticSearch documentation
  URL 31, 111
ElasticSearch-Head
  installing 275-279
  using 275-279
ElasticSearch logging system
  URL 40
ElasticSearch plugin
  URL 352
ElasticSearch thrift plugin
  URL 328
ElasticSearch transport memcached
  URL 328
entries field 196
epoch value
  URL 193
exchange_declare parameter 240
exchange_durable parameter 240
exchange parameter 240
exchange_type parameter 240
existing filter
  executing 167-169
exp(a) function 217
explain parameter 120
explanation() 312
explicit mapping creation
  using 42-44

F

FacetFactory helper 346
facets
  executing 180-182
facet search
  executing 313-316, 344-347
facets parameter 120
factor parameter 163
fetchsize 246
field parameter 185, 202, 366
fieldQuery 308
fields 313
fields option 118
fields parameter 103, 113, 120

field(String name) 313
files system data 268
filtered query 342
filteredQuery 308
filter facets
  executing 198-200
filter parameter 120, 234
filter_parameters parameter 234
flags parameter 167
floor(a) function 217
flush 90
fragment_size parameter 128
from parameter 120, 152
fuzziness parameter 157
fuzzyLikeThisQuery 308

G

generic data
  adding, to mapping 72
geo_bounding_box filter
  using 172, 173
geo distance facets
  executing 206-210
geo_distance filter
  using 174-177
geohash parameter 66
geohash_precision parameter 66
geohash value
  URL 66
geo_point field 208
GeoPoint field
  mapping 64-67
geo_polygon filter
  using 173, 174
GeoShape
  URL 68
GeoShape field
  mapping 67, 68
GET
  speeding up 111-113
GitHub repository
  URL 324
Glob pattern
  URL 57
Google Guice
  URL 367

Groovy
  about 213
  URL 213
gte parameter 152
gt parameter 152

H

hamcrest
  URL 361
handleRequest method 364, 365
has_child filter
  using 160, 161
has_child query
  using 160, 161
has_parent filter
  using 164, 165
has_parent query
  using 164, 165
heartbeat parameter 241
Highlighter helper 346
highlighting parameter 120
highlight option 118
histogram facets
  executing 190-194
hits option 118, 312
hostname 261
host parameter 234, 240
http 261, 268
http_address 262
HTTP client
  creating 284 288
HTTP protocol
  about 326
  advantages 15, 18
  disadvantages 15
  using 16, 17
HttpRequestRetryHandler method 287
hypot(x,y) function 218

I

ICU Analysis Plugin
  URL 74
id() method 312
idsFilter 309
IDS filter
  using 158, 159

ids parameter 159
idsQuery 308
IDS query
　using 158, 159
IEEEremainder(f1, f2) function 217
ignore_attachments parameter 234
ignore_conflicts parameter 82
ignore_retweet parameter 249
ignore_unmapped (true/false) parameter 124
include_in_all option 47
include_in_lower parameter 152
include_in_parent 59
include_in_root 59
include_in_upper parameter 152
incremental_factor parameter 163
index
　about 246, 334
　closing 80, 81
　creating 76-78
　deleting 79, 80
　existance, checking 91, 92
　flushing 87, 88
　mapping, putting 81, 82
　opening 80, 81
　optimizing 89, 90
　refreshing 86, 87
index() method 312
index aliases
　using 94-97
index_analyzer option 47, 56
index_boost parameter 120
IndexBuilder method 304
index_name field 49
index_name parameter 329
index option 46
index parameter 235
index property 69
IndexReplicationOperationRequest 371
index settings
　about 258
　managing 92, 93
index_settings 246
index value 341
indices
　about 257, 268
　managing 328-330
　managing, with native client 292-295

IndicesExistsResponse object 294
initializing_shards 253
in_order parameter 155
InstanceShardOperationRequest 371
InternalIndexShard object 374
interval parameter 197
IP field
　mapping 68
IPField 333

J

Japanese (kuromoji) Analysis Plugin
　URL 74
Java API
　URL 284
JavaScript
　about 213
　URL 213
JDBC river
　using 243-247
JDBC river plugin
　URL 243, 247
Jest
　URL 288, 289
Jetty plugin
　URL 287, 289
jsonBuilder method 297
jvm 262, 268

K

key_field field 205
key_field parameter 197
Kibana
　URL 68, 180

L

lat_lon parameter 66
lib directory 26
Linux systems
　ElasticSearch, setting up for 31, 32
ListBulker object 338
locale 246
log10(a) function 217
log(a) function 217
logging settings

changing 39, 40
lte parameter 152
lt parameter 152
Lucene documentation
  URL 47

M

mapping
  about 258
  deleting 84, 85
  managing 295-333
  obtaining 83, 84
  putting, in index 81, 82
master_node 257
MasterNodeOperationRequest 371
match 56
matchAllFilter 309
match_all query 341
matchAllQuery 308
match_mapping_type 56
match_pattern 56
matchPhraseQuery 308
match Query
  about 308
  using 156, 157
maven package command 360
Maven repository
  URL 285
max(a, b) function 217
max_bulk_requests 246
max field 202
max_num_segments 90
max_retries 246
max_retries_wait 246
max_rows 246
maxScore 312
mean field 202
MemcachedConnection 327
Memcached protocol 327
metadata 257
min(a, b) function 218
min field 202
minimum_match/minimum_should_match
    parameter 144
missing field 184
missing filter

executing 167-169
missing (_last/_first) parameter 125
mode parameter 125
MongoDB river
  using 236, 237
MongoDB river plugin
  installing, URL 236
  URL 238
moreLikeThisQuery 308
Morphological Analysis Plugin
  URL 74
multifield
  mapping 62, 63
MVEL
  about 213
  URL 107, 213
MySql driver
  URL 244

N

Nagios plugin
  for Elasticsearch, URL 281
Nagios server
  URL 281
name method 360
native client
  creating 289-292
  indices, managing with 292-295
Native protocol
  advantages 15
  disadvantages 15
  using 18, 19
nested_filter parameter 125
NestedObject field 333
nested objects
  managing 58, 59
nested_path parameter 125
network 262, 268
networking
  setting up 27-29
newRequestBuilder method 373
newResponse method 373

node
  about 8, 9, 257
  setting up 29-31
NodeOperationRequest 371
Node Services 9, 10
nodes information
  obtaining, via API 259-263
node statistic
  obtaining, via API 264-268
node types
  setting up 32, 33
not filter
  executing 169-171
notFilter 309
no_verify parameter 234
null_value option 47
number_of_data_nodes 253
number_of_fragments parameter 128
number_of_nodes 253
number_of_replicas parameter 77
number_of_shards parameter 77
numeric_detection option 56

O

oauth parameter 249
object
  mapping 49, 50
  properties 50
ObjectField 333
Object Relational Mapping (ORM) 72
one shot
  using 231
onFailure method 366
only_expunge_deletes 90
operator parameter 157
oplog (Operation log) 237
optimistic concurrency control
  URL 101
optimize_bbox parameter 176
op_type 100
order (acs/desc) parameter 124
order parameter 185, 205
or filter
  executing 169-171

orFilter 309
or parameter 144
os 262, 268
other field 184

P

params field 210
params parameter 194
parent parameter 100, 105, 110
pass parameter 240
password parameter 235, 245
path_match 56
path_unmatch 56
Phonetic Analysis Plugin
  URL 74
plain parameter 144
plugin
  about 262
  installing 34-36
  installing manually 37
  removing 38
poll 246
port parameter 234, 240
PostgreSQL driver
  URL 244
pow(a, b) function 217
precision_step property 69
preference parameter 103
prefix query/filter
  using 146, 147
pre_tags/post_tags parameter 128
process 262, 268
processAnalyzers method 379
processBulkIfNeeded method 387, 389
producer thread 232
protocol parameter 234
PyES
  on GitHub, URL 328
PyES online documentation
  URL 328, 343
Python
  about 213
  URL 213

Python language plugin
  URL 36
Python memcached library
  URL 328
Python thrift library
  URL 328

Q

query
  creating 305-309
query facets
  executing 198-200
query parameter 120, 161-165
query_weight parameter 123
queue_auto_delete parameter 241
queue_declare parameter 241
queue_durable parameter 241
queue parameter 241

R

RabbitMQ river
  using 238-243
RabbitMQ river documentation
  URL 243
RabbitMQ river plugin
  installing, URL 239
random() function 217
range facets
  executing 187-190
range filter
  using 150, 151
rangeFilter 309
range query
  using 150, 151
raw parameter 249
readFrom method 372
red status
  solving 14
refresh 90
refresh parameter 103, 110
regex_flags parameter 185
regex parameter 185
regexp filter
  using 165-167

regexpFilter 309
regexp query
  using 165-167
regexpQuery 308
relocating_shards 253
replication 100, 12-14
Request button 278
RequestsHttpConnection 327
rescore parameter 120
Response object 366
RestController parameter 365
REST plugin
  creating 362-367
results
  highlighting 126-129
ResultSet object 343
return fields
  computing, with scripting 218-220
rint(a) function 217
river
  managing 230-232
river plugin
  creating 379-389
round(a) function 217
rounding parameter 246
routing 99
routing_nodes 257
routing parameter 103, 105, 110, 113
routing_table 257
run function 389
run method 389

S

scale parameter 246
scan query
  executing 129-131
scan search
  executing 317-320
score() method 312
score parameter 163
score_type parameter 165
script
  used, for sorting 214-218
script_field parameter 187
ScriptFields helper 346

script_fields parameter 120
scriptFilter 309
scripting
  return fields, computing with 218-220
  search, filtering via 221-223
  used, for updating 224-227
script parameter 235
scriptType parameter 235
scroll parameter 121
scroll search
  executing 317-320
scroll=(your timeout) parameter 131
ScrutMyDocs
  URL 71
search
  executing 116-123
  filtering, via scripting 221-223
  sorting 123-126
search_analyzer option 47, 56
SearchHit object 312
Search object 346
search_type parameter 121
search_type=scan parameter 131
SemaText
  URL 280
SemaText SPM
  installing 279-281
  using 279-281
Sense
  URL 279
setIndices 311
setQuery 311
setScroll method 319
Settings parameter 364
setTypes 311
shard() method 313
Shard
  URL 12
sharding 12-14
shardOperation method 373
shard_size parameter 205
signum(d) function 218
simple plugin
  creating 352-361
sin(a) function 217
SingleCustomOperationRequest 371
SingleShardOperationRequest 371

sinh(x) function 218
site plugin
  creating 350, 351
size parameter 185, 205, 345
slop parameter 155
Smart Chinese Analysis Plugin
  URL 74
sniffer_timeout 327
sniff_on_connection_fail 327
sniff_on_start 327
Sorted helper 346
sorting
  script, using 214-218
sort option 118
sort parameter 120, 216
sortValues() 313
span queries
  using 152-155
sql 245
sqlparams 245
sqrt(a) function 217
standard search
  executing 309-313, 339-343
start function 381
start method 387
State 257
statistical facets
  executing 200-202
std_deviation field 202
strategy 245
suggest parameter 121
sum_of_squares field 202

T

tags_schema=*styled* parameter 128
tan(a) function 217
tanh(x) function 218
templates 257
term filter
  executing 139-142
termFilter 309
term query 341
  executing 139-142
termQuery 308
terms facets
  executing 183-187

terms field 184
terms filter
  executing 142-145
termsFilter 309
terms query
  executing 142-145
termsQuery 308
term statistical facets
  executing 203-205
testNG
  URL 361
thread_pool 262, 268
thrift_address 262
ThriftConnection 327
Thrift ElasticSearch plugin
  URL 21
Thrift protocol
  about 327
  advantages 15
  disadvantages 15
  URL 21
  using 20
thrift support
  for Python, URL 325
Tika library page
  URL 71
time() function 217
time_interval parameter 193
timeout 100, 253
time_out option 118
timestamp 100
timestamp parameter 110
toDegrees(angrad) function 217
took option 118
to parameter 152
top_children query
  using 162, 163
toRadians(angdeg) function 217
total field 184, 202

totalHits 312
transport 263, 268
transport_address 263
transport_class variable 327
ttl parameter 100, 110
Twitter
  URL 247
Twitter river
  using 247-250
Twitter river plugin
  URL 247
type
  about 246
  existance, checking 91, 92
type() method 312
type field 196, 202
typeFilter 309
type_mapping 246
type parameter 159-165, 235, 249
type property 61
type value 341

U

ulp(d) function 218
unassigned_shards 253
unit parameter 126, 176
unmatch 56
update operation 334
updating
  scripting, using 224-227
url
  about 245
Urllib3HttpConnection 327
user parameter 235, 240, 245

V

Validate button 278
value_script parameter 210
variance field 202
version() method 312
versioning 246
version parameter 105, 120
version value 100
vhost parameter 240

W

wait_for_merge 90
wildcardFilter 309
wildcardQuery 308
window_size parameter 123
writeTo method 372

Y

yellow status
  solving 14

Z

zero_term_query parameter 157

Thank you for buying ElasticSearch Cookbook

About Packt Publishing

Packt, pronounced 'packed', published its first book "*Mastering phpMyAdmin for Effective MySQL Management*" in April 2004 and subsequently continued to specialize in publishing highly focused books on specific technologies and solutions.

Our books and publications share the experiences of your fellow IT professionals in adapting and customizing today's systems, applications, and frameworks. Our solution based books give you the knowledge and power to customize the software and technologies you're using to get the job done. Packt books are more specific and less general than the IT books you have seen in the past. Our unique business model allows us to bring you more focused information, giving you more of what you need to know, and less of what you don't.

Packt is a modern, yet unique publishing company, which focuses on producing quality, cutting-edge books for communities of developers, administrators, and newbies alike. For more information, please visit our website: www.packtpub.com.

About Packt Open Source

In 2010, Packt launched two new brands, Packt Open Source and Packt Enterprise, in order to continue its focus on specialization. This book is part of the Packt Open Source brand, home to books published on software built around Open Source licences, and offering information to anybody from advanced developers to budding web designers. The Open Source brand also runs Packt's Open Source Royalty Scheme, by which Packt gives a royalty to each Open Source project about whose software a book is sold.

Writing for Packt

We welcome all inquiries from people who are interested in authoring. Book proposals should be sent to author@packtpub.com. If your book idea is still at an early stage and you would like to discuss it first before writing a formal book proposal, contact us; one of our commissioning editors will get in touch with you.

We're not just looking for published authors; if you have strong technical skills but no writing experience, our experienced editors can help you develop a writing career, or simply get some additional reward for your expertise.

ElasticSearch Server

ISBN: 978-1-849518-44-4   Paperback: 318 pages

Create a fast, scalable, and flexible search solution with the emerging open source search server, ElasticSearch

1. Learn the basics of ElasticSearch like data indexing, analysis, and dynamic mapping

2. Query and filter ElasticSearch for more accurate and precise search results

3. Learn how to monitor and manage ElasticSearch clusters and troubleshoot any problems that arise

Mastering ElasticSearch

ISBN: 978-1-783281-43-5   Paperback: 386 pages

Extend your knowledge on ElasticSearch, and querying and data handling, along with its internal workings

1. Learn about Apache Lucene and ElasticSearch design and architecture to fully understand how this great search engine works

2. Design, configure, and distribute your index, coupled with a deep understanding of the workings behind it

3. Learn about the advanced features in an easy to read book with detailed examples that will help you understand and use the sophisticated features of ElasticSearch

Please check **www.PacktPub.com** for information on our titles

Apache Solr 4 Cookbook

ISBN: 978-1-782161-32-5 Paperback: 328 pages

Over 100 recipes to make Apache Solr faster, more reliable and return better results

1. Learn how to make Apache Solr search faster, more complete, and comprehensively scalable
2. Solve performance, setup, configuration, analysis, and query problems in no time
3. Get to grips with, and master, the new exciting features of Apache Solr 4

Apache Kafka

ISBN: 978-1-782167-93-8 Paperback: 88 pages

Set up Apache Kafka clusters and develop custom message producers and consumers using practical, hands-on examples

1. Write custom producers and consumers with message partition techniques
2. Integrate Kafka with Apache Hadoop and Storm for use cases such as processing streaming data
3. Provide an overview of Kafka tools and other contributions that work with Kafka in areas such as logging, packaging, and so on

Please check **www.PacktPub.com** for information on our titles